# Red Flags or Red Herrings?

## Also by Susan Engel

*Real Kids: Creating Meaning in Everyday Life*

*Context Is Everything: The Nature of Memory*

*The Stories Children Tell: Making Sense
of the Narratives of Childhood*

# Red Flags
## or
# Red Herrings?

## Predicting Who
## Your Child Will Become

*Susan Engel*

**ATRIA** BOOKS
New York London Toronto Sydney

**ATRIA** BOOKS
A Division of Simon & Schuster, Inc.
1230 Avenue of the Americas
New York, NY 10020

First Atria Books hardcover edition February 2011

**ATRIA** BOOKS and colophon are trademarks of Simon & Schuster, Inc.

For information about special discounts for bulk purchases, please contact Simon
& Schuster Special Sales at 1-866-506-1949 or business@simonandschuster.com.

The Simon & Schuster Speakers Bureau can bring authors to your live event. For
more information or to book an event contact the Simon & Schuster Speakers
Bureau at 1-866-248-3049 or visit our website at www.simonspeakers.com.

Designed by Jill Putorti

Manufactured in the United States of America

10   9   8   7   6   5   4   3   2   1

Library of Congress Cataloging-in-Publication Data
Engel, Susan.
    Red flags or red herrings? : predicting who your child will become / by Susan
Engel.
        p. cm.
    1. Personality development.   2. Character.   3. Child psychology.   4. Child
development.   I. Title.
    BF723.P4E54 2011
    155.4—dc22
                                                                    2010016957

ISBN 978-1-5011-0807-5
ISBN 978-1-4391-5588-2 (ebook)

*For Tinka, Kathy, and Jenno*

# Contents

# Author's Note

You cannot dictate who your children will become. But you can get a pretty good sense of who they are and where they are headed. By noticing what they do, say, and feel, you can begin to see the story that is unfolding before your eyes. Like all good narratives, your child's story contains some red herrings—things that might alarm you but don't mean much. There's more good news. There aren't as many red flags in most children's stories as you might think. It's rare that any one thing a child does is a warning sign. More often, problems reveal themselves as a thread within the story, a thread that becomes visible over time. When there are problems, there are gentle ways to help. Every child's life tells a story. This book offers you a way of finding out what that story is and when you can revise the story just a little bit.

# Red Flags or Red Herrings?

# A Road Map to Your Child's Future

I got my first pair of evening slippers when I was three, a birthday gift from my six-year-old sister. They were sparkly gold plastic high-heeled mules, with little pink poofs on the toes. I'd sashay around the living room in them, listening to the click of the plastic, feeling glamorous. I liked to wear them to nursery school, along with a large black leather purse I dragged around with me. It had first belonged to an elderly relative and contained lots of things I might need during the day: lipstick, candy, pencils, stuffed animals, Scotch tape, and sometimes a book or two.

According to my family, from the time I was two years old, I'd spend hours by myself dressing up in other people's discarded fancy dresses, telling stories, and outlining, to anyone who would listen, my secret lives. On any given day, I might be a mother of fourteen who also managed a busy medical practice. I loved the part where I would get out of my station wagon, loaded down with grocery bags, my stethoscope swinging around my neck. I'd pretend to soothe one of my babies on my hip, while holding a phone cradled between ear and shoulder, giving a diagnosis over the phone. I was harried and competent, and so many needy people depended on me. But other days, I was an immortal princess who had been married to a handsome strong king for a thousand years. I could visit with him only now and then, when he appeared magically in the night, to court me all over again. Sometimes I was the maverick head of a major company, who managed a large staff and strode into meetings wearing black high heels, holding a clipboard. At other times, however, I was a starving orphan who lived in the woods and had only animals for friends. I could get very caught up in the pathos of that character. My fantasies weren't confined to marvelous identities acted out in the privacy and solitude of my bedroom, either. Sometimes I tried to bring others into my imaginary world.

My grandmother Helen lived in a small white farmhouse at the edge of a potato farm, her home since she married in 1927. I visited her almost every day, walking down a little dirt path that led from my house at one end of the farm to hers at the other end. She'd toast me Wonder bread, spread it with oleo, and I'd chatter to her. She was a wonderful audience, smiling and nodding, ready to sit there with me for hours.

One day, when I was about six, I arrived and plunked myself down on one of her blue plastic kitchen chairs. It was probably about seven in the morning. I explained that I had some bad news. In a mournful voice, I told her that I was suffering from a rare disease. I lifted my hands from my lap and laid them out on the red plastic checkered cloth that covered her kitchen table, so that she could see the odd semi-shiny veneer, cracked in places, that covered my skin. I explained that the disease required me to peel that top shiny layer of skin off my hands every few hours, even though it was extremely painful. I demonstrated by pulling at one of the edges, grimacing in stoic agony as the translucent material lifted from the top of my hand. Tolerant and adoring, she'd watch sympathetically, clucking her tongue at how awful it must be for me. It was Elmer's glue, which I had carefully painted across my hand and allowed to dry before walking down the path to share my condition with my grandmother. I can remember the disbelieving glee that I felt when she seemed to fall for my fabulous account. I loved temporarily inhabiting that suffering victim, and I loved the thought that others would fall for my story.

The joke in my family is that someone passing by my bedroom door would hear lots of people talking. Looking in to find out who my visitors were, an observer would see just one little girl, pale and thin, sitting alone, sometimes in a darkened room, creating an imaginary world peopled by admirers, comrades, enemies, and support staff.

However, this funny little story has a twist. Sometime during my teens, I found out that when I was little, my father was concerned that all of those imaginary friends foreshadowed schizophrenia. When I talked to myself, he worried that I had a fragile hold on reality. He was alarmed that I didn't know the difference between the real world and make-believe and that I spent too much time pretending. He anxiously watched for signs that my fantasy life was getting the better of me. His aunt had suffered from schizophrenia, although her diagnosis had been kept secret for most of his childhood. Perhaps my behavior triggered his fear that someone else in the family would also be afflicted with mental illness. Was my father right? Did those early escapes from reality presage something more debilitating?

As things turned out, I am riddled with anxieties and, perhaps as a result, almost unbearably controlling. I tell my husband what to say to the kids, I tell my grown children what to say in job interviews, and I wake my sixteen-year-old son, even though his alarm clock has gone off, just to guarantee he will get to school on time. When guests visit our home, I rush down to the kitchen before anyone else wakes up, just to make sure that breakfast goes the way I think it should. I have all kinds of fears. I cannot board a plane without Xanax. I don't like to be the passenger in other people's cars. I've never met a superstition I didn't embrace. Every single evening, I stop whatever I am doing so that I can wish on the first star and ensure that my children will stay healthy. Just as I did when I was young, I still mentally rewrite the sad endings of novels I like. I've had my share of troubles, too—estrangements, disappointments, and regrets. But other than my quirks and the neuroses from which they spring, my connection to reality is pretty solid. I've worked my whole adult life, been married to the same man for thirty years, and raised three sons. The usual barometers of mental health point in the right direction.

Those wild gatherings of imaginary friends and narrative performances when I was little predicted something, but they did not predict mental illness. My love of fictive lives stayed with me. I studied literature in college and am still an avid reader; I love novels most of all. Much of my research has concerned the stories children tell and the worlds they create in their play. I have spent plenty of time thinking about alternative worlds, but scientists tend to call this counterfactual thinking. Most researchers do it.

My vivid fantasy life in early childhood might have foreshadowed my interest in psychology, but it wasn't a red flag for mental illness. Although my father's prediction turned out to be wrong, it's understandable that he was uneasy. Most parents feel anxious at one point or another about how their children will turn out. In those uncertain moments, what are they to do? Often, parents feel lost, as if all they can do is read tea leaves. Some lean on folk wisdom they have inherited from others, and it might not, in fact, be very wise. Yet developmental psychology can provide parents with a helpful road map for identifying and interpreting clues about who their children will become.

## Finding Each Child's Pattern

I fell in love with developmental psychology when I was a sophomore in college. I was dazzled by the clever experiments that revealed how children thought. I loved the idea that there was a pattern and an order to development that could be deciphered through observation. I loved the contrasting theories that illuminated such different aspects of what children did and said. Seemingly small patches of behavior offered clues about how a child was thinking and feeling. Taken together, those clues provided a blueprint for growth and change. I had already spent years watching children play and talk (my much younger sister and the children I had taught in the summer program I ran during my teens). Now research was offering me a way to think about the patterns that governed what I had noticed.

Yet once I became a mother, the world of children looked very different to me. I no longer saw moments of behavior simply as a demonstration of a psychological principle. But I did begin to notice, with a sharpened focus, all kinds of details about my kids, and my friends' kids. One little girl I knew was high-strung from the moment she was born. She fell asleep crying and woke up crying. When she did sleep, she stuck one finger straight up in the air. She learned to talk with vehemence and rattled off long, breathless sentences about everything. Which of these things was an indication about her future, and how did the clues fit together? One little two-year-old friend of my son used to come home with us from the park and spend the afternoons at our house. From the moment he set foot in our loft, he would race around and around our kitchen table, letting out shrill screams for what seemed like hours on end, as if this were the most fun game ever. When he would eventually get tired, he would stop running, and a blank, inscrutable look would cover his face as he just stood quietly, watching whatever my son was doing. *What kind of a guy will he turn out to be?* I wondered.

As my immediate world became peopled with babies and children, my younger sister and I would play a guessing game. We would imagine the little boys and girls in our extended family thirty years later. What kind of grown-up would each of them turn out to be? One niece spent several years of her childhood dressed like her boy cousins, even wearing boys' boxers under her pants. She also insisted on peeing standing up. She was strong-willed and dynamic, a real bossy boots, and easily excited. My sister predicted that this niece would become the head of a big record company and would wear a pinstriped three-piece suit to work every day. Another niece had a quiet, beguiling manner. She was ultra-feminine, almost languorous, even as a little girl. She loved pretty things, and we guessed that she would grow up to be a fashion designer. We playfully thought we could see the seeds of their future selves.

For many years, my interest in children seemed to follow two parallel paths: the children I knew and watched, who seemed to be brimming with intriguing quirks, and the world of research, which was bent on lifting patterns from the confusing debris of specific children and particular situations. As a mother, I noticed the incidents and idiosyncrasies that made each child so interesting. As a psychologist, I thought about trends and benchmarks.

As strange as it might seem, I never thought my life as a mother and the friend of other mothers had anything much to do with my work as a psychologist. I lived among real kids, but I studied behaviors that proved and disproved general theories. I never dwelled on the possibility that I knew anything as a psychologist that could help me predict what my children or their friends would be like when they got older.

That changed suddenly in 2008, during a conversation with my sister. We were gossiping about the son of one of our childhood neighbors, a young man who had just celebrated his twentieth birthday. His early family life, we thought, had all of the ingredients that would surely lead to trouble. His father was a substance abuser with a spotty and troubled work life. His mother's hold on reality was tenuous. His parents had broken ties with many of their family members. They had few friends and were always feuding with neighbors. They mistrusted everyone around them. They seemed plagued by physical ailments that had no clear cause or cure. And when he was young, the son seemed muted, anxious, and often sad. We would have bet our bottom dollar that this boy would bear the marks of such problematic family life. Yet, against all odds, as a twenty-year-old, he was thriving. My sister reported to me how warm, smart, and engaged he now was. He was doing well in a good college, he loved his courses, he enjoyed the new friends he was making, and he was dating a really nice young woman. Who knew? On the face of it, his childhood had seemed filled with arrows pointing toward disaster.

As we discussed this, I laughed wryly and said, "Development is a mystery, isn't it?" This book starts with that comment, because it took me off guard and forced an idea that had been bubbling around in my head finally to take shape. I thought to myself, *Now, wait just a minute here. I've been a developmental psychologist for almost thirty years. Development is not a mystery. It's a crystal ball. But you need to know how to read it.*

When I thought about that neighbor, I realized that along with all of those worrisome signs were other, more significant qualities. The young man had had a very strong bond with his mother even as an infant. His parents had adored him and been very consistent in their attention to him. They were smart, and he was smart. He was good at things. The family had fun together, spent time doing things together, and showed love for one another. I shouldn't have been surprised that he seemed to have grown into a happy, able young man. I had let myself get distracted by red herrings and ignored equally clear signs that he would probably be fine.

The idea for this book came from that conversation, which led me to rethink the ways in which developmental research could help us see and understand the paths of real children. I wanted to show parents that the findings of well-done research could help them see their children with more subtlety and understanding.

The heart of the book comes from my experience as a mother and a friend to other parents. I have seen that each of us looks into the face of our little baby with joy but also with apprehension and uncertainty. What will her life be like? What will *she* be like?

A very close friend of mine had a little boy whom she worried about during nursery school. He spilled his milk every night at dinner, played too roughly with toys, and frequently broke lamps and dishes. His elbows were everywhere. He didn't sit, he bounced. Although he was kind and loving, he often clobbered other children or knocked them over. He played too hard, leaving tears and wagging fingers in his wake. In nursery school, he had only one buddy. He would often come home with his Charlie Brown mouth turned down, telling his mom that his friend had rejected him or that some little boy had been mean to him.

When it came time for kindergarten, his mother fretted that he would be the kid teachers wouldn't like, the rambunctious boy who found lessons difficult to concentrate on, and, on top of all that, a loner. As they were heading out the door that first morning of school in September, the little boy suddenly said, "Wait a minute. I need something." His mother stood watching as he raced to his shelf of toys, grabbed a small action figure that punched its fist when you pushed a button, strode over to her, and said, "I'm ready now." When they got to school, he walked in calmly, the small figure visible in his hand. Within thirty seconds, four little boys had gathered around him to admire the toy. He was off and running.

His mom thought to herself, *Phew. He's gonna be fine.* Then she called me on the phone and said anxiously, "Can I count on this? Does it mean he'll always know how to navigate a group?"

In the best moments of your child's life, you want reassurance that he will always be this ebullient/clever/determined/appealing. At the worst moments, however, you want reassurance that your child can change and is likely to. I recall going to visit a younger friend a few years ago, the mother of a smart and dynamic four-year-old named Rosie. Rosie was a handful. She had a big vocabulary and was a sponge for adult phrases. She often behaved as if others worked for her. As I walked through the door, she was thrashing around the house, screaming at her mother, "You are not the boss of me! I hate you. You don't love me, and you never have. Don't tell me what to do. I am the boss of myself!" Rosie's harried mother looked up at me with a stricken look on her face. "Is she going to be this way forever?"

I had to take some time to answer that question, because children are as complex as the adults they will become. Rosie was not simply bossy and stormy. She was also bright and highly attuned to what others were thinking. She was full of zest for life. She soaked up what was going on around her, and even at four, she was like a laser beam zeroing in on people's interactions, quickly learning what she should say to persuade others to do what she wanted. Which aspect of life was Rosie's mother trying to predict? As a grown-up, Rosie would probably come on strong—she might continue to put her own needs ahead of the needs of others. She might always tangle with people. But she would also have passionate close relationships, and no doubt, she'd use her vitality and intellect to become very successful in some career. But it's easy to see why Rosie's mom felt anguished. All of us gaze at our children in adoration or exasperation and can't help but try to envision the future that lies ahead for them.

My first son, Jake, was born when I was twenty-four. I thought

I had never felt that kind of love before. I couldn't stop kissing him and staring at him. I can remember holding him in a rocking chair, in our loft in New York City, and murmuring to him, "I knew I was going to have a baby. But I had no idea it would be *you*. I'm so glad it turned out to be you and not someone else, Jakey boy." Even as a tiny baby, he was, I realized, already a complex and distinctive person, brimming with qualities that, at that time, only peeked out but soon enough would define him.

He loomed so large in my life that first year. Everything he did seemed important and vivid. The way he nursed, his cries at night, the things that made him laugh, enthralled him, and terrified him, all seemed like crucial clues about who he was. It's just now, twenty-six years later, that I understand that some of the things I paid attention to when he was young were clues, and some were not. Other behaviors and qualities were pointing toward his future, but I didn't know it.

I also felt awed by the responsibility of being his mom. At three months, Jake still wasn't sleeping through the night, as my mother and Dr. Spock assured me all good babies would. He was still waking up in the middle of the night when he was six months old, still not sleeping well at nine months. When he was twelve months old, I let him cry for an hour and a half before bringing him to our bed. Was it bad that I picked him up in the middle of the night, or was it worse that I had let him cry for ninety minutes? Would either have a lasting effect? When he was two and a half and happily snuggling into our bed each night for a good night's sleep, a colleague at the school where I taught shook her head, sucked her teeth, and said knowingly, "If you don't get them to sleep alone when they're babies, you'll never get them out of your bed." I felt sick. Had I already screwed him up for life? Would he ever become independent? Would I ever again sleep alone in bed with my husband? Then my pediatrician, a slightly older mother, said to me, "Eventually, almost everyone figures out how to get through the night alone. Not that anyone ever wants to." With those casual words, she helped me shake off the emphatically dire predictions others had so eagerly offered me.

People's common hunches about human development are often wrong. We carry around strong intuitions, often based on nothing more than our own experiences, about children and their likely paths in life. Many of us have ironclad views on just what a child must have, or be, in order to turn into a healthy and good adult. One parent thinks good sleep habits are the key to a happy childhood, another thinks constant adult attention is the only way to ensure well-being, and a third parent is certain that if you allow a child to give up on things, he is doomed to a life of failure.

You might think that children must have discipline in order to grow up as productive members of society, or you might think that as long as a child is swaddled in love, nothing else can hurt her, and she will turn out to be a happy, caring adult. You might think that children who get lots of positive feedback are going to be confident grown-ups or that children with serious illness are certain to be riddled with neuroses later on. We make assumptions about which characteristics will follow a child as he or she grows up and which are simply passing phases of development. We assume that a defiant fifteen-year-old boy is just going through adolescence but an unsociable nine-year-old is in for trouble. Most people think they can spot the kid headed for turbulence and the one bound for success. But those intuitions are often wrong.

## Red Herrings

A mother recently told me that the summer when her son Nate was seven years old, they went on holiday with extended family. Nate got into an argument with his five-year-old cousin, Tess, and smacked her across the back. Tense and disapproving, the little girl's father, Bill, warned with absolute certainty that Nate showed clear signs of developing into a violent teenager. Bill was a teacher who had worked in tough neighborhoods in Harlem and the Bronx, and he "knew" that kind of kid. By college, Nate had grown into a shy, cerebral literature major, with a small group of close friends who demonstrated against the war in Iraq. He loved violent movies and wrote his thesis on the horror-film genre. But as far as anyone knew, he hadn't hit anyone since before puberty. It can be hard to know, except in hindsight, when a child's unusual behavior is just a quirk with little long-term significance and when behaviors provide signposts for what's to come.

People mispredict children's futures all the time, and not everything can be determined. Exposing our mistaken assumptions about stability is an equally important part of the story that this book will tell. For instance, as new research shows, obstreperous behavior in early childhood does not predict academic difficulty in elementary and middle school. In one study, teacher and parent reports on three-year-olds were compared with various measures of school adjustment when those same children were in middle school. The children described as being difficult and loud and having low impulse control or in other ways being disruptive were no more likely to have problems in middle school than the other children. By the time she is in seventh grade, a rowdy three-year-old will not look different from other children, even though many teachers assume that the unruly preschooler is throwing up a red flag.

When my son Jake was three, his nursery-school teacher told me that he frequently seemed to have trouble finding something he wanted to do and sticking with it. It was a Montessori classroom, and the teacher set great store by the children's ability to choose a set of materials and play with them for a sustained period of time. It seemed to her that Jake was drifting through the room, picking up something for a few moments, putting it down, and moving on to something else. I began to wonder whether this meant he would lack self-direction and motivation. Would he be able to stick with things? Would he always need someone telling him what to do? His teacher's concerns sent me into a small tailspin, casting a slight shadow that I couldn't quite shake off.

A year later, in kindergarten, his teacher told me that she was concerned because he didn't pay attention when they sat at the table learning numbers and letters. A few weeks after I got this worrisome feedback, my mother visited his classroom for Grandparents' Day. She came home, shook her head, and said, "No wonder he drifts away during lesson time. It's boring."

I began to rethink my earlier worry. He was a child whose passions already consumed him. He could spend hours developing elaborate imaginary games involving his favorite superhero, Green Lantern. He spent whole summers directing his siblings and cousins in an extended and complex game of something they called "Baby Animal." Years later, he would direct them in even more complex films that he planned, filmed, and edited for large groups of friends and family to view. Meanwhile, he became an artist, working alone for months on end on a single sculpture. It wasn't his lack of self-direction that explained his vague wandering in the Montessori room. It was the lack of materials that really grabbed him.

Jake, like all of us, has had his struggles. But concentration, perseverance, and involvement are not among them. These were red herrings. The clues about his future were lying there, right next to the red herrings. They often are.

## The Vital Clue

My youngest son, Sam, could already tell a wickedly funny dirty joke at two and a half. Precocious and outgoing, he stood up one night at a beach picnic and delivered a joke about three mice: "The three mice are sitting around talking about how tough and strong they are. The first one says, 'Ya know those poison pellets they put out for us to eat, so we'll die? I eat 'em up all the time. They're better'n candy.' The second mouse says, 'Well, you know those mousetraps they've left all over the house? I do bench presses with 'em every morning and night.' The third mouse gets up and starts to walk away. The two others call out, 'Hey, you didn't say anything. Where you going?'" At this point, my toddler turned and sauntered from the fire on his sixteen-inch legs, delivering the punch line over his shoulder, in his high, clear voice, " 'I'm going to fuck the cat.'"

My stepfather, a farmer who was raised a Methodist, laughed till tears squirted out of his eyes. And from that day on, he called Sam "The Reverend." Here's the catch. Sam, now a teenager, frequently gives public lectures around the country. His talks are inspirational, and in them, he urges young people to do good works in their communities. His grandfather saw his command of the audience and his urge to communicate. Although the nickname was a joke about a two-year-old child's profanity, it also captured a vital clue about a quality that would last through his adolescence and beyond.

Underneath our hopes and worries, we parents want to know which signs predict the future and which do not. We also want to know which of our own actions will have an influence on our children's lives and which will not. We're not the only ones trying to figure out the paths that connect our children's lives to their future. Psychologists have spent the past one hundred years trying to figure this out as well.

## Children Are Clay

The American behaviorist John Watson famously claimed in the early twentieth century, "Give me a dozen healthy infants, well-formed, and my own specified world to bring them up in and I'll guarantee to take any one at random and train him to become any type of specialist I might select—doctor, lawyer, artist, merchant-chief, and, yes, even beggar-man and thief, regardless of his talents,

penchants, tendencies, abilities, vocations, and race of his ancestors."
He boldly asserted an idea that lay buried in the minds of many: that
you could mold a child's future by the way you raised him. Countless
people still believe this, although they might not even know it.

A few years ago, an old friend was complimenting me on my
three sons, how well they had "turned out." She said this with some
surprise and admitted that when they were little, she thought they
were totally out of control. "You had no rules at all. Sam swore in
the grocery store. He never wore clothes. They ate candy morning,
noon, and night. You let them fight. I thought they were totally wild."
I disagreed, suggesting that my rules might not have been about
things like swearing or keeping their clothes on or saying thank you
to a grown-up but had more to do with working hard at things and
being kind. She thought about that for a moment and then said,
"But what? Did you punish them when they weren't kind? Did they
have a consequence when they didn't throw themselves into a project?" I was baffled. What was she talking about? Then I realized that
her implicit model of development was showing through. Perhaps
without even knowing it, she was basing her ideas on a behaviorist
theory of child development: the traits that will emerge over time in
a child are the ones that are regularly rewarded, while undesirable
behaviors that are punished will disappear.

Although most psychologists no longer think Watson's undi-
luted behaviorism provides a good account of development, many
researchers have shown that experiences in early life do shape the
future adult—and not just in the obvious ways most of us assume.
For instance, studies have shown that the number and kind of
conversations children have with their parents when they are toddlers and preschoolers have a formative influence on the ability to
read at five or six. Thus, we now know that a measure of a young
child's family conversations allows us to predict something about
that child's long-term academic success. But not every experience
leaves an indelible impression on a child.

A friend who is a young mother of two recently confided in me, "You're not going to like this story. Finn came home from school the other day and walked straight through the kitchen onto the patio outside. He opened his book and began to read. No snack. No chatter. I finally asked him whether something had happened at school. He reluctantly admitted that he had gotten in trouble for throwing a candy wrapper across the room at snack time. It seems another little boy, something of a rabble rouser, had been egging Finn on to try to toss it into the garbage and make the basket. But Finn knows they aren't supposed to be rowdy at snack time. I don't want him to be the kind of child who gets into trouble with the teacher. He needs to learn how to control those issues. We are giving him a consequence. I told him how glad I was that he told me the truth but that there would be no play dates for a week."

She was right. I didn't like the story too much. That was partly because I think throwing a candy wrapper into a garbage can as if he were playing basketball is pretty harmless and was probably funny at the time. And it was partly because I think lively, exuberant children should be allowed their unpredictable moments. Mostly, however, parents can't mold a child's personality to fit their preconceived notions, no matter how consistent and carefully thought through their parenting style is.

Finn might be the kind of kid who likes rabble rousers and who periodically bursts out. Little his mother does will change those qualities. As I told her, "You can't make him exactly what you think he should be. You might be able to control him, but that doesn't mean you can control who he will become."

## Children Are Seeds

Sometimes it is not that the conditions of a child's life hold the key to his or her future but rather that the child already contains his or her future self. In the old musical *The Fantasticks*, a frustrated father bewailing the way his almost grown child is acting thinks wistfully of how much more predictable and easy it is to grow a garden. He sings, "Plant a radish, get a radish." This view says that if you know what you start out with, you will have a good idea of what you'll get in the long run. As it turns out, there is some truth to this with human beings as well as with radishes.

Research has identified several characteristics that show up early in infancy or childhood and don't change much over a child's life. In contrast to Watson's view, these characteristics predict the future precisely because they are fairly impervious to features of the environment such as child rearing or schooling. Certain kinds of information about a baby provide us with a pretty good picture of what's in store for that child later on.

Take, for example, the way a young child plays. Whether a child prefers to turn small objects into characters and use them to enact a scenario or prefers to use small figures to make patterns tells us something about the kinds of conversations she will have when she is older and even what kind of reader she will be. Researchers have also found that the way a child plays offers a glimpse into her ability to think about other people's perspectives and imagine alternative outcomes to situations. One psychologist, Daryl Bem, has argued that a child's play style is the first indicator of his sexual orientation. Boys who play more like girls spend more time with girls, thus making boys the exotic objects of their erotic interest. Taken together, numerous studies have suggested that a child's play offers intriguing clues about specific aspects of her future self. Moreover, there is little a parent can do to affect her play style.

Some predictors are more mysterious than others. Consider Thomas Bouchard's research examining the role of biology in shaping a child's intelligence. Bouchard and his colleagues studied a group of twins who had been given up for adoption. They assessed the children's intelligence when they were in preschool, in middle school, and again in adolescence. The researchers also collected the IQ scores of the children's adoptive parents. When they were little, the children's IQ scores were more similar to those of their adoptive parents than to those of their twin siblings to whom they were genetically similar. However, by the time a set of twins were teenagers, their IQs were similar to each other and less like the IQs of their adoptive parents.

The most compelling explanation for this finding, and the one most researchers accept, is that IQ is driven by genes. In other words, a great deal of the variation among people's IQs can be traced to variation in the IQs of their parents. Very young children reflect the influence of the parents raising them, but as they age, the influence of their immediate environment wanes, and the genetic influence of their biological parents gains the upper hand. Along some dimensions, information about a biological parent provides an excellent forecast of the child's future.

## The Alchemy of Genes and Environment

Yet even when we are able to identify genetic information about a child, it rarely provides a straightforward or simple blueprint for predicting psychological development. For instance, one important new study has found reliable links between the number of books, tools, art objects, and spaces for free play found in a child's home and a child's academic success in grade school. In this case, the physical environment, and what it might convey about interactions at home, is a crucial ingredient in shaping a child's intellectual capacity.

The current preoccupation with pinning down the relative contributions of nature and nurture has led to a mistaken notion that whatever is genetic is unchangeable and whatever is environmental is changeable. Yet research has consistently demonstrated that most attributes reflect a complex and dynamic interaction between genes and environment. The psychological effects of the environment can often be intractable, while expression of a genetic trait can be powerfully molded by experience.

When the Major League baseball player Jerry Hairston Jr. was two years old, his father, Jerry Hairston Sr., who had played in Major League baseball, and his grandfather, Sam Hairston, who had played in the Negro League, were having their photograph taken. Sam Hairston stopped the photographer. He said, "Bring Jerry Junior over here. I want my grandson in this picture. He's going to play for the Major Leagues someday." Sam Hairston was right. In 2009, Jerry Hairston Jr. was hired to play for the New York Yankees and helped them win the 2009 World Series.

What made Sam's prediction come true? He might have assumed that his grandson had inherited certain characteristics that would give him the same outstanding ability his father and grandfather clearly possessed. But which characteristics? A strong arm? Exceptional hand-eye coordination? Huge ambition? It's also just as likely that Jerry's baseball success came from the fact that he grew up in a family immersed in and dedicated to baseball. He probably saw, heard, and played more baseball than most children. His same strengths and talents, if he'd been born to a family of dancers, would have expressed themselves quite differently. And someone with those same strengths and talents whose family had no athletic ability or connections within the sports world might have ended up working as a gym teacher.

## Unsimple Patterns

It's easy to think that some kids are lucky enough to have it all, while others will face one struggle after another. And it's true that during a child's first eighteen years, there are certain qualities that set the child on a happy pathway. Success and happiness often seem self-perpetuating, and so do failure and sadness. The cranky child stirs up conflict, often doing or saying something that rubs others the wrong way. He brings out the worst in others, and before you know it, he has every reason to believe that other people just aren't nice to him. The good-looking child who gets along easily with others and is sunny keeps encountering nice people who want to help him—enough to make anyone feel cheerful most of the time.

If you take even a cursory glance at the psychological characteristics found to be most stable, the ones that can be measured in a baby and remain pretty much the same over the next twenty years, it would be easy to think that forecasting a child's future is fairly straightforward. It might seem at first that a few good qualities predict everything wonderful, and a few limitations predict a lousy life. Take, for instance, the research on agreeability, a highly stable characteristic not hard to decipher. Agreeable people are easy to deal with, they take things in their stride, and they have a generally upbeat outlook on things. It seems obvious that children who are very agreeable, on the whole, are better off than children who are not. The agreeable child attracts friends. Having friends gives her a chance to become good at having friends, which ensures that she will always find friends. Being agreeable makes it easier to get along with your parents. And the better you get along with your parents, the more benefit you'll get from family life.

But development is a little more complex than that. We all know someone who has risen to the top of her field but spent years in unhappy love affairs. We all know someone who has a lasting, loving marriage but feels like a failure at work. Although a few characteristics are very important and surprisingly stable, each of us is made up of myriad qualities, and each of us lives in a particular set of circumstances that shape those qualities. Imagine three kids, none of whom makes friends easily. One of them has three close siblings and spends a lot of time with her family. The second is an only child whose parents don't have many friends of their own. The third, on closer inspection, does have strong friendships, but the friendships are rife with conflict. These three kids are on different paths leading to very different adult lives—and it's probably only the second child who will be lonely later in life.

This book is about figuring out which clues mean something and which do not. Every child's life contains patterns that point toward the future. But each child's pattern is quirky, not quite like anyone else's. This book offers a way to read the clues and decipher the pattern.

Each of the following chapters examines one central quality—an aspect of life that can seem hard to decipher when children are little and yet is of central importance as they grow up. Chapter 1 discusses how to spot your child's intelligence. This is a dimension of human behavior that has been hotly debated in recent years but almost always in the context of politics and educational policy. However, intelligence is not just a subject for policy makers and those concerned with social justice. Everyone values intelligence in their daily lives. It matters to all of us whether we are very smart or not so. This is as true for the bricklayer as it is for the mathematician.

Chapter 2 looks at the other quality that most worries parents during the early years: their child's ability to make friends. Like intelligence, sociability seems to have enormous stability, but, also as in the case of intelligence, there is more to making friends than meets the eye. There are different ways to make friends and different ways not to. Some young children spend a lot of time alone and will be fine as they grow up. Others might have an unhealthy friendship, throwing up a big red flag for later difficulties.

Chapter 3 examines a quality most people believe they value, even if you wouldn't know it from the way they behave: goodness. Very few parents feel that their children were just born bad, but if you have a child who is mean to others, cheats in sports, or lies to you, there might well come a day when you wonder whether she is going to be a good person when she grows up. Of course, there are different levels of goodness. Some people simply don't break rules and try not to be cruel, while far fewer of us consistently put other people's well-being ahead of our own. From a very early age, some children seem attuned to the needs of others, while others seem to have a keen sense of justice. But there are also several ways parents can have a powerful impact on how moral their children become.

In chapter 4, I head into somewhat trickier territory. Some of the things we yearn for and dread about our children's futures are not so easily defined or measured, but they matter a great deal. Even if we rarely admit it, most of us want our children to be successful, and we might consciously struggle with what that means. When my children were little, I imagined them doing great deeds. Now, as they enter adulthood and I peer at old age, I think of this somewhat differently. I care much less about their great deeds and not at all about fame or fortune. My longings have been tempered by age and the vagaries of real life. Now I want my sons to do well at something they love. What do I mean by doing well? Earning money, finding acknowledgment, and seeing the value of their labor. Mostly, I want them to be able to wake up most days happy to go to work. I want them to find pleasure in the work they do day in and day out. And I want them to earn money at whatever that is. The signs of someone bound for success are there in childhood if you know what to look for. But just as intriguing are the things you can do to encourage success, and these are not altogether obvious.

As your children enter adolescence, you begin to think about their love lives. My youngest son first fell in love at an early age. Sam was four when he was stricken by a six-year-old named Macy. He would blush every time her name was mentioned. He wrote her notes. He dreamily recalled their two-minute interactions on the playground. I myself almost got married at five, to a next-door neighbor, but at the last minute, I couldn't go through with the wedding. However, the roots of love don't lie in these early crushes. Love is a snowball that you begin making with your mother. Chapter 5 describes the nature of this snowball.

Parents I talk to worry about specific things—whatever has been troublesome for them or whatever has raised a red flag in their child's young life. But eventually, most parents will say, "I just want him to be happy." And life is agony for those of us who have watched our child be deeply unhappy or sad over a long period of time. The very worst moments of my life have been when one of my children was devastated by disappointment. If I could find a potion that would buffer my children against crushing defeat or give them the strength to rebound from setbacks, that's the potion I would pay big money for. Most of us want desperately to know what it would take to ensure that our children will be cheerful and content as they grow up. It turns out that although you cannot change a person's basic outlook on life, you can nudge it in a sunnier direction. I examine this in Chapter 6.

Two types of people will probably read this book. Some of you, I hope, are simply interested in the fascinating patterns that make us all who we are. You might even find yourself or your childhood in these pages. But many of you are reading this book because you have young children and want to know what lies ahead for them. You might also want to know what you can do to change the course of your child's future.

Children are born with certain powerful tendencies that shape their future. In addition, each child is born into a family, a neighborhood, and a set of circumstances that exert an equally powerful (and often unchangeable) influence. But none of this means that a child's path is set in stone. In each case, there are ways a parent can respond that will help a child draw on her strengths and minimize her weaknesses. Yet you cannot custom-tailor your child's personality.

In recent years, a dangerous myth has sneaked into our collective consciousness. It's a sophisticated modern version of John

Watson: we think that if we just do things well enough with our kids (use the right punishments, choose the right schools, encourage at the right moments), we can make them all into smart, successful, happy individuals. That is not the case. There is no perfect parent, and there is no recipe for parenting. Development, just like relationships, is complicated and unruly. Every gardener knows that you can put three plants in the same patch of the garden, feed them the same plant food, water them on the same schedule, and they'll still come out differently. The same is true of children. Thank God.

When babies in the United States are born, they are given a score, called the APGAR. That score rates them on several important dimensions (skin tone, sound of cry, and so on). In theory, the higher the score (from one to ten), the more likely it is that the child will thrive and grow in the days and weeks following birth. The APGAR score is an excellent predictor of early health. We don't have a psychological APGAR, especially not one that will predict a child's long-term development. Nor do babies come with labels that say, "Makes friends easily, smart but unmotivated." What we do have is a wide body of research that indicates the experiences and behaviors that are stable and those that are not. We know more than ever about which aspects of a child's early circumstances matter and how they matter. We know quite a bit about the things parents can do to influence their children, for better or for worse. There are plenty of good data telling us what clues predict a child's potential, when we shouldn't worry at all, and what we can do to nudge a child off a bad path and onto a healthier path. Each child's life contains clues that, when put together into a story, point the way toward her future.

# Intelligence: As Smart As the Day You Were Born

At three, Stevie was jubilant and inventive, a lively little guy. He had a wiry, lithe body, brown, cheery eyes, and wide cheeks. In a photograph taken of him when he was four, he is lounging on the limb of a tall tree, his arms draped casually and comfortably over a branch. He looks spry and savvy, as if he knows what the photographer sees and gets a kick out of it. What doesn't show is any sign of the fierce intensity that later became such an integral part of his intelligence—for better and for worse.

His nursery-school teacher wrote this about him in his midyear evaluation: "Stevie loves to paint and enjoys experimenting with new techniques. Last week, he tried using two paint brushes at once. He is an avid block builder and often spends hours making complicated structures. He enjoys helping our janitor clean the room at the end of the day and almost always helps move the chairs and sweep the floor. Stevie needs to learn that teasing is not a good way to make friends."

A year later, the art teacher from the same school sent home a note to Stevie's mother: "I would like to talk to you briefly about Stevie. Until now, he has always loved arts and crafts so much. He's been one of the most prolific students in the woodworking area, but recently, he seems to have lost interest. He appears completely indifferent to what he makes. He seems like a different child—even his hand-eye coordination has slipped backward. He doesn't seem to have the interesting ideas for projects that he did just a few months ago, and his wood projects are carelessly put together."

Stevie's mother, Francis, was concerned. Highly intelligent, well educated, and extremely ambitious, Francis assumed that all three of her children would excel at school. It was a given, from her perspective, that her children had superior intellectual ability. Both she and her husband were smart and came from academically oriented families. Her husband was a well-regarded doctor in Boston, with a medical degree from Johns Hopkins University. Francis was a freelance book editor who had been the president of her class at a top women's college. They read constantly, discussed the news at dinner, went to art museums, and traveled. Stevie's older sister and brother were top students. What was wrong with him? Perhaps he just wasn't as smart as the rest of the family.

## Who's Smart

Is there anyone who doesn't want his or her child to be smart? Whether you live in a family of schoolteachers or a neighborhood of factory workers and farmers, everyone values intelligence. There are few jobs where it doesn't matter, and most of us intuitively know that smarter people do better in all kinds of settings. They get more done, have better ideas, learn things more quickly, are better at their jobs, are often more fun to be with, and can solve unexpected problems.

Years ago, psychologist Robert Sternberg set out to learn what ordinary people think about intelligence. He sent his students at Yale out into the streets of New Haven to ask passersby what they thought were the essential characteristics that make someone intelligent. In particular, he wanted to know if people from different walks of life would agree or disagree about the qualities that make up smartness. It turned out that almost everyone found it easy to answer the question. To a great extent, at least within our culture, people tended to agree.

Whether we are highly educated or not, whether we work in offices or factories, almost all of us feel, even if we don't admit it, that we know whether someone is smart or not soon after meeting him or her. On what do we base this? We look for humor, savvy, verbal skill, competence within a domain, and a general air of "quickness." And as it turns out, our collective intuition about who is smart, and why, falls for the most part right in line with what psychological research has to say on the topic.

Herbert Crovitz, a social psychologist at Princeton University in the 1960s, used to tell his students, "Theories do two things: they account for the data, and they make people happy." As it turns out, theories of intelligence do one or the other but usually not both. And in the past two decades, theories that make people happy have gained some ground over theories that best account for the data. Many people in our society resist thinking of intelligence as a narrow, quantifiable characteristic. They find the traditional view of intelligence, conveyed by IQ tests, to be too restrictive. In my psychology classes at Williams, few students will say openly that intelligence is the ability to do math and comprehend texts, the very abilities that got them into a college like Williams. They worry that such a definition is elitist and are quick to point out that one can be intelligent in many ways. My students are like many across the country who are drawn to the idea that being "book smart" is only one way to be intelligent.

Howard Gardner, a psychologist at Harvard University, provided an alluring alternative to traditional views of intelligence when he published *Frames of Mind* in 1984. In it, he railed against the narrow-minded idea that the full range of people's mental acuity could be measured by something as academic as a traditional IQ test. He argued that there are not one but seven kinds of intelligence (logico-mathematical, spatial, verbal, musical, bodily kinesthetic, interpersonal, and intrapersonal) and that there are a range of ways to express intelligence. A child who is wonderful at dance but has a small vocabulary and trouble with numbers would be considered to have high bodily kinesthetic intelligence but low logico-mathematical and verbal intelligence.

As Gardner's idea began to take hold, teachers embraced the idea that they could use it to identify the particular kind of intelligence each child had. Teachers felt that Gardner's scheme helped them fine-tune their curriculum to fit the particular kind of intelligence each child possessed. As the theory got diluted within schools, some teachers simply used the idea of multiple intelligences as a way to help each child feel smart, even when he or she didn't excel at traditional school tasks. This egalitarian conception of intelligence has taken hold like wildfire, and in every town in America, you can hear teachers talk about the specific kinds of intelligence their students possess. "He might not be good at math, but he sure is smart when he's on the basketball court." "She struggles with English class, but she's so artistic; her visual intelligence is outstanding." Or the most common form: "He might be book-smart, but he's street-dumb." The theory of multiple intelligences makes people happy. But does it explain the data?

## The Smartness Thermometer

Ever since psychologists began formally measuring things, they've been trying to measure intelligence. Until Howard Gardner introduced *multiple intelligences* into the common lexicon, people tended to use the term *IQ* as a stand-in for *intelligence.* The intelligence quotient is a mathematical expression, devised in France at the turn of the twentieth century by Alfred Binet. He developed the test to help the French school system identify children who were retarded or significantly slower than others in their age group. His goal was to make sure that "slower" children were not punished for their inability to learn. The original IQ (as well as almost all subsequent forms of it) was based on a very simple concept in psychological assessment: Ask children of a certain age a series of questions. The number of questions they get correct is then divided by their chronological age. Thus, although a given ten-year-old might answer more questions than a seven-year-old, the younger child might well have a higher intelligence quotient. Using the test to compare children depends on a much-trusted practice among researchers: norming. This means that in order to evaluate a given child's IQ, you have to compare it to the average (mean) score of children that age. As a result, each child of a given age is being compared with what is considered normal or typical of all the other children in that age group.

What kinds of questions do IQ tests involve? The test is divided into several components, each asking questions that tap into a specific kind of thinking. In one part, children are asked to say what is missing from a picture (a door knob from a picture of a room that includes a door, for instance). Another component requires children to recall a string of numbers. Another involves moving around a collection of colored blocks so that they form a pattern presented on a card. Another asks children to answer questions about famous books, presidents, the weather, and different parts of the country. Although the test has been criticized for favoring children who live certain kinds of lives (if a child looks at a picture of someone riding a horse and doesn't know that the missing piece is the stirrup, it might well be because the child has lived her whole life in the inner city, with little access to books about riding). On the other hand, many of the questions test more content-free abilities, such as memory span. However, even these supposedly content-free questions might well favor children with certain kinds of experiences.

In the early 1960s, Sylvia Scribner and her colleagues set out to show the invisible bias in intelligence tests. Scribner was sure that something about school experience was helping some children do better even on parts of IQ tests that had been considered relatively culture-free. Her previous work in nonliterate communities had shown her that children who go to school regularly seem to acquire, without even realizing it, specific techniques that might help them do well on the kinds of memory tasks used in IQ tests. Sure enough, when she and her colleagues asked students to recall a fairly long list of words, such as *apple, banana, desk, hat, plum, shoe, chair,* and *sweater,* the children who had missed a lot of school days because of poverty, migrant work schedules, and segregation seemed to struggle. Scribner knew, from her literacy work, that learning to read leads people to conceptualize in a different way. Thus, the school children were using categories to chunk the items, making it easier to remember them: first the fruits, then all the furniture, then all the tools. Unschooled children didn't have this strategy at their disposal. However, when Scribner provided the category names ("Tell me all the kinds of fruit on the list, now all the pieces of furniture, now the clothing"), the children with little schooling performed similarly to the others. It seemed, then, that memory span per se did not differ between the two groups. Instead, what differed was the savvy to use category labels as a mnemonic, a skill found in school.

Scribner's research, which was really so simple, dealt a serious blow to the notion that any aspect of the IQ test, even the most seemingly culture-free part, was the same for all children. However, for all of its weaknesses and built-in biases, it taps into something pretty steady and real. But it's been hard for psychologists and lay people to put their finger on just what the test measured.

That is, until psychologist Joseph Fagan published a paper in the 1980s arguing that traditional IQ tests, the kind developed by Binet and modified by David Wechsler, created the illusion of coherence where there wasn't really any. That is, traditional IQ tests measure concrete knowledge ("What is the capital of Pennsylvania?") with more basic processing skills (remembering a list of words). Researchers have found again and again that while each person taking the test might do better on some parts of the test than others (For instance, I always do terribly at creating a visual pattern to match a picture, but I do well at analogies), there is, generally speaking, a lot of consistency—in other words, a high correlation between components of the test. The person who gets a higher score than others her age on one part is likely to get a higher score than others on most of the other parts of the test. It is easy to see how scientists, and ultimately the general public, came to think of this test as actually measuring a particular quality of mind or even a physical part of the brain.

Psychologists have even given this imagined underlying quality a name: g (for "general intelligence"). If you're high in g, you are smart, and if you are high in g, you are likely to do well on many components of the test. Fagan didn't disagree that intelligence might ultimately be a single quality of mind, but he wanted a test that would actually focus on just that quality, the ability that produces g. So he zeroed in on the single characteristic he thought underlay the myriad of abilities we push together and call intelligence.

Fagan argued that what makes one person do better on an IQ test and seem smarter in real life as well is what he called speed of processing. We are all familiar with that concept from our computers: the faster the processor, the more the computer can do. It's the same with the human brain. The faster it can take in information, the more information it can take in. Hence two children might be exposed to the same environment, but the one who can take in more will know more. Fagan's point was that speed of processing is a much simpler, more precise, and more value-free characteristic, which might actually explain the correlation between items on traditional IQ scores. But how do you directly measure something like speed of processing?

This is pretty easy, as it turns out. From birth, babies stare at something until they become used to it—in other words, until they have processed it. Then they look for new stimuli. Fagan showed babies two pictures projected onto a screen in front of them. Then he measured how long it took them to absorb (become familiar with, or process) the first picture before turning their heads to look at the second picture. Of course, it's possible that some children simply have shorter attention spans than others. And yet the important thing about Fagan's test was that there was enormous consistency between his infant test and more traditional IQ tests. Babies who processed visual information quickly on Fagan's test also did well on IQ tests when they were in elementary school.

Fagan's IQ test cannot be bought over the counter, but that doesn't mean parents aren't looking for signs of their babies' intellectual potential. Most parents think their baby is smart unless they see signs of trouble. In particular, there are two points when parents tend to worry about their children's intellectual acumen: when they learn to talk and when they start getting evaluated in school.

Stevie learned to talk at the usual age for a third child and a boy. By the time he was two, he could name many familiar objects, and by the time he was two and a half, he could speak in phrases, and he learned new words rapidly. So far, he seemed as smart as the other bright pennies in his family. He only began hitting a snag when he went to school. When your child has trouble with schoolwork, it's only natural to wonder, even if you don't admit it, if it's a sign that he's not as smart as you had hoped.

Recently, my husband was skiing at our local slope in Great Barrington, Massachusetts. It was a Wednesday, and usually on weekdays, the only other skiers are local people sneaking in a few hours or children coming en masse from one of our nearby public schools. But on this day, my husband found himself riding up on a chairlift with a man in his late forties and his twelve-year-old son. They had taken time off from work and school to celebrate the day the son was adopted from Korea. As they glided up the side of the mountain, the boy and his father began discussing what trail they would ski on next.

The boy said, "Let's try the triple after this."

The father answered, somewhat uncertainly, "OK. But I am not sure I know how to get over there."

The boy quickly replied, "I know how to get there."

The father said skeptically, "How could you possibly know? We only have been here once before, and that was a year ago."

The boy answered, "I memorized the map."

The father smiled and shook his head. "How is it that you can memorize a whole map so easily, but you can't seem to do math in school?"

The boy said, "Because school is boring."

Here was a clear example of a child whose intellectual abilities weren't in sync with school tasks. When a child has trouble in school, does it mean he isn't bright?

## Do Smart Kids Get Good Grades, or Do Good Grades Create Smart Kids?

Here we come to a dicey problem. On the one hand, school success is caused by intelligence. If two children come from the same socioeconomic background, have roughly similar childhood situations, and attend the same school, the one who is smarter is likely to do better—in school and in life beyond school—than the one who is less smart. And yet the caveats to this prediction are important. Some very bright children don't do well in school because they have specific learning disabilities, emotional problems get in their way, or, like the boy on the chairlift, they find school boring. In any of these cases, a very bright child can underperform in school.

On the other hand, if your son scores well on a math test when he is five or six, he is likely to get good grades in fifth grade. Equally important, if he scores better than most of the children in his kindergarten class, he is likely to get better grades than his classmates in fifth grade. The research is very clear on this, and it should come as no surprise. A child who is bright and comfortably applies himself to a math test as a five-year-old is not only going to be just as bright when he is eleven years old, but he is, in all likelihood, still going to be interested in doing well on tests, able and eager to focus on the task at hand and follow instructions. The Peabody Picture Vocabulary test, used to assess the verbal skills of preschoolers, is a very good indicator of a child's grades in elementary school. There is no mysterious trail leading from a good evaluation in kindergarten to high grades in middle school. The same abilities and motivation that led to the good kindergarten performance also explain the good algebra grade. But do those good scores in preschool and high grades in elementary school tell us anything about a child's intelligence?

The answer is a bit complicated. Early math and verbal scores predict later academic success, and academic success is correlated with IQ. But that doesn't necessarily mean that the five-year-old with the good math score is going to be smarter than the five-year-old who doesn't get as high a math score. For instance, some children do well in school because they are highly attuned to the expectations of adults—they are dutiful, eager to please, and able to focus on achieving the things expected of them in school.

Take, for instance, a young biologist named Elise. She graduated magna cum laude from an Ivy League university and received her PhD in sociology from a top graduate program. She was awarded tenure at one of the best colleges in the country when she was only thirty-two years old because she was successful as a teacher and did high-quality research that got published in the better journals in her field. However, she insists that this is much less because of her intellectual powers than her determination to do everything she needed to succeed. When she was a child, her parents made it clear that they expected good grades. Her mother insisted on looking over every assignment before it was handed in and made her fix mistakes. She had no interest in challenging the assignments or trying something outside the requirements. She was aggravated when other students distracted the teacher from the planned lecture. She hated vague assignments. But she was diligent and highly attuned to figuring out what each teacher wanted from her. She was a perfectionist and had great attention for detail. Good wasn't good enough for her. She felt compelled to do whatever it took to get the highest grade. She behaved well in class. She was a teacher's dream. At each stage of her career, she replicated that approach.

Robert Sternberg, the psychologist who asked the man on the street what it meant to be smart, has also argued that there are three kinds of intelligence: analytic, practical, and creative. He would probably find that Elise scored high in two of his three kinds: analytic (her ability to learn information and use it to solve new problems) and practical (she knew how to figure out what was required of her to reach her goal). In the end, that practical intelligence is as powerful for Elise as her analytic intelligence. But the point is, Elise's experiences in school pushed her forward. By the time someone is in college, it's not always easy to figure out whether academic success is rooted in intelligence or in earlier academic success. In other words, being smart might cause children to do well at school, but doing well at school also causes children to continue doing well at school.

For many children, the desire and ability to conform to expectations is as big a part of their success in school as their intellect and might well carry them even farther. Academic success tends to be self-perpetuating. And by the same token, the child who does not do well in school might continue to have trouble. She might not do her homework. She might question every assignment. She might skip classes. She might act surly in school. All of these qualities can affect her grade, and yet she might in fact be very smart. On the one hand, you can say she is bright but just doesn't do well in school. However, over time, a child who is not treated as if she is bright might begin to function as if she is not bright. As a result, by the time she is an adult, she might not have the knowledge and skills she could have acquired by participating more fully in school, which in fact would allow her to do the things intelligent people do. In other words, by the time a person is thirty years old, her functional intellect is no longer simply a matter of potential—it's a matter of what she has actually learned and done.

IQ might or might not capture all we would wish about the ineffable but powerful quality we call intelligence. However, it predicts a lot, and it's surprisingly stable—it doesn't change much over a person's lifetime.

## The Resilient IQ

One of the simplest and most compelling facts about IQ tests is that the measure is so sturdy. If you give a child a proper IQ test (say, the Stanford-Binet or the Wechsler) when he is five and test him again when he is eighteen, he is likely to get a similar score. More important, if you give a group of ten children the test when they are five, each of them is likely to get the same score, in relation to the others, when he or she is eighteen. In other words, even though children know more as they get older and change in significant ways (double their size, learn to read and write and do math, and acquire whole bodies of knowledge about topics such as baseball, dinosaurs, car mechanics, or American history), whatever it is that is captured by an IQ test remains pretty much the same. Kids think they get smarter in school. They don't. They just acquire knowledge and skills.

One of the most thorough and elegant demonstrations of the stability of IQ was conducted by a group of scientists in New Zealand in the late 1960s, although that is not what they set out to study. Obstetric medicine and care had improved dramatically in the previous decades. Many more babies were surviving childbirth, particularly babies who experienced problems just prior to and during delivery. Doctors began to worry, however, that these children were prone to greater problems as they grew up. Perhaps by decreasing infant mortality, new medical practices had led to increased childhood morbidity. The theory was that the problems that might have caused difficulties during birth were now creating problems later down the road when these babies were a bit older. In an effort to track the well-being of this new population of babies, a group of doctors and psychologists in New Zealand decided to try to follow a large cohort of babies all born in one place at one time. The researchers followed the fate of 1,037 babies, all born at the Queen Mary Hospital in Dunedin between April 1, 1972, and March 31, 1973. Almost all of the babies chosen for the study have been visited, observed, and tested every few years right up to the present. Many of those babies now have babies of their own who are being observed and interviewed. One of the extraordinary features of this endeavor is that so many of the children remained in the study.

As anyone who has ever done longitudinal research will tell you, the hardest part is keeping your subjects in the study. Most studies of this kind suffer from attrition. Say a scientist recruits one hundred babies for her study. By the time the babies are ten years old, fifty of the families might have moved away, twenty more might refuse to be part of follow-up assessments, and before you know it, the researcher has only thirty subjects to work with and, as a result, can say almost nothing about broad trends. So it is particularly impressive that when the Dunedin kids were twenty-one years old, almost all of them were still around and happy to answer the researchers' questions, take the required tests, and participate in interviews. Ninety-three percent participated in a daylong assessment. Only nineteen refused to participate, and another nine couldn't be tracked down.

In the Dunedin study, doctors were able to learn a great deal about the health patterns of the children as they grew up. They began to see which kinds of illnesses were the sequelae of improved pre- and perinatal care. But as it turned out, they also learned quite a lot about the children's intelligence.

They first assessed the children's IQ when they were young, as part of a complete battery of baseline measures. Then, to be consistent, they measured the children's IQ every three years, through adolescence and early adulthood. And here's the simple but startling fact: when it came to performance on an IQ score, the overwhelming majority of the children (930 out of 1,037) stayed pretty much the same. The researchers first thought that they had found straightforward evidence that IQ does not change. However, the beauty and difficulty of large data sets is that you always get some noise.

The psychologists couldn't ignore the 107 children whose IQ seemed to fluctuate wildly across a twelve-year time span. Was this evidence, after all, that IQ is not so stable? To complicate matters more, the fluctuations in children's scores did not follow a simple pattern. Some scores dropped precipitously, while others seemed to surge upward. Perhaps IQ was more malleable than people thought. Then the psychologists took a closer look.

They realized that most of the kids whose scores got markedly better or worse during the study actually ended up about where they started. Among those 107 were children whose scores rose between the time they were five and eight but then dropped between the age of eight and adolescence. By the time those 107 children were in their teens, they had almost all returned to their original baseline scores. If you had tested a child only twice, you might see a surprising gain or loss in IQ. You might think you had found proof that children can lose their intelligence or get smarter. But the beauty of the Dunedin study was that researchers showed that over the long haul of childhood and adolescence, while there might be peaks and valleys, kids pretty much test where they began. If a child's IQ stays the same, the question is why. Is it because, like eye color, intelligence is inherited, or is it because, like taste in food, what you experience when you are little becomes imprinted on you? Just the fact that something is resilient doesn't tell you much about where it comes from.

Anyone who has adopted a child knows the quiver of uncertainty, however subtle, that makes you wonder whether your baby will "turn out" like you or like the biological parent neither of you will ever see. Karen had given birth to two children with her first husband and now wanted to raise a child with her second husband, a powerful creative director of television programs. They adopted Maude before she was even born. Karen was there for the birth and cut the umbilical cord, wrapping Maude up and giving her her first bottle. Neither Maude nor Karen saw the biological mother again. When Maude was little, she was full of energy, and she learned her first words before she was fourteen months old. She had a sparkle in her eye and a loud, happy laugh, and she seemed surprisingly like her father. She even looked like him. They doted on Maude, filling her life with toys, interesting trips, stories, friends, good food, and books. When Maude was a preschooler, she seemed every bit her parents' daughter. So Karen and her husband weren't sure what to make of it when Maude began to have trouble in school. She loved the work, was eager to try everything, and carried herself like someone who thinks she is at the top of her class. Then it was time for her to be tested, because her parents wanted to send her to a private high school, which required an aptitude test. Although she had seemed so bright and adept during her first years of school, her parents were confused and dismayed to learn that Maude's scores were very low, much lower than their own or than those of Karen's biological children from her previous marriage. Although in so many ways she was like her parents, her IQ was not. How could this be?

The most compelling explanation comes from a study of twins separated at birth and given up for adoption. When these children were tested in early childhood, their IQs tended to match the IQs of their adoptive parents. The subjects were more like the people they lived with than the people with whom they shared genes. But by the time the children in the study had become teenagers, they more closely resembled their identical twins than they did their adoptive parents. The researchers' explanation was that environmental influences of parents temporarily lifted the children's IQs but that this influence didn't last. As the children aged, the expression of their intelligence seemed less dependent on what was going on around them day to day (the conversations people had, the activities they were encouraged to engage in, the kinds of schools they went to). Instead, it seemed that biology was taking over, and their IQs inched toward a level that much more closely resembled the long-lost siblings with the exact same genetics, even when the two had been raised in very different circumstances. Maude probably had an IQ more similar to the IQs of her biological parents than to those of her adoptive parents, but the disparity only showed up as she entered adolescence.

The research on IQ tells a pretty unambiguous story: children's IQs and the intelligence IQ tests measure are stable and heavily determined by a child's genes. And yet, as we have seen, there are factors that can either temporarily disguise a child's true intellectual ability or in some way inflate or depress it. If you think your child is more intelligent than tests or academic performance suggest, what might explain the discrepancy?

## What Gets in the Way

Many years ago, when I was teaching at a fairly progressive independent school in New York City, there was a four-year-old boy, Alec, who came in for the usual interview and admissions assessment—a combination of a shortened IQ test and some open-ended play in the admissions office. Alec had been touted as very bright, and his parents were sure this was the right school for him. And yet he did miserably in all aspects of the admission process. He did not get a high score on the test, he was uncommunicative in the interview, and his playing seemed immature, lacking the kind of complexity that is often seen as an expression of intelligence. Alec was denied admission. However, a teacher at the school later learned from a friend of the family that when Alec had gotten home that day, he had complained bitterly to his mother about his sore feet. It turned out his mother had mistakenly put him in a pair of shoes that were two sizes too small. The poor little boy had spent the whole time at the new school thinking about his aching feet, not old enough to realize that he could let someone know something was wrong. His performance in that interview was not a good measure of his real abilities. Anyone's intellect can be temporarily masked by some glitch of circumstance, and in the long run, such momentary setbacks won't alter the path of a child's intellectual development. A very smart teenager who does poorly on the SAT because he has a headache will do well the next time he takes it. And yet some glitches can have a long-lasting impact.

Hank, a four-and-a-half-year-old boy with bright red hair and an impish face, was exactly the kind of bright child bound to get into trouble at school. He had lots of physical energy and enormous physical skill. Let him outside with some mud puddles or put him near a climbing toy, and he'd be happy for hours. The first time he saw snow (on a visit to Massachusetts from California, where he lived), he spent four hours outside inventing different routes from the top of the hill to the bottom and constructing different kinds of jumps for the sled. If anyone handed him a complicated toy that involved moving parts, he would focus on it quietly for long stretches of time, trying out the different ways the toy could work. But he was also the little guy who unwittingly knocked over the glass of juice at the lunch table every single day. He often got chastised by other parents for things like pushing another child off the sandbox ledge in a moment of exuberance, although he did it not from anger but out of boisterousness. He was the little boy who tapped his pencil against the edge of the desk as the grown-up read a story aloud, fidgeting restlessly in his seat. As his mother said about him, "He can be rough, but he's never mean."

Hank had all the signs of high intellect. He took in information quickly and synthesized bits and pieces of knowledge he'd gathered from different settings. He could look at a picture of a shape and make the same shape using small plastic pieces, create a new kind of slingshot from branches, and devise a new set of rules for a dart game. As Howard Gardner would say, Hank could solve problems and make things that were interesting and valuable to the people around him. And Hank wasn't always fidgety and restless. He listened carefully when he was interested in something and seemed to zero in on the important information. A child like Hank shows his intelligence in slivers, like small fish darting through a stream of more unruly behavior. The signs can be easy to miss. Once when he was two, he sat on a couch watching television with his aunt Laura. She leaned toward him to ask a question about the cartoon on the screen but saw that he was gazing intently at her mouth.

"Laura, you're old," he said.

She laughed, a little thrown. "What?"

"You're old. Your teeth are lello. Lello means old."

It would be easy to miss the mental acuity that went into his logic, which in form resembled a syllogism. Yellow is a sign of age. Laura's teeth were yellow. Laura must be old. Hank's ability to analyze information and think logically was a clear sign of his sharp intellect. But those flashes of intellect were often obscured by his bouncy, slightly clueless energy.

He was just the kind of kid who could seem naughty and over time, because of that, be seen as not smart by a teacher. One day when Hank was four and a half, his aunt was trying to help him put his winter boots on. She kneeled down in front of him. As she began to tug at the first boot, Hank, looking down at her bent head, began to tug at her hair.

"Hank," she said in a slightly exasperated tone, her head bent in the effort of getting on the boot, "that hurts. Stop pulling my hair."

Hank tugged harder.

"Hey," Aunt Laura said sharply. "Cut it out."

Hank kept a steady tension on her hair for another two seconds before lowering his hands.

"Listen, Buddy. I'm helping you get ready to go sledding. But what you're doing really hurts." An experienced mom, Aunt Laura looked him right in the eye. "If you pull my hair one more time, I won't help you put your boots on."

Slight, lovable, goodwilled Hank looked her steadily in the eye and gave a hard yank.

One can easily see how behavior like this alienates grown-ups. Once alienated, they back away from a child, offering less help, less encouragement, less of the very attention that seems to help children make the most of their potential. It is easy to see that teachers would be aggravated by Hank's physical energy. When other children were happily filling in the questions on a worksheet, Hank would be looking out the window at the bird fight happening on a limb of a nearby tree.

Most teachers and many parents worry when a child is obstreperous. The young child who won't sit down when the teacher rings her little bell, who stares off into space when the other children are filling in worksheets, who talks during a group discussion or jumps up and starts fiddling with the thermometer during a meeting can look like trouble. But on its own, unruliness in kindergarten does not predict academic trouble later on. Research shows that all other things being equal, these children are just as successful as other children when it comes to grades in elementary school. However, those kinds of unruliness can lead to trouble if they frustrate teachers enough.

Years ago, in a pivotal demonstration of how this can play out, Harvard social psychologist Robert Rosenthal and his collaborator Eleanor Jacobsen, a schoolteacher, showed how malleable a teacher's view of a child really is. Rosenthal and Jacobsen gave children in a Chicago public school a paper-and-pencil test that is closely correlated with IQ. However, they told the teachers that it was part of a subtle and obscure test of children's thinking. They then mentioned casually that some of the children were real intellectual "bloomers," likely to make substantial intellectual strides in the coming months. Amazingly, those children, who had actually been chosen at random, did make significant intellectual strides.

When all of the kids were tested again at the end of the year, the children who had been tagged as "bloomers" had made significant gains on the IQ test. So, lesson number one: when teachers expect children to be smart, for whatever reason, children often become smarter. It's important to note that Rosenthal and Jacobsen spent a great deal of time in those classrooms and could detect no obvious or concrete difference in the way those bloomers were treated. In other words, there was no simple explanation for the phenomenon—teachers didn't give harder work to those kids or spend more time at their desks or even call on them more often. The expectations adults have of a child are, it seems, both enormously powerful and somewhat invisible.

You will recall that when Joseph Fagan tested the speed with which infants could absorb visual information, he had an excellent idea of how smart they would seem as seven-year-olds. But Fagan's test had an advantage over the more traditional scores. Whereas IQ tests seemed to favor certain ethnic and racial groups, Fagan's test did not. Some babies were quicker to turn their attention from one picture to another, but there were no differences as a function of what racial group a baby belonged to. This stands in stark contrast to the persistent finding that the average IQ score of a group of black children is almost always lower than the average IQ score of a group of white children. Keep in mind that the overall correlation between Fagan's test in infancy and more traditional IQ scores when the children were older was high. Yet the correlation did not hold up for all of the children. Either some of the white children were doing better as they got older, or some of the black children were doing worse as they got older, hence the group differences among older children, where none was found in infancy. What might explain this confusing pattern?

We're beginning to find out why the IQ test might be a weaker measure of intelligence for black children than it is for white children. In the past ten years or so, psychologists have learned something very important about what might depress the IQ scores of some students and how to remedy it. The gap between the average score of a group of black students and the average score of a group of white students has diminished somewhat in recent years. But it hasn't gone away or even halved. There are only two explanations for this, broadly speaking. The one promoted by Charles Murray and Richard Herrnstein in their book *The Bell Curve* is that underlying differences in ability account for the gap, and nothing will change that. But many psychologists (as well as geneticists) doubt this explanation, not simply because it is politically and socially distasteful but rather because it represents bad science. To begin with, we know next to nothing, so far, about the genetic underpinnings of intelligence. Intelligence might well be the expression of a cluster of abilities and skills caused by a wide variety of genes, rather than a single attribute determined by a single gene. Second, we know very little about the relationship between the genetic basis of race and intelligence. In other words, even though skin color is inherited and IQ also seems to a great extent to be inherited, those two facts tell us nothing about whether intelligence and skin color have any underlying genetic relationship. The difference in IQ between racial groups might be a result of something altogether different. This point is so important and so often misunderstood that it is worth illustrating with a few examples.

If you compare men who have had heart attacks with those who haven't, it turns out that the average height in the group who had heart attacks is lower than the average height of those who haven't. Does this mean that short men have more heart attacks than tall men? Does it mean that the gene for height comes hand-in-hand with a gene for blood pressure, cholesterol levels, or a predisposition to heart attacks? No. It means that older men are more likely to get heart attacks than younger men, and men shrink as they age. So what looks like a clue to an underlying genetic link is, in fact, nothing of the kind. Take a second example. People who live in temperate climates tend to get more colds in the winter. Thus, many of us come to believe that the cold weather actually causes sickness. Climate and colds are related, but not because one causes the other. Instead, one leads to the other. In cold weather, we spend more time with other people in close, unventilated spaces. Our immune systems become weakened because of the stress of staying warm. The winter weather does help explain our increased sickness, but it doesn't cause the common cold. Having black skin might mean you are less likely to get a high score on an

IQ test, but that doesn't mean that black people are not as smart as white people.

We are a long way from knowing what it is exactly about intelligence that is genetic and just as far from knowing what gene or genes might explain a person's intelligence. But imagine that you are a researcher who doubts that the lower IQ scores of black children can be explained as a genetic difference. What would you do? You'd begin to try to identify other explanations for the difference. And that is just what researchers have been doing in the past fifteen years or so.

Some of the causes of group differences in IQ have been hidden in plain sight, just waiting to be identified. Claude Steele, from Stanford University, knew that stereotypes not only influence the behavior of the stereotyper, but they also have a huge effect on those who have been stereotyped. He reasoned that a powerful social stereotype affects people in the stereotyped group, even when no stereotyping or prejudice is active or present. In other words, stereotyping is "in the air" and shapes people all the time. When it comes to students taking important tests that measure their ability and might determine their future, the threat of potential stereotyping is particularly menacing. Steele and his colleagues reasoned this way: black students might worry, when in a testing situation, that if they do not do well, they will strengthen people's erroneous stereotypes. Worrying about this keeps them from doing their best on the test. In the kind of demonstration every researcher longs for, Steele tried a very simple manipulation. He removed the threat by telling students at the beginning of the test that this particular test had never shown any differences between groups. He learned a few startling and important things. Removing the threat in that simple way dramatically improved the scores of black students taking the test.

Thus, while an IQ test might in fact accurately reflect a white student's intellectual ability, it might not be as good a measure of a black student's intellect. The fact that the black students' test scores could be improved with such a simple yet specific intervention is quite stunning. Since Steele's early studies showing this, researchers have followed up with equally important findings.

Steven Spencer and his colleagues reasoned that even if you assume that black students are not showing their true potential in a standard testing situation, that doesn't explain why those students continue to underperform in school. Spencer and his colleagues decided to try to remove the "threat in the air" from students' ongoing academic experiences. If those kinds of threats make it hard for a student to show his true ability on a test, why wouldn't they also hinder his performance in classes throughout school? Spencer contacted black students who had been accepted at Yale and told them that if they came to Yale, they would be part of an honors group within the college. During the next four years at Yale, the students in this group spent time together, talked about the issues facing black students on campus, and stayed connected. He tracked their success at Yale, compared with other black students with similar entering test scores who were not included in the group. Lo and behold, the black students in the group fared better when it came to grades than the others.

In a second version of this intervention, conducted at a junior high school in Connecticut, students were asked four times during the year to write a story about a personal value. These students also did better than students matched on race and test scores who did not write the essays. It seems that by supporting a minority student's sense of identity, you reduce the impact of stereotype threat.

Many students might not show their true potential during a test of their cognitive ability. Black students are not the only ones to experience stereotype threat. And there might be other invisible threats that depress a child's expression of cognitive ability. For those who run schools and design college admissions requirements, identifying those kinds of inhibitors and removing them are hugely important. But here's the twist: barring any powerful interventions, the same conditions that might influence a child's test score or his apparent intellectual ability when he is four years old are likely to go on shaping him throughout childhood.

People tend to think that internal characteristics are constant and somewhat impervious to change—the more biologically rooted the characteristic, the more resilient we think it is. For instance, although it is something of a fashion for adults to trace their neuroses to the kinds of parents they had, you rarely hear anyone suggest that the relationship a baby has with his mother might have something to do with how smart he will be. Yet it turns out that it does. Recent studies have shown that babies who are cuddled, touched, and even massaged as infants become smarter than babies who are not handled this way. Adele Diamond, eager to pinpoint exactly how important cuddling and touch might be to healthy development, found that keeping a mother rat from licking her pups for even an hour increases the pups' stress, causing the release of hormones that seem to inhibit their ability to learn. Simply put, rat pups who aren't licked are not as smart as pups who are. Does this mean that the more you cuddle your child, the smarter she will be? No, but it does mean that certain kinds of deprivation depress or limit a child from realizing her full potential. These kinds of studies remind us that what seems purely biological is not. Even the most intrinsic capacities are influenced by specific experiences, and biology is not set in stone. The inverse is also true. It would be wrong to assume that environment is always flexible. Biological characteristics can be changed, but environmental influences are often resistant to change.

As you will recall, psychologists Rosenthal and Jacobsen tested all of the children before identifying some as intellectual bloomers. Some of the children who had not been in the randomly selected group labeled as bloomers did make gains over the year in their IQ scores. These children were rated less favorably by the teachers at the end of the year. Teachers don't like to have their expectations violated. Again and again, educator Lisa Delpit encountered white teachers frustrated by the unruliness of their black students. Behavior that might otherwise be interpreted as engaged and enthusiastic is seen by the teacher through the lens of low expectations. Suddenly, an eagerly waving hand becomes a sign that a child cannot contain herself. A long, enthusiastic story about an adventure at home becomes a sign of a chaotic family or evidence that the child hasn't learned at home how to construct a good story. When a teacher responds to a child as if she is incapable, it is not simply that the child might feel bad about herself. The teacher often doesn't give that child the feedback she needs to expand her skills.

Sarah Michaels provides devastating examples of this in her research looking at how teachers respond to the stories children tell at circle time. When white children in a Boston classroom told stories, they conformed to the white teacher's idea of what a story should be. As a result, the teacher would nod and smile as the child spoke and then ask interested questions such as "Really, and what did your parents say when you popped out from behind the couch?" or "Did your brother know he was going to be alone in the boat?" Just the kind of questions that would lead the child to try to expand her thinking skills by filling in details, adding linguistic complexity, and providing perspective. On the other hand, when black children told stories that didn't fit the teacher's model of a story, the teacher would frown and hesitate. Sometimes, not knowing how to build on such an unfamiliar type of story, a teacher would say nothing at all. In some cases, rather than asking questions or showing interest, the teacher would simply correct the child's grammar. Michaels's research showed how these seemingly casual activities were providing white children but not black children with opportunities to expand their skills. It is easy to see how a teacher's mindset can, in turn, shape and mold a child's ensuing academic experience. So, although IQ is sturdy, negative expectations can become self-fulfilling prophecies. Race is one big source of negative expectations. So is poverty. On the face of it, research seems to indicate that rich kids are, on the whole, smarter than poor kids. But if you dig a little into the research, a slightly different picture emerges.

## Are Rich Kids Smarter?

Charles Murray of the infamous *Bell Curve* argued that smarter people have better jobs and make more money. Thus, from his perspective, it is not that wealth leads to certain behaviors or benefits that help children do well in school and maximize their intellectual potential. Instead, he argues, smarter people will always be richer than those who are less smart, because their intellect brings them success. But this is a ridiculous argument, since it is premised on the notion of a completely fair society in which intellect alone leads to professional and economic success. And yet researchers have found again and again that children who live in families with more financial resources have higher IQs. Why would this be true?

One large-scale study showed that children with more books, more art on their walls, more rooms, and, strangest of all, more *tools* in the home are likely to have higher IQ scores and do better in school. That should mean that if you go into a toddler's home and find lots of books, tools, and rooms, it's a good bet that the child growing up in that house will get higher scores on school-readiness tests at age five and get better marks in third grade than a similar child growing up in a house without as many books and tools. But does that mean that if a parent, eager to help her child flourish, buys more books, hangs more paintings on the wall, and borrows some tools, her little girl will get better test scores? A close look at the data suggests that those objects are a proxy for a kind of behavior that does explain differences in IQ—and that behavior is conversation.

Children who live in homes with more wealth talk differently and more with their parents than children who grow up with less money. Todd Hart and Betty Risley compared middle-class families to families living at or below the poverty line by tape-recording the interactions of forty-two families from the time the children were nine months old until they were three years old. Children whose parents were well educated and held professional-level jobs heard about 2,100 words per hour. Welfare children heard about 600 words an hour. By the time the subjects in the study were four years old, the middle-class children of professional families heard as many as 48 million words. In contrast, children in families on welfare heard as few as 13 million words.

The difference in language environment goes beyond sheer numbers. Children from families with more money heard a different kind of talk from that heard by children with less money. Parents from the wealthier families were more likely to talk about the world around them, to identify what was interesting, and to discuss what was worth noticing and worth remembering. Some parents seemed to provide their children with a running narration of experience and also encouraged their children to narrate experience. This measure, which Hart and Risley called "extra talk (non-business talk)," taken when children were three years old, had a 77-percent correlation with the Peabody Picture Vocabulary test at third grade. In other words, families that engaged in a lot of "extra talk" had children who were much more likely to succeed in school.

It is not clear why families with greater wealth do this more than families without money. It might be because families with more money tend to have gone to better schools and to have spent more time in school. Or it might be that families with more money are more likely to have jobs that involve a higher level of education and require more conversation, more exchange of information, and possibly more time in deliberation.

In one of the oddest theories about intelligence, Robert Zajonc argued that birth order was the single strongest determinant of a person's IQ. Firstborn children, he argued, are likely to be smarter than later-born children. At first blush, this seems almost silly. How could your position within a family explain anything about your intelligence? Do a woman's eggs get weaker as she produces more babies? But Zajonc's explanation for his prediction makes some sense and fits with other data.

Zajonc argued that the firstborn is likely to have the highest IQ within a family because he or she benefits from a richer intellectual environment than subsequent children. Imagine, he argued, that the average combined IQ of two adult parents is 200. The firstborn child received all the benefit of that combined IQ. But the next child, and those who come after, have to share that intellectual environment. So the firstborn gets to grow up in a 200 IQ environment, while the later-born children are developing in a 100 IQ environment (200, the parents' IQ score, divided by two children). The formula is so simple it's almost hokey. But the logic behind it is backed up by other research. It is not that somehow the parental genes for intelligence get thinner or weaker with each child. Instead, each child, in theory, experiences a more diluted intellectual environment. Think of it in terms of any big family you know. The parents probably talked quite a bit to their firstborn, discussing what their little boy could see out the window, answering his questions about why his milk turned pink when he ate Lucky Charms, and asking him what was going to happen to the ice cube if he left it lying on the floor. But the third or fourth child in a busy household is much less likely to hear and be part of those kinds of exchanges. So, in fact, later-born children grow up in a somewhat weaker intellectual environment.

Interestingly enough, Zajonc's formula predicts that a child who is born a long time after the last one benefits from his position in the family. Why would this be so? Because if you have three much older siblings, your intellectual environment reflects the IQ of five grown-ups, not two diluted ones. Your much older brother and sister talk to you the way an adult would.

Zajonc's research is so parsimonious it is hard to accept. Everyone can think of exceptions—the twenty-four-year-old who is brighter than her twenty-five-year-old brother, the one born eight years later who is not as bright as his three much older siblings, and so on. But the logic behind his formula fits perfectly with all of the data showing that children benefit from conversation. When parents use talk as a way of reflecting on and making sense of the world around them, a child's intelligence benefits. And the data suggest that families with economic resources engage in more of this kind of conversation. So being rich does not make you smart, but having more wealth might be tied to having more conversation, which contributes significantly to a child's intelligence. In other words, the bank account itself does not explain wealthier children's advantage in school—what the bank account provides explains it.

Children do benefit from the intellectual environment created at home—and for children who grow up with their biological families, that environment tends to be an expression or an amplification of their genes. As I described earlier, smart families are likely to create smart environments. This is not only true for parents. Developmental psychologist Sandra Scarr followed adopted children as they grew up and found that children create their own environments—she called it "niche picking." Imagine two children within a family who seem, from day one, to be really different. One child, Emmanuel, learns to talk at an early age and loves words. It is clear almost immediately that he is attuned to the conversations around him and quick to use new vocabulary, try out verbal expressions, and tell stories. His brother, Dwight, seems more visual right from the beginning. Whenever he can, he uses toys to make patterns, buildings, and other visual displays. He seems to notice details in whatever room he enters. Even if Emmanuel and Dwight share the same parents and the same bedroom, go to the same family celebrations, attend the same nursery school, and spend their weekends on the same playground, they will experience substantively different environments. While Emmanuel listens to his parents' conversation, sits in rapt attention while his uncle tells a story, and creates elaborate stories when he is with his playmates, Dwight is oblivious to the conversation, spending his time instead taking all of the silverware and making a giant pattern with it, watching his grandfather repair the cabinet, and making patterns with colored blocks. These two children are, in effect, creating their own intellectual environment. Whatever it was they were born with, in terms of cognitive ability and style, leads them to notice, seek out, and immerse themselves in particular facets of the world around them. Emmanuel will grow up in a more language-rich environment than Dwight, who, in contrast, will grow up in a more visually rich environment than his brother.

Understanding what makes up a child's intelligence does not require parsing out the genetic component and the environmental component. Genes only express themselves within a particular environment. You can't be smart without questions, tools, and people to be smart with. But the questions, tools, and people you pick up on are shaped, in part, by your intelligence. Especially in the case of children who are raised by their biological parents, the IQs they get through their genes are often merely amplified by the IQs that surround them in their homes. The smart mom who has a large vocabulary provides her child not only with her genes but also with the kind of language-rich environment that enhances her child's native capacity.

## Sign of Intelligence

What does this all mean for your child? To begin with, it means that your child's intelligence is likely to be similar to yours (and by the way, most research shows that people are likely to marry someone of similar intelligence, so you needn't fret too much about whether your child will get your wonderful IQ or your mate's lowly IQ).

It also means that in many ways, you need not try to disentangle what your child brings in the way of intellectual capabilities from what you provide her with. All things considered, these are likely to be of a piece. There are some dramatic exceptions— children who might have tested very highly on Fagan's test of infant speed of processing but who grow up without fundamental resources such as adequate nutrition or regular attendance at a reasonable school are likely to seem less intelligent than they otherwise would. After a while, if you seem less intelligent, you are less intelligent. IQ is not simply a capacity; it is a pathway. Each step leads you farther in one direction and away from another. The child who feels smart seeks out stimulating aspects of the environment. The child who feels that others don't think he's smart begins to inhibit his performance, further lowering other people's expectations, and so on.

I have said a lot about the stability of a child's intelligence. But I have said little about how a parent knows whether his child is smart or not. After all, as I mentioned earlier, many, if not most, children *seem* smart to their parents, and few people have their child's IQ tested, nor should they. It rarely helps. If your child is very bright, the chances are that you and his teachers already know it. Getting a number can only send you into a tizzy of needless enrichment activities, pushing teachers in ways that don't help, or aggravating your friends by finding subtle ways to tell them how high your child's IQ is. If your child's IQ score is lower than yours, or than most kids', you might unwittingly transmit that information to your child. And as we have seen, lowered expectations usually only make matters worse. For most kids, most of the time, IQ tests aren't necessary. You usually can tell if a child is smart, if you know what to pay attention to. Children who learn new information easily, can solve problems, can create objects and ideas, and can understand complex situations are smart. Children who struggle with more than one of these challenges are less smart.

The one caveat to this is when a child is having trouble in school and you want to know whether it is because she has a learning disability. IQ scores, handled properly, can sort out the difference between a problem learning to read and a general intellectual deficit, which brings us back to Stevie.

Stevie took in information quickly, especially visual information. He could look at a structure and quickly build one just like it. He could watch someone put a toy together and quickly take over adding new parts himself. He could walk into a room and tell you, hours later, the color of the furniture or a picture that was hanging on the wall. When he wanted to make something, if he didn't have the right materials, he could find a substitute and finish his project. That is, he was quick to process information, he could solve problems, and he could fashion products valuable to his community. But this was only when he was interested in the problem he needed to solve or cared about the thing he was making.

Only recently have developmental researchers begun to take seriously the idea that interest is a crucial component of the learning process. When babies are given objects to play with, they spend more time and, more important, use a wider variety of gestures to explore an object for which they have shown a prior interest. In another study, children who got to read stories about domains in which they had demonstrated a sustained interest actually learned more about and from the story. Teachers often try to elicit interest in academic tasks by making sure stories and activities relate to things that are, in general, child-friendly (a story about a kid who gets hooked on drugs for the preteen, a math activity that involves counting koala bears instead of colored rods for first-graders). But scholars who focus on interest are talking about something that goes beyond making a topic lively or superficially relevant to children. Research has shown that from a very early age, children often show intense and sustained interest in one activity or domain (bridges, puzzles, or bugs, for example). And it's also becoming clear that children actually behave in smarter ways when they are using the materials or engaging in the activities that most interest them. In one elegant demonstration of this, Suzanne Hidi gave toddlers objects to play with. Some of the children were given objects in which they had shown a prior interest (cars, dolls, various puzzles), while others were given objects in which they had shown no particular prior interest. When the toddlers were allowed to play with things in which they had a prior interest, they played for longer and used a wider range of gestures. So, it's not just nice to let a kid learn what she is drawn to. It's the best way to help her develop her intellect and make use of her intellectual potential.

Unfortunately, Stevie didn't find it easy to focus on the things that interested him. But it wasn't because he had a hard time focusing. It was because everyone around him was telling him he should do better in school, read more, apply himself, and talk more. His teachers and his parents wanted him to excel at things that didn't interest him and disregarded the activities and materials that did interest him. If a child seems highly motivated and intelligent in some domain, trying to push him to be well rounded or to excel in a more obviously marketable or appealing arena probably won't do any good and might just keep him from pursuing the activities in which he really does shine. In Stevie's case, his stubbornness was his best friend and his worst enemy. He began to act as if he didn't care what teachers said about him. He began to channel his resistance into rebellion and a determination not to follow the conventional path the adults in his life preferred. By the time he was seven, his parents were extremely alarmed that he hadn't learned to read. His mother gave him a dictionary for his birthday, even though he showed a clear disinterest in reading and writing. "For our little scholar," her card read. Then she transferred him to a stricter school, a school he hated.

Stevie was smart. And he was also stubborn. He resisted his parents' rules. One school day, it snowed, and Stevie didn't have boots that fit. His mother insisted that he wear an old pair of his sister's ski boots. He felt ashamed—he'd look silly arriving at his fourth-grade class in cumbersome ski boots. He walked out the front door as if he had agreed to his mother's injunction. But instead of continuing the five-block walk to his school, he wandered slowly around the block several times. After he had calculated that it was too late for him to go to school, he came back home. He had won. But his mother's sense that he wasn't up to snuff permeated the atmosphere. His teachers agreed, and Stevie began his journey away from anything with the whiff of schools or books on it.

With each year, his grades went down. Stevie became quieter, both at school and at home. A teacher in fourth grade wrote, "Steven needs to get hold of himself if he intends to achieve anything." His interests went underground, but they didn't go away. He began college at a conventional school—not the Ivy League school his parents would have preferred, which by then was inaccessible to him, but still a conventional academically oriented college. He hated it and transferred to art school. His parents refused to pay, appalled by his lack of academic focus. So he began working in a graphic design shop. By the time Stevie was twenty-five, he had succeeded on his own terms. He was an expert in graphic design, cabinetry, and printmaking. His intellect had taken the shape of the things he cared about. Along the way, however, the barrage of conventional expectations kept him from exploring things he might otherwise have delved into. The wall he built to keep out his critics also kept out interesting sources of information and inspiration and the expansion of his repertoire.

Stevie was smart when he was four, and he stayed smart. A child cannot get smart. Nor can he lose his smartness. However, a child's intellect takes shape in the company of other powerful forces. Some of those forces are inside the child (specific interest, motivation, and a sense of self-efficacy). Other forces exist outside the child (poverty level, social dynamics, and family events). If you had met Stevie when he was six, you might not have known that he was smart. You might not have known which clues to pay attention to. The clues about Stevie are buried in the stories of his childhood, but his parents missed those clues, which had repercussions.

Stevie's mother had been thrown by how different he seemed from her other children. And he could be so stubborn, so unwilling to do the things the other children seemed happy to do. When he didn't like what an adult asked him, he'd say, "Aren't talking," and fall into a long silence. To his mother, this was just more proof of Stevie's lack of verbal acumen.

When his kindergarten teacher noted that he had lost his steam for woodworking, his mom was dismayed. She believed that children need high standards, that even at five, it meant something when a child didn't do his best. And she was not sure what Stevie's best was anymore. The next afternoon, when he came home from school, she told him about the note.

"Miss Allen says you have lost interest in the woodworking area. That you don't try hard. She says you just smash two pieces of wood together and don't even hammer in the nail carefully. I know you are good with the hammer. What's going on?"

Stevie shrugged and looked away. He didn't like being questioned this way. "Nothing," he answered.

His mother felt sure that he just needed to be pushed, held to high standards, and she had a sharp tongue. She didn't believe in talking down to young children. She herself had been guided by a mixture of behaviorism and Dr. Spock (be firm and reasonable, and your reasonable child will accept your rules).

"Stevie, you have to try your best at school. I can't believe you are satisfied doing such shoddy work."

Stevie paused, still looking away. His mother came on strong, and he had learned to recede within, to disconnect from her. He answered diffidently, "I said I wanted to make a dog house for Sparky. Miss Allen said I couldn't. She said that was too big a project. So every day, I just tack together two pieces of wood and bring them home. Soon I'll have enough wood here at home to make the dog house."

## Red Herrings

What would you do if you were Stevie's parent? His mother saw worrisome signs: disinterest in his work, a detachment from school, an unwillingness to cooperate with the goals adults set for him, and difficulty with reading. But the reassuring signs were there, too: Stevie was born smart. He had intelligent parents. He lived in a house filled with books, art, and tools and the conversations for which those things are a token. He had the stubbornness to seek out access to the activities and materials in which he had an interest.

A child who is fundamentally bright is very likely going to stay that way. And it would have done Stevie's parents a lot of good to relax a little about him—focusing on his great strengths instead of the red herrings. In fact, to the extent that their worry expressed itself as a low expectation ("Stevie's not that smart"), it might have become a self-fulfilling expectation for Stevie. Let's put it this way: the best thing for a child is to be around adults who think he is likely to bloom intellectually. Most of the time, when parents feel disappointed in a child's performance in school, what comes across to the child is the disappointment, not the sense that he or she is actually capable of more. What children often seem to sense is that their parents are worried that they are not smart. Teachers who think a child is not smart are also likely to have a dampening effect on a child's future academic success. And this brings us to the heart of the matter. For all intents and purposes, whether your child is smart or not, she's likely to stay that way. But how adults respond to her can make it easy for her intellect to find avenues of expression. This can lead her down a path of intellectual realization or can put roadblocks in her way that make her feel, and then behave, less intelligently than she might be capable of.

And why does it matter if your child is smart? Remember that the first intelligence test was created simply to make sure that children who were unusually slow were not punished for having trouble learning. Geniuses almost always announce themselves—you don't need to be tested to show that you are forty points smarter than other people. And as Malcolm Gladwell has argued in his book *Outliers,* above a certain level of intelligence, the difference doesn't, for the most part, matter when it comes to outstanding achievement. Children who get the highest IQ scores are not necessarily destined for a life of greatness, and children who have average intelligence are not doomed to an average life.

As I will explain in Chapter 5, success depends on a lot of things besides intelligence. However, it would be silly to discount intelligence altogether. In our society, the child who has an IQ score of 140 is going to be attracted to math or books in a way that a child with an IQ of 115 might not be. But the point is that you don't need to subject your child to an expensive and tiresome test to find this out. Most children who have an IQ score of 140 act as if they do. They seek out information, they like learning things, they solve problems more easily and creatively than others, and they analyze situations with acuity. Parents might simply learn what that looks like in the six-year-old, for two reasons. First, if your child is subjected to negative stereotypes, you can push against those stereotypes. Hank's mother had better make sure his teachers know the difference between unruly and stupid. He might knock the glass over, tap his finger during a lesson, or defy an adult's request, but none of these has anything to do with his intellect. A teacher had better know that her unconscious negative stereotype about black children needs to be examined and that she needs to take concrete steps to counteract that stereotype.

Second, on the positive side, the more aware you are of your child's expressions of intellectual liveliness, the more likely you are to encourage her, giving her a chance at a positive self-fulfilling prophecy. But here we need to draw a line. There is currently an epidemic, particularly in the white middle class, of parents eager to identify their children as gifted. Everyone wants his or her child to be in the program for gifted and talented children at school. It's not always clear whether it's because these parents think their children's needs are not being met in the regular classroom, whether they have a hunch that livelier and more engaging activities, things that would be appealing to any child, are going on in the gifted and talented program, or whether they want to make sure their children have an edge over everyone else when it comes to college. But in truth, not that many children are gifted, if gifted means exceptional. By definition, there are few exceptions. Few children fall outside the normal range of intelligence. Moreover, focusing on your child's exceptional ability encourages a kind of preciousness and competitiveness that isn't good for anyone.

Whether a child is of average intellect or on the high end, providing him with chances to pursue his interests, offering plenty of "nonbusiness" talk, and surrounding him with books that you and he actually read are the best support you can offer. The rest will take care of itself.

## 2

# Friendships: The Fate of Lonely Children

One day when she was six years old, Abby came home from school and handed her mother, Meg, a picture she had made. Her drawing showed two large hearts and several smaller ones. She had drawn different kinds of lines connecting the hearts—some were solid, some jagged, and some broken.

"This is my heart," she said, pointing to one of the figures. "And this is Selena's," she continued, pointing to the second large heart. "The other hearts are our friends. These lines show you what my life is like."

All of the smaller hearts were connected by strong lines to Selena's heart. But all of the lines connecting the smaller hearts to Abby's were broken lines. The one line that directly connected Selena's heart to Abby's had a spear point on the end, and it was piercing Abby's heart, which was divided by fractured lines.

"My heart is shattered. Even if we make up, it can't be glued together again."

Abby was a smart and precocious little girl. Like her mother, who was an epidemiologist, Abby was quick to analyze a situation, detect inconsistencies, and construct a complex argument about something. She learned new information easily and excelled in her class work. Devastated by the social dynamics of first-grade girls, she used her keen mind to try to figure out her friendships. Her drawing offered a vivid picture of how Abby perceived her social world, which had always been vexed.

When Abby was little, she was not one of the cute, popular girls, and that didn't change much in the next few years. Even by eleven, she hadn't yet outgrown a slightly ungainly physique. Her hair lay flat against her neck, and when she spoke, you could tell she was self-conscious about her overbite. She often spoke a little too loudly at the dinner table, going on after others had lost interest in what she was saying. Her mother would remind her to let others have a chance to talk.

She did not have an easy time with other little girls. And to little boys, she was just invisible. In second and third grade, she was often left out at recess time, or she'd be invited to a party and then, when she arrived, excluded by the other girls. One friend, Gretchen, organized a yearly summer talent show where the girls competed against one another with song, dance, and other acts. Abby was always invited and then told by the other girls that her acts were lousy. Eventually, she began to believe them, but she still prepared an act each year, as if her life depended on it.

As is often the case with social dynamics like this, she was part of the problem. Quick to point out her friends' moral lapses, she would get visibly angry when they didn't treat her well. When she was ten, she was given the job of putting away the tennis rackets at the club where she took lessons and played. One day, she left a note in large capital letters on the blackboard in the tennis shed, addressed to a slightly older girl, one of the best and most popular players at the club: "JESSICA: YOU SHOULD TAKE BETTER CARE OF YOUR EQUIPMENT!"

It seems obvious, looking at this from the outside, that publicly chastising the older, more powerful girl was a bad way for Abby, a younger girl fairly new to the club, to break into the group. But Abby either didn't realize this or didn't care.

Abby's mother couldn't decide whether to point out to Abby that the blackboard message would probably backfire. And she wondered how significant it was that Abby had made such a blunder. Did the abrasive message on the board foreshadow an ongoing problem for Abby? Would Abby always have trouble with friends?

From the moment your child can walk and talk, you look for signs that she can get along with other kids. Some parents, probably the gregarious among us, simply expect that their children will like other children and be liked by them as well. Some parents, the shy or socially awkward, are a little more anxious and watchful than that. They monitor, out of the corner of their eyes, whether their child is invited to swing at the park or is standing at the center of the liveliest group at a birthday party. Any parent might feel a little twinge of anxiety if she arrives to pick up her three-year-old son at day care and finds him standing off by himself while the others are happily building blocks together. Is he destined to be a loner? Why don't the other kids invite him to play? Why does he isolate himself?

If you are a parent who feels that little twinge of worry when your child doesn't seem to be in the center of action, you're not alone, and you're not off base. Having friends is a hugely important part of childhood and one of the key indicators of a child's future well-being. A vast array of research has shown that children who have trouble with other children are more likely to have trouble as adults. Lonely and rejected children are at much greater risk for depression when they get older and, in fact, are at heightened risk for depression even when they are young. Aggressive children are at much greater risk for various kinds of problems with society when they are older. In other words, a child who doesn't have friends as a seven-year-old is less likely to have friends as a grown-up. She's also more likely to become depressed and/or to get into all kinds of trouble in adulthood.

If you have a child who is never chosen to be on a team during school sports, is often the one not invited to the birthday party, or has no one to sit with at lunch, it's pure agony—both for her and for you. As one eleven-year-old who was excluded, again and again, from the group of girls at her school said to her mother, "I'm not going. I'm not going to school ever again. I don't care if I can't go to college, if I never get a job. You can just forget it. Nothing would make it worth going back in to face those kids again. I'd rather die."

Not every child is so honest and articulate about his or her social struggles. And it's not always easy to know when a child is simply going through a difficult stretch with his friends and when his behavior indicates a real problem. You may think that when he comes home sad or mad about his friends, he's overreacting or that his frustration will pass quickly. If he's made similar complaints since he was very little, you might just assume that this is what happens to all little kids. You might even vaguely remember it happening to you and wonder why he cares so much. You seemed to get through it, and you're OK, so you assume he will be, too.

Every child has fights now and then with friends or goes through a brief period when he feels left out or unfairly targeted by others. But for some children, this problem becomes persistent—a defining characteristic of daily life. Somewhere between 10 and 30 percent of all school children are chronic victims of peer aggression. Even more worrisome, as it turns out, about 25 percent of the children who are continually victimized are also physically aggressive toward others.

Is there any objective way to know whether a child is just having a bad day or really has trouble with friends? The concerned parent faces two obstacles in answering that question. The first is that it can be difficult to see your own child objectively. A six-year-old comes home sad because he wasn't chosen for the kickball team at recess. One father might be outraged and worried, immediately certain that his little boy is doomed, destined to be left out of the group of cool boys for the rest of his school days. Another father, faced with a son who seems quickly to drop out of each group he tries to join, year after year, in summer camp as well as school, explains away each incident as an isolated event.

But parents face a second obstacle when it comes to understanding what is going on in their children's social lives. How does an adult find out about a child's social standing? You hear about your child's day only from your child. You have no real way of knowing how she is viewed by others. And it's not just parents who find it hard to scope out a child's social position. Psychologists face the same challenge. If being liked by others is so essential to a child's well-being, how might researchers find out who is liked and who is not?

## Measuring Friendship

Unfortunately, the most obvious method—asking—is not the most reliable way to find out. Children are not necessarily good sources of information about their own popularity (any more than adults are). Although moderately well-liked children usually know that they are, certain kinds of children who are not well liked seem oblivious to the fact. So self-reports might gloss over the very kids you'd most want to know about.

A second, seemingly obvious source of information about a child's social skills is teacher evaluations. It makes sense for a concerned parent to ask a teacher if the child seems to have friends at school, and good teachers often do have an accurate feel for who is liked and who is not liked. However, there are limits to this source of information. For one thing, plenty of teachers are not that in touch with their students and don't really know what's going on. For another, a lot of the social dynamics of school-aged children happen outside the teacher's view. Knowing this, Canadian psychologist Debra Pepler and her colleagues placed a video camera in a playground at a suburban school and fitted the school children with tiny microphones attached to their clothes. The kids kept this equipment on for days, no matter what they were doing, until they had forgotten they were wearing it. Pepler and her colleagues were able to gain a sneak peek into how kids really treat one another when they aren't being supervised. When it comes to finding out about children's fights, this seems incredibly important. Kids, like adults, are much less likely to pick on another child when they know an adult is watching. Pepler and her colleagues found that the most aggressive children (based on separate measures of social behavior) said mean or incendiary things to other kids once every three minutes and hit or physically taunted other children once every eight minutes. Mind you, the more popular, sociable children were no angels—engaging in verbal aggression once every five minutes and physical aggression once every eleven minutes. It's pretty clear that kids are mean to one another and that some kids have more trouble than others (as victims and/or as aggressors). But this only provides information about the most external level of the problem, the kinds of aggression that come out in moments of conflict on the playground. Clearly, there are subtler dynamics at work throughout the day, which might help explain the relationships Abby so vividly diagrammed in her drawing of hearts.

For years, psychologists were stumped. How could they get an objective measure of something as subjective as how much a child is liked or disliked by others in her classroom? The solution, it turns out, is reminiscent of James Thurber's classic children's book

*Many Moons.* When the king is desperate to fulfill his daughter Lenore's sickbed wish for the moon, he asks all of the kingdom's wisest men what to do. They come up with lots of complicated yet absurd solutions. Finally, the court jester makes a suggestion that seems ridiculously simple: ask Lenore how to do it. Sure enough, asking Lenore solves the problem. In the 1980s, researchers, eager to know how children were viewed by one another, came up with a similar solution: ask the children what they think about one another.

In the past twenty years, psychologists have developed an intriguing and somewhat controversial way to measure a child's social standing, called sociometrics. To some extent, the measure just transforms what most kids naturally do anyway into a formal procedure, gauging a particular child's social worth by computing just how much the other kids like him or her. The experimenter asks each child in a given classroom to name the children he or she likes best and least. As it turns out, there is often a pattern: children in a group tend to agree on who is most likable, who is least likable, and who isn't worth rating at all.

But this popularity measure is not without its critics. Two potential weaknesses stand out in particular. First of all, there is a statistical weakness. What if a child is very popular with some kids and not at all popular with others? She will get pretty much the same score as a child who is moderately popular with everyone. And it doesn't take much knowledge of children to know that those two kids have a very different experience of daily life.

The other problem is a bit harder to get a handle on. Some parents (and ethical review boards) worry that gathering these data stirs up trouble and encourages kids to label one another. Perhaps when the experimenter asks a child who is really popular in her class, some little girl will begin to ruminate on how unpopular she is. However, the worry that such research stirs up problems ignores the reality of children's social lives. Most children don't go a full morning without thinking about and discussing who is good-looking, who is smart, who is gross, and who is cool. Children evaluate one another all the time. And of course, even if conducting such a study causes passing discomfort to a few children, it's worth it if it allows researchers to figure out how to keep bullies from bullying and rejected children from getting left out.

## The Loner

Studies using sociometrics have revealed some striking, though not altogether surprising, patterns. Children who are consistently rated as unappealing and unpopular by their classmates have real problems—problems that persist. If your daughter is rejected by the other children at school again and again, she is not only likely to be miserable while she is enduring such brutal rejection, but she is also at risk for emotional problems later in her life. Children who are rejected are more likely to become seriously depressed as they get older.

When Sasha's third-grade teacher would look out the window during recess to check on his students, the first thing he would check to see was whether Sasha was finally playing with some of the other children or still standing alone. Each day, he would spot her, leaning on the pole of the swing set, twirling the rope on one of the swings. It wasn't easy to tell whether she was lost in a daydream, idly enjoying the breeze and the movement of the swing as she twisted it, or waiting, tentative and anxious, for one of the little clusters of kids to invite her in. When the children paired up to work on a mosaic project, there were just enough for twelve pairs. Yet the twenty-third child joined another pair rather than work with Sasha.

The teacher, Mr. Sanjit, had been talking with Sasha's mother all year. Sasha's parents knew she didn't have friends and felt angry that the school allowed her to feel so left out. Mr. Sanjit didn't quite know how to handle it. In his eight years of teaching, he had come to feel that you couldn't do much to change a kid's style of interacting. Watching different groups of children year after year, he saw that some children seemed to have a built-in mechanism for doing or saying just the wrong thing to other kids.

Mr. Sanjit had suggested to Sasha's mother that Sasha didn't seem to know how to connect to the other children. She would say things that just missed the mark. The other kids found her odd. When you are nine years old, being funny, energetic, and clued in to the reactions of other children is your ticket of admission. But it was as if the group was singing in C major and Sasha was singing in D minor. One day, after a difficult math lesson, Mr. Sanjit put on a CD of "The Macarena" and suggested that they enjoy the music for a little while. The children jumped up with glee and began dancing. Many of them knew the specific moves for the music and began to dance in unison. Even the ones who didn't know "The Macarena" got the beat and began swinging their butts, mirroring one another's moves. To the other kids, this was an invitation to party, something they had in common. But it was as if Sasha didn't recognize the invitation. She twirled around with a gentle sway to her body, as if she were hearing waltz music, slightly apart from the others. Mr. Sanjit would never have allowed the other children to make fun of her. But they didn't need to. They just ignored her. And that can be almost as bad.

Sasha's parents were very frustrated with Mr. Sanjit. Why didn't he do something to make things better for Sasha? And that raises a big question. Can teachers change the way children treat one another?

## Can Teachers Fix Friendships?

There is no question that a teacher can create a certain atmosphere in his classroom. He can make it clear that overt meanness is not tolerated. Vivian Paley, the legendary nursery-school teacher and author from the Lab School in Chicago, made a rule one year in her preschool classroom: You can't say you can't play. A teacher widely known for encouraging play, imagination, and the free expression of children's inner thoughts, Paley decided to tell the children there was one thing she insisted on that year: the children could not exclude anyone from their play. If two children were in the dress-up corner playing Mommy and Daddy and another child wandered over hoping to join, they had to find a way to include her. It took a lot of time and energy not only to enforce the rule but also to help the children figure out how to resist exclusion and incorporate others into their stories and games. Paley claimed that by the end of the year, the children were kinder and more inclusive to one another. By creating a simple but dramatic rule, one that spoke in actions, not in talk, she created a norm and changed the way the children related to one another. Perhaps most teachers expect children to be mean and therefore subtly tolerate it in ways that perpetuate the meanness. If, on the other hand, a teacher assumes that children want to be decent to one another and simply need some gentle steering along the way, it can have a big impact.

The fifteen children in the second-grade class at the Hoboken, New Jersey, public school were a harmonious bunch. They seemed to like one another, and they liked their young teacher, Catlin Preston. He described them as a focused group, ready to plunge into school life. They held lively discussions during meeting time, solved problems, shared tasks, and worked at the wide array of projects and materials available to them in his small chock-filled classroom—observing the pet rats, making muffins for snack time, solving math problems, building with blocks in the block area, and writing poems on a computer.

"They were not an unruly group, as I've had other years, and they seemed unusually cohesive, right from the start," he said.

That is why he was so surprised when, in November, he became aware of the "Mortal Enemy Club." About six of the kids had formed a club during their daily recess time outdoors, away from Catlin's watchful eye. The primary purpose of the Mortal Enemy Club was to spy on and exclude one particular child. To be honest, the teacher couldn't see much ill will or fighting stemming from the club. But parents knew about the club, and they were upset. They called him to complain. He agreed that exclusive clubs could lead to no good.

Catlin typically used the children's work time to wander around the room, offering a word of advice or a helping hand, but mostly, he used this time to observe. Holding a clipboard and a digital camera, he walked from one activity area to another, jotting down what children were doing and talking about. Sometimes he photographed their work (for instance, a tall block skyscraper, a marble maze constructed from small plastic interlocking pieces, or a painting) so that they could show the other children what they had made during the meeting time that followed work time.

After learning about the club, Catlin did a little extra nosing around, asking the kids a few questions, listening to their conversations, and watching. He learned that a little boy had started the Mortal Enemy Club several weeks earlier because he was sure that one of his buddies had stolen a ship made from Legos while playing at his house. The members of the club would spy on the accused thief by following him around to watch his activities. If the little boy spoke to any of the spies, asking what they wanted, they would turn and quickly, silently walk away. Catlin said the club was not obvious to a casual observer: "You had to have heard about it, or pay careful attention, to see it in action."

Three thoughts guided Catlin as he mulled over how to end the club. Because the class had seemed to be such a well-functioning group in the first place, he felt confident that they could get past the problem without too much intervention. He also knew that the little boy who was the target of Mortal Enemy Club was "forceful, a gung-ho kid, not fragile." Finally, Catlin reminded himself of a premise he felt was central to working with elementary-school children: each of them is a "reasonable person." From what he had seen and heard, the club members were just "caught inside their own motivation." To them, it made very good sense to organize together against a "Lego thief," to show their solidarity with one another and express their disapproval of the other boy. "It just hadn't occurred to them to think about the effect their club might have on the outsider," Catlin said. Seven-year-olds can be inconsistent. When a child acts aggressively, that doesn't mean he actually wants another child to feel bad.

Catlin decided to count on their reasonableness and talk with them. But he wanted to surprise his students a little and make them think in a new way. "So I called a meeting of the club members and invited the 'enemy' to join us. I might not have done that," he said, "if the boy himself hadn't seemed so sturdy."

Once they were gathered on the rug in the meeting area, Catlin asked the boy whether he was aware of the club.

"I knew about the club, and I knew why they started it," the second-grader said. When asked how it made him feel, he shrugged and answered, "It made me feel lousy." But he didn't seem overly upset. Then the little boy looked directly at the other kids and added, "I didn't steal the ship. I only took it apart. If you had ever asked me, I would have told you."

Catlin addressed the club members: "What would you do if I told you right now that there was a new club, whose whole point was to keep you out?"

That was all it took, Catlin said. The kids seemed a bit taken aback by his question, and they readily agreed to dissolve the Mortal Enemy Club.

Things were fine for about six weeks. No clubs. Then a new little girl, Shonda, joined the class. She had played with some of the kids in an after-school program and was already friends with quite a few of them. However, within a week of her arrival in the class, Catlin found out that a group of students had started the "I Hate Shonda Club." They didn't actually exclude her from anything. They just periodically reminded one another of their club membership. Once again, a meeting was held, and the outsider was invited in. That was in January. During the spring, some of the children formed rock-finding clubs and animal clubs. But as far as Catlin could tell, there were no more enemies.

The children in Catlin's classroom seemed to lapse periodically into the kind of ganging up that many of us remember or read about in *Lord of the Flies*. With some well-timed intervention by a teacher the children loved and admired, the kids were easily guided toward a more gentle and inclusive way of operating. The Mortal Enemy Club incident was a red herring for those in the club and those outside it—it signaled little about the club members or their victim.

But Sasha, on the other hand, was left out again and again. And while a skilled adult can steer a group of kids away from bullying, that doesn't mean a teacher can make children like a kid they don't like. And here is one of the most painful truths for parents of a child who is left out: almost invariably, the child is doing something that is causing her to be left out. But what do children like Sasha do that makes other kids exclude them?

With some kids, like Sasha, it's not easy to put your finger on the behavior that pushes other children away. She wasn't mean, she wasn't loud, she didn't look for trouble in any way. She just seemed tuned out. Psychologists refer to these children as rejected-withdrawn. When teachers have a student like Sasha, they often have a hard time knowing whether she pulls herself away from the group or the other kids keep her out. The bad vibe is subtle for kids like Sasha. But the effects are not subtle. As they get older, children like Sasha are at a much greater risk for depression. What researchers haven't figured out is whether underlying depression causes the problem in the first place or the social isolation they suffer causes the later depression. However, some preliminary work with interviews and diaries suggests that children like Sasha experience real sadness and isolation even when they are young. She might have seemed unaware of what was going on around her, but she probably was very much aware of how her separation from the group was making her feel. Even when Sasha wasn't wandering around the edges of the classroom, she seemed droopy and slightly sad.

Mr. Sanjit encouraged Sasha's parents to invite a child over after school to play with her. Sometimes a kid like Sasha can forge a bond with one child, which acts like a bridge when they are back in school—a passageway to more group interaction. But—and here's the kicker—as often as not, a child who has trouble relating to other children has a parent who also has trouble relating to other people. Often, they don't even know how to help their child make friends.

Steve Asher described a parent who approached him after he gave a public lecture on children's friendships. The father was concerned because his child was being left out at school, and the teacher had recommended that the parents try to help their son make friends.

Asher said to the father, "So, what does your son like to do when he's with other kids his age?"

The father said, "How would I know that?" He seemed perplexed about how one would go about making such a judgment.

As Asher talked to the father more, it became clear that he had no clue about his son's social life and little idea about what might go into finding new friends or developing interests that would attract new friends. How could he help his son when he wasn't so sure how to make friends himself?

Sasha's parents made a few attempts to invite other little girls over. But those dates didn't seem to extend themselves. When I asked Mr. Sanjit about it, he said the parents seemed to invite kids at random, not necessarily the ones Sasha might actually get along with. He got no sense of what the girls did at Sasha's house, partly because the parents didn't have a sense of it, either. Sasha didn't become better friends with those girls in school, and she didn't seem to change her way of operating in the classroom. The get-togethers didn't change anything. Sasha remained alone. Eventually, she left the school. The last Mr. Sanjit heard, she was having similar difficulties in her next school. And she went on seeming depressed.

If Sasha's parents had created situations in which she could become friends with another little girl or two, away from the school environment, it might have helped. If they had found out from Mr. Sanjit who might become a friend for Sasha and invited that child over for projects and small outings, situations where they could gently guide the girls to become closer, it might have created a scaffold on which Sasha could build. But because they were somewhat clueless themselves socially, such help was not in the cards. In their situation, the best thing probably would have been to take Sasha to a child therapist, someone warm and skilled at forging a bond with children. It's possible that by creating a friendship with a therapist, Sasha would build up a base from which to connect to other children.

## Lonely Bullies

Not all children who are left out are sad and quiet like Sasha. Some rejected children also behave, oddly enough, like bullies. And these kids have even bigger problems in store for them. Harold was big for his age—athletic but also kind of thick—the type of kid who would knock over a chair rushing to get to the seat he wanted. When he was in preschool, he always had long columns of green mucus streaming from his nose. His hair flopped over his eyes, and his shirt always looked as if he had just been rolling in the mud. Harold made other kids cry at least twice a day. It seemed to his second-grade teacher, Miss Levin, that just when another child might make a friendly overture, Harold would instead begin to threaten and intimidate some other child, often one who seemed obviously smaller or more timid than he. He was what psychologists call rejected/aggressive. Children didn't want to play with him, and he, in turn, antagonized them. Kids like Harold don't have many friends and they're not popular or admired. They are not the tough, cool guy, like the character Iceman in the movie *Top Gun*. They are just mean and scary, and they are disliked by the others. When Harold was sixteen, he was arrested for driving under the influence. When he was seventeen, his girlfriend got pregnant. When he was eighteen, he was arrested for beating someone up while traveling across the country. Bullies who are also rejected have around a 70 percent chance of getting in trouble with the law by the time they are young adults.

Kids with these problems aren't difficult to spot. Any teacher worth his or her salt knows exactly who is left out of the game at recess, who isn't chosen to work on the science team, and who eats lunch alone. Any teacher can identify the Sashas, quiet and withdrawn, and the Harolds, creating constant friction and trouble.

## Invisible Trouble

Plenty of kids are not well accepted in school, and yet no one sounds the alarm bell. These kids can be emitting signs of trouble that no one is picking up. Unfortunately, this can lead adults to miss a vital opportunity to help a child.

Andy was just that kind of kid. Even at four, while he liked other children and they seemed to like him well enough, he was beginning to show signs of the trouble to come. Once, at a friend's house, he and his buddy wanted to build a tree house. They found a hammer and some nails. While his friend diligently, if unsuccessfully, tried to hammer a strip of wood to the trunk of a tree, Andy became absorbed in wildly smashing the nails into the dirt. It was as if he lost sight of the shared goal and lost interest in being part of a duo—two attributes essential to making and keeping friends when you are young.

But Andy was one of five siblings, with only two years between any two of them. Their parents were loving but slightly overwhelmed and distracted. They loved their own casual style. Once at a birthday party, a toddler's mother reached out to keep her eighteen-month-old from careening over the low edge of the deck. Andy's mother gently and authoritatively held her friend's hand. "Don't jump in. Let him explore. Let him find out for himself," she said. In the abstract, her advice seemed calm and wise. Relax. Let kids be who they are. But her impulse was not in the abstract. It was in the context of a son who already was showing subtle signs of social isolation.

As Andy got older, he seemed bright but out of sync with others. However, he didn't get into fights, and he didn't complain that children were mean to him. He raised no red flags. If he had been in a classroom where a psychologist had been collecting sociometric data, he surely would have come up as a neglected child—not the kid other children seriously disliked and not the one they loved or admired, just not someone other kids sought out. In Andy's case, this mild lack of acceptance might have been a wrinkle that got ironed out with time, if it weren't for his other difficulties.

Years later, as a sixteen-year-old, after he had been caught stealing a pair of basketball shoes from a local store, his mother recalled that when he was young, he would wander away from her. With no warning, he'd slip away, taking off by himself down the street. At the time, she thought it was the sign of an independent spirit. It went with his almost translucent skin and black curls. He was spritelike, quirky, and a bit dreamy, she thought. But she also recalled that the few times she sent him to his room for misbehaving, he'd climb out the second-story window and lower himself to the ground with ropes he'd found and tied together.

When Andy was caught with the stolen shoes, his mother happened to be shopping next door at another store. The policeman, who knew her, came and got her and explained what had happened. She promised she'd deal with her son, and the policeman agreed to let it go. Andy put back the shoes, and she and Andy left. Once they were in the car, Andy turned to his mother and said, "But now will you buy me the shoes?"

It's not hard, now that Andy is in his twenties and struggling mightily, to see that all the signs were there when he was young. But one can also see how easy it would have been to miss those signals. He didn't get into a lot of trouble when he was young, he wasn't a bully, and he wasn't picked on. The red flags were fleeting and obscured by daily life, which washed over his family and kept them from zeroing in on his emerging difficulties.

Andy's odd behaviors, once slight and easy to pass off as eccentricities, became more than that as he entered adolescence. By the time he was fifteen, he had been arrested, caught again and again with liquor and drugs, and had had several car accidents. But his parents thought, "Lots of teens drink too much and take risks with cars. His judgment isn't the best, so he gets caught while others get away with it. But he's not really all that different from other kids, right?"

They were comforted by the fact that he had a close relationship with a girl and had one really good buddy. Here is where they misread the cues altogether. The research shows that for kids who are not accepted by other kids, having one or two intense friendships might guard against future depression, but it doesn't necessarily indicate that things are OK. In fact, a rejected kid who has one good friend is more likely than other rejected kids to face future problems with the law. Kids who get into trouble and are outside the mainstream often gravitate toward other kids who get into trouble. And that's just what happened to Andy. He made close friends with a boy who loved to get high and skip school.

In another study of children who were either unpopular or had no friends, Asher found that often when a rejected kid has one good buddy, the quality of the friendship is fairly low. What does that look like? Good friendships, even among preadolescents, involve a fair amount of validation, help, exchange of intimate information, and low levels of conflict and betrayal. But when an unpopular kid makes friends with another unpopular kid, the same social problems each has with others begin to bubble up between them.

Andy's parents were grateful that he had a buddy—they spoke about how reassuring it was that Andy had an ally, a friend with whom he seemed close. It never occurred to them that Andy's friend was making things worse.

By the time Andy was sixteen, he was in so much trouble that his parents dropped him off at a rehabilitation program for teens in California. He spent the next few years moving from one program to another—three in all. He finally made his way to college, although he continued to get into serious trouble with the law for drugs, speeding, and disorderly conduct. This trajectory is classic, cited in study after study. Children who have trouble with peers tend to have other kinds of trouble as they get older. What, if anything, could his parents have done differently had they interpreted Andy's childhood behaviors as the red flags that they were?

## Friendship 101

Asher has been studying children's friendships for thirty years. He's looked at kids who are kept out of the group and kids who simply are not sought after. He's looked at close friends, and he's looked at kids who have lots of friendly acquaintances. He's watched children interact, and he's questioned them one by one. He's observed kids' friendships evolve and dissolve over a period of years, and he's tried to intervene and change the course for kids with problems. And that brings us to the million-dollar question for those who do research on peer relations: Can children who have trouble with peers be coached? Can they change?

As Asher and others have shown, kids who are chronically rejected often do things that seem to get them rejected. They tease inappropriately, they promote themselves in just the wrong way, their timing is off, and they push when they shouldn't. Sometimes their difficulties are hard to change. Kids who are not athletic are less popular than kids who are, and kids who are funny are more liked than kids who are not. These are not qualities one can coach into a kid. But as John Coie has argued, a lack of these qualities is not in itself the kiss of death. Some plain, unfunny kids seem to make the most of their best qualities, read the pulse of the group, and find a way in. The kids who have trouble are typically the ones who don't know how to read the group. The kid who really has trouble often is the one who handles an initial experience of exclusion badly. Popular kids pay attention to signals from the others, and they adapt their behavior accordingly. Rejected kids do not. Children who are liked tend to be interested in what other kids are doing and saying. They share information about themselves and solicit information about the other kids. They are interested in making joint activities fun. Kids who don't seem to have these skills make a bad beginning worse. Thus, what begins as a slight difficulty meeting others or joining a group leads to other problems. Because they misread cues and miss opportunities to connect to other kids, they end up missing opportunities to practice friendship, which leads to further isolation and unhappiness as they get older.

However, Karen Bierman, among others, has found that kids can get better at becoming part of the group in just a few coaching sessions, especially when they are young. They can get better at showing interest in what other kids say and think. They can learn to focus more on having fun with other kids and less on proving themselves. They can learn to let the other kids know they are having fun. In one study, Bierman and her colleagues set up so-cial training sessions for children who were unpopular. Each child who was unpopular (based on sociometric scores and on reports of teachers and the children themselves) was teamed with two well-accepted children from the classroom. These three kids spent a total of ten sessions together engaged in a variety of activities (drawing, talking, and so on). Half of these groups also received direct coaching from an adult. For the other half, an adult was present and supportive of their interactions but offered no spe-cific directives about how to interact.

The coaching consisted of teaching children how to say posi-tive things to the other kids, how to listen and acknowledge what the others said, and how to suppress the urge to be disagreeable and argumentative. Children who interacted with more popular peers and were coached by an adult did seem to become more ac-cepted over time, even after the study was over. However, it wasn't clear that they actually became more popular or had more friends. Taken purely as research, this sheds light on what might go wrong for some kids and suggests that there are two critical factors for improvement: the chance to interact with more popular kids and some direct instruction in the behaviors that seem to cause the problems. But it's not clear what this offers to parents, because, as it turns out, it's often not only the kids who need help.

Marlene Sandstrom has been studying friendships since she was eight years old and in the third grade. She vividly remembers when a new boy joined her class in a public school in suburban New Jersey.

"Oh, boy," she said. "He was kept out from day one. He never got in. I could see that the other kids weren't all that nice. But it wasn't just that. I could tell, even then, even though I was only a kid myself, that he was just slightly off in every encounter. It was fascinating yet painful to watch. What was keeping him from fit-ting in? I couldn't stop thinking about it."

Fifteen years later, as a doctoral student in clinical psychology at Duke University, she worked with one of the founders of the study of peer relations, John Coie, and did her doctoral research on how parents might influence their children's peer status. Like others in her field, she got all of the children who were her test subjects to nominate classmates who were most liked and most disliked. Then she followed the kids who were most disliked. Those students whose parents got involved—by helping them join after-school activities and other kinds of groups—were much more likely to be accepted by peers one year later. The quick answer from Sandstrom's work: kids can get better, and parents can play a role. But her research highlighted a puzzle. Do the kids whose parents get involved do better because they get the chance to practice new skills or because if you're that kind of kid and you're lucky enough to have a parent perceptive enough and involved enough to help, you're already in better shape than the kid without that kind of parent?

Asher's research has something to say about this. In one set of studies, he and his colleagues actually involved rejected kids in some training groups. The children were taught how to ask other kids about themselves, how to make someone feel welcome when he or she came into the room, how to suggest a new game, and how to share interesting and appropriate information about themselves. A year later, rejected kids who had been part of his training groups were more well liked by other children in the classroom, suggesting that you can help a kid become more popular.

Asher is quick to say that we don't yet know if you can also help a kid make stronger, better friendships. A socially awkward child can learn to do the things that come naturally to the other children, and it has some payoff. These children get higher ratings on sociometric measures after the training and might well find themselves more accepted. It's not clear, however, that this kind of training leads to a change in the quality of a child's friendships.

You can learn how to act in a group, but that doesn't necessarily mean you can learn how to be a friend. But since being accepted and having close friends are not the same thing, the training is worth something. While everyone assumes that all good things befall the popular kid and all bad things befall the kid who is not popular, the data show something different. Children who are not popular but are also not rejected by the group seem to do pretty well over time. They report a fair amount of satisfaction with their daily lives. They can do well in school, and as they get older, they often get better at making and keeping friends.

One of the problems for kids like Sasha and Andy is that without help, they begin to identify themselves as unpopular—they feel like losers, and then they act even more like losers. But therein lies a good avenue for intervention. When kids can be made to feel that their interactions with other kids have gone well, they become more appealing. Coie and his students demonstrated this with a startling experiment. Children who had been identified as rejected through peer nominations were introduced briefly to two boys with average peer status. A few days later, some of the rejected boys were told that those two boys they had met a few days before really liked them and were looking forward to getting together again. Other rejected boys were not given that positive feedback. Then each of these rejected boys was given some time with the two boys again. Kids who were given the positive feedback were subsequently rated as more likable than the kids who were not given that feedback. In other words, when rejected kids are given the sense that they have made a good impression on others, they behave in a more appealing way. This should come as no surprise. In a similar study of adult attractiveness, a team of social psychologists asked subjects to talk on a phone to a stranger (another subject in the study). The stranger was shown a photograph of the telephone partner, but some were shown a picture of a very attractive member of the opposite sex, while others were shown a photograph of a very unattractive person. Those conversations were recorded. When a third subject listened to the original subject's voice during that conversation and rated how much he would like to meet the person whose voice he was listening to, he was much more interested in meeting subjects who had been talking to someone who believed they were attractive. Bottom line: if you feel attractive, you act attractive. And if others think you are appealing, it leads you to be more appealing.

Matt always had one or two good friends at a time. He was the kind of little boy who loved to have the same friend over each weekend. Together they would develop elaborate play scenarios involving superheroes and bad guys. They ran lemonade stands and made fortresses in the woods near their home. When he moved to a new school in third grade, Matt again made a few best friends. In fifth grade, those buddies gravitated toward soccer and hockey, things Matt had no interest in. So he found himself two new friends—kids who liked to talk, draw cartoons, and plan movies. But by the time he was in middle school, Matt felt lonely and unhappy. He was the only Jewish kid in the class. He read more than the others. The questions he asked the teachers were different from those the other kids asked. He got into feuds with a few classmates over things like gun control and the president. By the spring of his seventh-grade year, he felt isolated from everyone in his grade. In the winter of his eighth-grade year, a girl with whom he had had some conflict gave a party and invited everyone but him. He felt he had not one real friend in the whole school, and he was downright miserable.

Research shows that kids who feel rejected at school and who also don't have a close friend suffer a kind of loneliness that dominates their every waking moment. Many adults who were rejected either still feel that loneliness or can easily recall a time in their own childhood when they did. It's one of the most negative and powerful of all childhood experiences. Parents often don't even realize what their kids are going through. And even if they do, they aren't always sure how to help.

## The Parent Steps In

Matt's parents began to look into other schools for him—the two nearby public schools to which he had access and a few private schools. His grandmother suggested that maybe it was something about him that was causing the problem, that perhaps he was rubbing the other kids the wrong way and would carry this problem with him wherever he went. His parents, worried and distraught to see him suffer, wondered how they would know if the problem was simply a bad fit between him and the group or something he would cause in any class.

Not knowing what else to try, they sent Matt to a different public school in a nearby town with a different demographic. The school had more kids from families who read books and more kids with parents who had white-collar jobs. There were more Jews and more kids who did as well as Matt at schoolwork. Most important, there were kids who hadn't known him in the seventh grade, which meant, among other things, more kids with whom he felt he could make a fresh start. He had a new buddy within a week. He had a new group of friends within two months and a steady girlfriend within three months. With a new peer group and a fresh start, he had a chance to shift his self-concept, and in his case, that made all the difference.

But switching schools is not the answer for every child suffering with social problems. Researchers have long wondered what many parents have wondered. Is it possible for an unpopular kid to change his reputation once he's been cast out? Do rejected kids repeat history wherever they go? Coie and his colleagues devised an ingenious method for disentangling the chicken-egg problem of a child and her social group. First, they went into the fourth-grade classrooms of a public school district in Durham, North Carolina, to find out who was popular, who was rejected, and who was neglected. Each boy who was characterized as rejected or neglected by the sociometrics was then recruited to participate in a six-week after-school program. Each child was placed in a group of unfamiliar children—all of the other children had received a neutral or positive rating in their original classrooms. Thus, each child who was chronically ignored or rejected was spending time playing with a new group of kids who were fairly popular. After each playgroup session, a different adult gave a ride home to the kids in the group. In the car, the driver would casually ask how things were going with the after-school activities. This gave the researchers a chance to gather information about the social dynamics without making the children too self-conscious or aware of the purpose of the program. What they found was both discouraging and encouraging. Ignored boys were able to turn over a new leaf—they used play time with this new small group as an opportunity to change their own social profiles. Kids reported liking the ignored boys, finding them interesting, and often noticing them more than kids in their regular classroom. However, rejected children didn't find the same success. They seemed to repeat the behavior that had made them unpopular at school, and the other children in their after-school groups reported the same kind of negative reactions that rejected children tend to get from their classmates. This study explains why a kid like Matt blossomed with a change of schools but why other children might not.

For instance, it had no effect on Abby, who moved to a new school for sixth grade. Not only did she continue to have conflict with friends, often feeling hurt by the girls she liked the most, but as the new girl in sixth grade, she found herself with a whole new set of problems. She wanted to be friends with the cool girls in her new classroom. But they hadn't really invited her to join them yet;

they were still thinking it over. Meanwhile, a girl in the class who knew Abby from the tennis club was eager to be her best friend. However, the cool girls made it clear that if Abby hung out with the "loser girl," they would never allow her into their clique. Abby had come home distraught over this plight.

Her mother, Meg, was in a quandary. "I don't want her to suffer. It's breaking my heart to see her so worried about who her friends will be. I can't stand to see her excluded yet again. I want to give her advice that will help her be more popular, but my own mother is appalled that I would do such a thing. She keeps telling me not to worry so much about her friendships. She warned me that I should worry more about whether Abby grows up with a strong moral compass. My mother says this is the time to teach her to put the welfare of others ahead of her own, to stick up for the weak. She's sure Abby's social life will sort itself out but that if I don't guide her to be selfless now, she'll become callous and self-interested. Help me. What should I tell Abby?"

The problem Meg faced will ring a bell with many parents. Who wants to see their child excluded or put down? And who wants to push a young child to behave in ways that might lock the child into unpopularity for years to come?

Meg hedged it. She encouraged Abby to find a way to be friendly to the loser girl but to explain that she was eager to make friends with lots of kids and wanted to spend time with that other group as well. As the year progressed, Abby forged ahead, finding herself deeper and deeper in what some have called "girl world"—filled with heated IM exchanges, changes of alliance, bad rumors, and ecstatic gatherings in town.

Toward the end of Abby's eighth-grade year, Meg was at a meeting of parent volunteers for the school. One mom called out, "How are Abby and Julio doing?"

"Who?" Meg asked.

It seemed that everyone but Meg knew that Abby had a boyfriend. Julio was a boy in her grade. They walked down the hall together between classes. They were known as a couple, a topic of discussion during nightly IM sessions. Once at a school dance, they kissed—a quick peck on the lips (all this Abby told Meg when she finally learned about it). When Meg asked Abby why she hadn't told her, Abby said, "When I asked you how old I had to be to have a boyfriend, you said eighteen. I thought you wouldn't let me go out with Julio."

What is most striking about this piece of the story is why Abby asked her mother how old she had to be. Many kids would not. Abby cared what her mother thought. She might have been trying to open up the topic when she asked her mother the question. Meg said her answer of eighteen gave Abby an out if Abby didn't feel ready to date. Meg didn't recognize the question for what it was. But that didn't really matter. What mattered was that Abby, highly aware of rules, both the ones she conformed to and the ones she circumvented, cared about her mother's rules.

I told Meg that I thought it was great that Abby had a boyfriend in eighth grade. It gave her bankable currency when it came to the other girls. Meg seemed happy to hear my interpretation. She smiled, relieved to think that Abby was no longer facing heartache each day.

"Yup" she said, with a small smile, "Abby is slowly but steadily working her way up the social ladder." She paused, and a rueful expression veiled her smile. "And she's becoming more conforming every minute."

But not all children can simply decide to do what it takes to become more popular and then do it. In one of the clearest pieces of research to emerge in the last fifty years, Jerome Kagan at Harvard has shown that shyness is one of the most persistent and long-lasting of human characteristics. But his story begins in the 1960s, when Stella Chess first argued that not all of a child's personality depended on the mistakes parents made. In response to the Freudian zeitgeist, in which parents were sure that their children's every foible was the result of some invisible but powerful interaction with them, Chess, a child psychiatrist, began to explore the possibility that babies arrive in the world with some pretty powerful characteristics, which play a big role in determining a child's future life. Chess and her colleagues asked parents to keep diaries of their babies, noting things such as the baby's response to a new food, how the baby fell asleep and woke up, and how she dealt with changes in routine (remember, this was in an era when modern U.S. parents were told again and again that a routine was essential to a baby's well-being).

In their classic book, *Your Child Is a Person*, Herbert Birch, Stella Chess, and Audrey Thomas argued that from birth, each baby has a temperament, a style of responding to the world, which influences every experience she has. Birch, Chess, and Thomas said that every child could be characterized as one of the following three temperamental types: easy, difficult, and slow to warm up. The easy baby falls asleep calmly, responds to new experiences (such as a new food) in a relaxed and open manner, and in other ways goes through the day with equanimity. Difficult babies, on the other hand, seem fussy and tense about any kind of change— waking up, tasting a new food, or entering a new place. The slow-to-warm-up classification is fairly self-explanatory, describing the baby who cautiously sticks her tongue out and warily tastes a new food, perhaps pauses, tries it again, and finally eats it. It's not hard to see how these basic ways of interacting might shape a child's experience. And any parent knows that you tend to respond differently to the calm, open baby from how you respond to the one who seems to get upset and tense again and again. In other words, the baby's temperament not only shapes her own behavior, but it also ends up shaping her emotional environment.

Forty years after *Your Child Is a Person* was published, Kagan picked up the thread of temperament. He began to tease apart what Birch, Chess, and Thomas were on to. From Kagan's experimental perspective, what parents say about their children was notoriously unreliable. The mom who says her baby cries all the time is just as likely to be exaggerating as the mom who says her baby loves every new experience. So, to find a more rigorous measure of a baby's temperament, Kagan invited mothers to bring their babies into the lab. After placing each child in one of those tilted baby seats that can be set on a table and rocked gently, he filmed them. After the baby had a chance to settle in, the experimenter dangled a toy that hung from a rod, sort of like a hand-held mobile. This type of toy is pleasing and interesting, the kind that parents often attach to their children's cribs and strollers. But this was a brand-new toy, one the baby had not seen before. In films of these babies, it is quite easy to see how differently each baby responds to the new toy. Some sit in the chair calmly. When the hanging toy is brought into their view, their eyes might widen for a moment, and they halt their character- istic exercising motions (the ones that make many four-month-olds look as if they are in a perpetual aerobics class). Little bands placed on their wrists show that their pulse temporarily changes, and their skin might produce slightly more moisture—the new toy makes them sweat. But after a few moments, most babies settle back down, their pulse returns to normal, and their kicking resumes. They might visually explore the mobile, but after those first moments, they are not overly perturbed by it. Kagan called these children "low reactive," meaning that they are relatively relaxed and able to take new experiences in stride. Some number of babies, however, have a very different response to the new toy. They become agitated, and instead of quickly settling back to normal, their agitation seems to be self-perpetuating. Their initial surprise and tension worries and upsets them, and before you know it, they are crying and unable to calm down. Kagan called these babies "high reactive."

When Kagan and his students observed the babies four years later, the two styles were still quite apparent, although they mani- fested themselves somewhat differently. Low reactive babies were the ones who eagerly entered a new classroom, joined a group of children playing on a playground, and seemed interested and happy when approached by a new child. The high reactive children, however, were the ones to stand back reluctantly at the door of a new classroom, hesitant to enter, unwilling to jump into the fray. In a host of follow-up studies, Kagan and others have shown that the babies he called high reactive become shy children. He wasn't talking about a little bashfulness at a big party. He was talking about children who are overwhelmed by new experiences, particularly ones that involve other people, children who would remain on the edge of a playground, even when the kids were doing something really fun, rather than have to talk to children they don't know.

Anyone who is extremely shy or has a shy person in his or her family knows that shyness can govern a person's life. A shy child finds it hard to meet new friends, terrifying to change schools, and overwhelming to have to talk to the teacher. Walking into the cafeteria can create dread day after day. Shyness can keep children from pursuing their deepest interests. A casual look at the narratives teachers write about children will show that most adults (except for those who suffer from extreme shyness) expect children to grow out of this kind of timidity. "We hope Jack will try to be more outgoing next year." "Sara should get involved in more group activities at school." "This year, Carlo has spent an awful lot of time alone. Next year, we hope to work on this with him." And yet, by and large, shy children become shy teenagers and then shy adults. Expecting a child to outgrow shyness is sort of like expecting a child to outgrow eye color.

## If You Can't Change the Child, Change the Path

Knowing how to help your child deal with social problems depends a great deal on what the story really is. Often, the most valuable thing a parent gets from talking to a therapist is the chance to piece together a detailed narrative. But you don't necessarily need a therapist in order to watch and listen and then put together a story for yourself, one that conveys what your child is experiencing. A quick glance, coming up with a summary view in which the conclusions are drawn first, often misses the most revealing elements of the narrative. Find someone to tell your story to—a friend or colleague who doesn't know too much about your child's daily life. Knowing what clues to include in your story makes a big difference.

Patrick's journey testifies to that. Patrick came from a family that seemed to have stepped right out of a story about modern middle-class America. His mom was a schoolteacher, his dad a social worker. They lived in a small rural area in upstate New York. Patrick's parents met in college, married, and proceeded in an orderly fashion to have a daughter, Meghan, and then Patrick. When someone called their home, the message said, "We can't come to the phone right now. We're either out at work or busy doing a kid project. Please leave a message for Catherine, Tim, Meghan, or Patrick." Their home had a modest and perfectly manicured garden, a different welcome sign for each season, and portraits of the family taken by a professional. Everything about their life seemed measured, planned, and moderate. Their social life revolved around the children's interests, church, and their extended family.

When Patrick was little, he attended day care and immediately made friends with a small cluster of other little boys, all of whom had siblings who went to school together and whose parents worked as teachers and social workers. As a four-year-old, Patrick's dark, shiny hair was cut in a perfect bowl shape around his head. He looked sweet and well kept and completely conventional.

The little gang of boys eventually moved on to elementary school together and began to play against one another in Little League baseball and on community basketball teams. That's when Patrick's troubles began. The charming roundness that had suited the page-boy haircut was suddenly a liability as the boys began to compete for traveling teams, shortstop position, and starting positions in basketball. Even at four, Patrick seemed slightly more sensitive and reactive than the other boys in the group. On a trip with one of them to a haunted house for kids at Halloween, he ran screaming from the display, terrified. On a flight home from a family vacation in Florida, he became so anxious he almost couldn't bear it. In the weeks following that trip, he became hysterical when he left a sweatshirt at a buddy's home, calling several times to make sure the sweatshirt was there and insisting that his mother drive him over to pick it up the very next morning. At the same time, differences among the kids in academics and athletics began to show up. Patrick wasn't chosen for the traveling team in basketball. And although he loved shortstop, he was made second baseman.

Despite this, his buddies still played with him, and he was invited over to their homes. The birthday parties always included him. And he made it onto every team. But the other kids began to rib him, often quite mercilessly, for his fears. When his feelings were hurt, he'd tell them so, and they teased him for that. They were in the process of adopting a tough-guy jock manner—most of them wouldn't drop that until their midteens, some never. Patrick took on no such mantle. By the time these boys were eleven, he was often getting the short straw. It seemed as if he wore a "Kick me" sign on the seat of his pants. When he invited one of the crowd to his house for a Memorial Day picnic, the friend stood him up, lured by the more appealing last-minute invitation to the cool boy's house. Patrick, easily wounded and longing for inclusion, cried and stayed in his room for the whole afternoon.

In sixth grade, his buddies were starters for the basketball team. He spent the season on the bench, too pudgy and slow to help the team. In eighth grade, two of the four boys ran for class president. Patrick was one of them. He lost in the first round. When his friend Ed made it to the final election, Patrick had a meltdown. He became so furious that his eyes bulged out and his veins popped on the side of his head. He fumed at Ed, shouting about how furious he would be if Ed won the election. His rivalry pushed him to go around the school for days lobbying against Ed, persuading other children not to vote for Ed, an act of betrayal Patrick would bitterly regret. Ed didn't invite Patrick over for weeks after that and discouraged other friends from including him. Patrick's rage at being bested only caused him further trouble with his friends.

One night, when Patrick was thirteen, all of the boys were at one house, engaged in their usual string of entertainments—a little Xbox, an hour or so on the blacktop playing basketball, breaks for chips and juice, periodic bursts of IM-ing various girls, time out for a movie they had watched twenty times before. At some point while roaming around his friend Elliot's basement, the boys discovered an old set of boxing equipment. Delighted by a new form of entertainment, they quickly put on the masks, mouth gear, and gloves and rushed outside to go at it. By this time, it was 11:00 on a warm summer night. Just before going to bed, Elliot's mother peeked outside to see if they were okay. Patrick, wearing one set of the gear, was sobbing with great ugly gulps, while one of the other boys, Keith, was jabbing and punching at him, taunting him, "Can't take it, can you? What are you, afraid? You a sissy? Huh? Huh? Afraid to get hurt?" The other boys sat by, watching with mean passivity. What had begun as a rowdy but innocent pastime had become a cruel chance to make Patrick feel terrible. And Patrick's response seemed to embody the larger problem. He stood there wailing, refusing to give up or leave the group but unable to shift the tone or turn the tables on his tormentor. He seemed stuck in the role of loser.

Watching Patrick struggle was agony for his parents. His mother offered encouragement and sometimes pointed out to him what he might have done that made things worse. His father struggled with Patrick's woes. He was desperate for Patrick to be good at basketball and baseball. Those were things he had loved when he was a boy. Those were things that made you stand out when you were young. So he got Patrick special baseball coaching after school. He sent him to summer sports programs. He offered to help coach the teams. He got mad at the coaches when Patrick wasn't given enough time on the court or a position in the batting order. Middle-class parents from the United States often think that when they do those things, they are simply advocating for their children. But most of the time, they are just making things worse. Patrick's "Kick me" sign seemed brighter than ever.

What Patrick needed was support to do the things he liked and that made him feel competent, because in those settings, he was likely to find friends and feel good about himself. One of his problems was that because he felt insecure in many of the activities he was supposed to love and be good at, he behaved in ways that irritated the other kids. When they showed their irritation, it only agitated Patrick more and made him perform worse, which further put off the other kids. And while kids need to feel supported when they are upset with other kids, it doesn't help them if their parents are always angry at the bad coach, the bad teacher, or the bad friend. Such "support" only encourages kids to feel resentful and misunderstood.

For better or for worse, Patrick didn't back off from his group of friends. He kept spending Saturdays with them, joining the same teams, and inviting them over. It seemed like a recipe for disaster. If you had skimmed over the details of Patrick's social biography at this point, it would have been easy to label him as socially at risk. He seemed headed down a bad path, doing all the things that made the original difficulties worse. The signs seemed to point clearly away from popularity and social success. But his life, like every child's life, was more complicated than that. Buried inside the big picture were small details that turned out to make all the difference. During those years, as he seemed to move farther into the category of "loser," he was still invited to the parties, he still played on the teams, and, perhaps most important, he still had a strong and happy friendship with one of the kids in his original group. Meanwhile, he began to focus seriously on a new skill, something those boys didn't share. He began to play the saxophone.

He also made a few friends who were not part of the original group. And although the group of friends never fully embraced him, his friendship with the one boy, Wilson, persisted and deepened. They got together in the summer, when the group wasn't a group. They did things together on weekends that didn't involve sports or those other boys. And Patrick got older. He lost weight. The bonds that held the boys as a gang loosened, and what remained was his close friendship with Wilson. Finally, being great at baseball and basketball didn't matter so much anymore. His interests lay in music. He developed an intense crush on a beautiful girl. He would never be the captain of the football team. He'd never be the cool boy who had kissed every girl in the class. But he was good at things, he had close friendships, and he knew who he was. He had weathered the storm.

Patrick was like a lot of kids—he had some trouble with friends. But he was never totally isolated. And although he might have had moments of frustration and rage at the way he felt treated by other kids, he also had fun with them.

A child doesn't need to be the king of the castle to thrive socially. Not all children are the most popular, and not all children have lots of friends. Your child doesn't need to be the first one chosen on the team or be the queen bee. If she is part of a group some of the time or has made a good friend, she is probably going to be fine. She will be fine even if at some point she has felt lonely in a new school or gone through a rough time in her early teens. Those kinds of momentary dramas can be very painful, but they don't last, and they don't predict much. They're just one of the perils of growing up, at least in our society.

But if you are worried, what can you do? Start by trying to get a fuller picture of what your child experiences and how she feels. Listen carefully to her descriptions of her day. The most valuable clues are probably buried in her stories (or her avoidance of certain kinds of stories, for instance, if she never mentions experiences that involve friends).

You don't have to hover and pepper your child with questions to find out if she feels connected to other kids. But if you have any reason to be concerned, watch and listen. Does she talk about particular friendships? Do you get any sense of what your daughter and her friends like about one another or like to do together? Does she play with kids outside of school? Does she look forward to eating lunch with a certain child each day? Do her friendships last more than a few weeks?

Parents of neglected or rejected children are often themselves somewhat tuned out and might be somewhat cut off from their children's everyday experience. If you are not used to creating intimacy with others, it can be hard to become intimately familiar with your child's daily life. On the other hand, there are plenty of parents in our society who treat their children's daily experience like a job to be mastered, and this doesn't help much, either. Interrogation usually doesn't work very well. The goal is to get a rich picture of your child's friendships, fights, and quandaries, not to become an investigator or take a deposition.

If, after watching and listening, you feel that your child is seriously lonely or constantly left out of the social scene at school, you can help in three ways. First, you can try to create situations in which she can make new friends. She can get involved with a different group of kids (preferably a small group) for some after-school activity, something she really likes and wants to do. Invite children she likes to do things with over on the weekends, outside of the dynamics of the regular classroom. Sometimes these bonds carry over into the school week and shift the social dynamics in class.

Second, if you have the sense that she continually makes the same mistakes in the way she approaches kids or deals with others in groups, you might consider getting her some help, the kind of peer intervention that has been successful in experiments. Finding a good version of this might not be so easy outside of university towns, however. Don't despair if your community doesn't provide such programs. A good counselor might work just as well. Family life, too, can help make up for what she isn't getting out of social life. One of the sad ironies of early peer neglect and rejection is that what these children miss out on is the very thing they need for later friendships. Research shows that making friends takes practice. Early experiences of intimacy and friendship lead to greater social skills later on. If your child isn't getting a chance to practice those skills at school, she will need plenty of opportunities to have fun with others, share confidences, work out conflicts, and be close to others while at home.

The third thing you can do might be the hardest of all. Be aware that life in groups is tough for her. Remind yourself that she doesn't mean to get into trouble with the other children. She can't help it that she puts people off. How does it help to know this if you can't do much about it? Parents underestimate the power of simply understanding what their children are going through. You can give her the compassion and support to buffer against those negative experiences.

Having compassion for your child's social difficulty does *not* mean justifying her actions when she is mean to other children. It is important to let her know that it is wrong and hurtful to bully others. Make it clear, in your own behavior with family members and friends, that thinking about the perspectives and feelings of others is extremely important. When it comes to social behavior, kids model themselves after their parents quite strongly.

What you can't do is simply turn your child into a kid who makes friends. So far, there isn't much evidence that a child who is chronically rejected can change all that much. Marlene Sandstrom tells the following story from her days as a graduate student working with John Coie, who was recording the behavior of some children in an elementary-school classroom. He could not help but notice one little boy who personified the geek and was always left out of everything. One day, this boy had a sign on his desk: "I'm a wild and crazy guy." Violating his usual rule of scientific disengagement, Coie wandered over to the little boy and said in a quiet voice, "I don't think that sign is such a good idea. If I were you, I'd take it down. I don't think the other kids will react well to it." The next day, when Coie returned to collect more data, he looked over and saw that the little boy had put up a new sign: "Pay no attention to that other sign." The poor little guy had only made matters worse. No research has shown that a child with such offbeat social instincts can be taught or lured into becoming socially attuned or better at making friends.

As Kagan's work has shown, a really shy kid is unlikely to become a party animal. One of the worst things parents can do, in their anxiety or disappointment that their child is not surrounded by friends, is to try to force the child into social situations. But that doesn't mean you have to give up on your child's social life or that she is doomed to unhappiness because of problems in her elementary years. The most important way to help is to understand that even if you cannot change her, you can change her path.

# 3

# Goodness:
# Bernie Madoff's Mother

Goodness comes from somewhere, and so does badness. In 2009, Bernie Madoff was arrested for bilking thousands of people out of billions of dollars. That was the year lots of people turned out to be selfish and immoral, many of them working in high-profile jobs at big corporations such as AIG and Morgan Stanley. What made Madoff stand out is that he not only duped faceless strangers, whose only connection to him was as a name on an accounts page, but he also cheated employees he had worked with and invited to his home, and he stole money from friends who had known him and trusted him for years.

In their quest to figure out how this charismatic and successful guy could have engaged in such a massive wrong, journalists began to poke through his childhood. What they found was that Madoff grew up in a tight-knit Jewish community, Laurelton, in Queens, New York. He hung out with the other kids, having the same kinds of fun they had. He came from an intact family. He did well at school and had extracurricular interests (one schoolmate remembered Madoff's hilarious turn as a sheik in a school play, wearing his parents' bedsheets for a costume). He attended the University of Alabama for a year before transferring to Hofstra University, and he married his high school sweetheart, Ruth.

"Mr. Madoff spent the next year at Brooklyn Law School, attending classes in the morning and running his side business—installing and fixing sprinkler systems—in the afternoon and evening, recalled Joseph Kavanau, who attended law school with Mr. Madoff. When Mr. Kavanau married his wife, Jane, who was Mrs. Madoff's best friend from Queens, Mr. Madoff was the best man. 'Bernie was very industrious,' Mr. Kavanau explains. 'He was going to school and working at the same time. Mr. Madoff was never interested in practicing law,' Mr. Kavanau says. Instead, Mr. Madoff left law school and, using $5,000 saved from being a lifeguard and from his sprinkler business, joined the ranks of Wall Street in the 1960s."[*] Nothing seemed to foretell the massive immorality that lay ahead.

But one detail about his childhood stands out as a huge red flag. Madoff's mother, Sylvia, was also involved in finance. During the late 1950s and early '60s, she had her own brokerage firm, Gibraltar Securities. In 1963, the Securities and Exchange Commission investigated her firm, along with several others, for failing to file financial reports. Before they could revoke her registration, Sylvia withdrew it, and matters ended there.

When people speak of a person's moral fiber, they would be more accurate to imagine a moral braid, a twisted rope of several different strands. And there is no question that one of those strands is the behavior a child sees in his home. Sylvia Madoff

---

[*] Julie Creswell and Landon Thomas Jr., "The Talented Mr. Madoff," *New York Times,* January 24, 2009, p. B1.

might well have told her son to say thank you when a neighbor gave him dinner and to get up and give his grandmother a chair when she came to visit. She might have lectured him sternly if he ever got caught cheating on a spelling test. He was known for his periodic generosity to friends and employees, and it could well be that Sylvia praised her young son when he was kind to the little boy down the street who got teased by other kids. All of this is possible. Meanwhile, she herself might have been defrauding customers, sneaking past the regulatory commissions, or cheating the government, and if so, there would be a good chance it was rubbing off on Bernie.

Although the roots of immorality can be found growing in a child's home, the roots of goodness can be found growing right within the child.

## The Good Egg

Oliver had a difficult start in life. His father walked out on his mother months before Oliver was born, leaving her on her own throughout her pregnancy and childbirth. She was from a middle-class, educated family, but by the time she had Oliver, she was so poor she was living in a shelter for unwed mothers. She had a difficult labor, and with no access to decent medical care, she died shortly following childbirth.

Oliver, a slender, pale boy, short for his age, spent his early years in a group home. When he was nine years old, he was taken in as a foster child by the kind of family that should never qualify as foster parents. His foster father was rough, demanding, and cruel. By the time he was nine, Oliver had had very little experience of kindness or parental affection. Most of the adults in the surrounding neighborhood believed that harsh punishment was the best way to discipline children. In his early years in the group home and then later in his foster home, there was not one adult who provided Oliver with the warm, authoritative parenting we now know is best for children. There wasn't one adult or friend who provided him with a role model in thoughtful or altruistic behavior.

Although the neighborhood was rough, it was also a community in which there was a lot of talk about godliness. There was a great deal of ranting and railing against sin, and when children misbehaved, they were often chastised for being sinners. But the truth was that the adults around Oliver rarely behaved in decent ways. What he saw, day in and day out, were grown-ups who put their own self-interest ahead of others, who were mistrustful of one another, and who assumed the worst about children.

When Oliver was ten years old, he met a slightly older boy named Jack. Jack, too, had had a rough childhood, but he seemed to have weathered it well. He was full of life, good at things, and savvy, and he seemed genuinely interested in who Oliver was. Oliver felt for the first time that he had a friend. Jack invited Oliver to his home, shared confidences with him, hung out with him, and introduced him to other kids and to his family. But here, too, Oliver came face-to-face with the duplicity and selfishness he had seen everywhere in his foster home. Jack's father, it turned out, was a petty thief who encouraged Jack and his friends to help him out in his nefarious schemes.

During his early teens, it seemed that Oliver couldn't get away from the very situations that have been shown, again and again, to push people toward immoral behavior. He had every motivation to lie and steal and little encouragement to do the right thing. The adults in his life provided perfect role models for cheating, and his peer group was every parent's nightmare, low achievers who had already chosen easy money and thrills over conventional accomplishment and community engagement. Oliver was surrounded by badness—the kind that often seems to shape a child. If you had known Oliver during these impressionable years, you might have predicted that he was doomed to the same kind of sordid, low life of those around him.

And yet, from the moment he could talk, Oliver seemed different from the people around him. He was honest and kind. He went out of his way for other people. He not only knew what was right, but he also did what was right. Although he hung out with kids who stole and committed other petty crimes, each time he was supposed to demonstrate his own prowess, he found a way not to steal. When he was about eleven, he fell in with a gang of kids trying to rob a house. All Oliver could think of was how he might warn the family that owned the house. He got caught doing it, but he succeeded in stopping the crime. Again and again, he behaved in ways that were good for others, even when it cost him personal comfort. No matter what pressures he faced to engage in selfish and hurtful behavior, Oliver's inner goodness steadily shone through. By the time he was a young teenager, it was clear that nothing could have thrown young Mr. Twist's moral compass out of whack. Some strands of the moral braid are part of the basic human architecture, and Charles Dickens dramatized that truth in his novel *Oliver Twist* as well as anyone could. But most children aren't as good as Oliver, who seemed immune to every sinister influence, with an unshakable urge to do the right thing.

Yet most of us don't turn out to be like Bernie Madoff, either. In real life, children aren't villains or heroes. Annie, for instance, was an inscrutable mixture of the two. Annie was the eldest of three children. Incredibly pretty, with slightly tilted blue eyes, a wide lush mouth, and almost white blond hair, she was as smart as a whip, brimming with talent and energy of all kinds. She spoke early and seemed eager for big, new words. At age four, she chastised her one-year-old brother for tasting her food when she was sick. "Hal, don't eat it. It might be confectionary."

She was adored by her parents, who loved her feistiness and precocity. She was the kind of exuberant and animated child teachers are drawn to. But she was also headstrong from the get-go. When her babysitter insisted that they leave the zoo one day, Annie sat down on her haunches and growled. She spoke to adults outside her family as if she were their peer. And somehow her willfulness seemed to go hand-in-hand with a determined sense of sneakiness as well.

Annie's aunt tells the following story: "We were sitting at the picnic table in the yard. It was early August, and the whole extended family of fifteen people was eating dinner together on one of the first nights of our annual summer reunion in Maine. Just as the adults and older children were leaning back to enjoy their second helping more slowly, I noticed that my two-year-old niece, Annie, had left the table. Where was she? We rushed to check the dangerous places (the road or the lake near the house) and then began to wonder where on earth she could have gone. Who knows what led me up the stairs to the bedroom where I was staying? There was Annie, busily doing something she didn't want me to see. She must have heard my steps on the wood stairs, because by the time I walked through the door, she was sitting on the floor near the bed, looking at me with an expression of furtive innocence. 'Annie,' I said, 'what are you doing up here, sweetie pie?' 'Nothing,' she answered. Her blue eyes were wide with feigned blankness and surprise at my question.

"I don't know what inkling drew me into the bathroom to peek inside the small cloth case in which I had brought my jewelry when I visited my parents' home. Empty. By then, my sister Jodie, Annie's mother, had joined me in the bedroom. 'Annie,' she said with some force, 'what are you doing up here?' 'Nothing,' Annie answered, shaking her head vigorously, her voice slightly raised, reflecting her surprise that we were questioning her. It was clear that she took umbrage at our suspicion. 'Nothing, Mommy.' I whispered to my sister, 'I think she took my jewelry.' Jodie peered down at her little daughter. She had only been a mom for two years, but she already had a bead on her little girl. Annie's eyes darted toward the hiding spot—her underwear. Sure enough, we saw a small bulge with sharp edges and little gold fasteners and a few beads peeking out of the hem of Annie's underpants. Jodie put out her hand, saying, 'Annie, give them to me right now.' I could hardly hold in my laughter. As we left the bedroom with Annie trailing behind, Jodie leaned over and hissed to me, 'My daughter's a jewelry thief.'"

What can you tell from a toddler's misdeeds about her moral fiber? Would Annie's naughtiness turn out to be a sign of things to come or just a red herring?

Each baby arrives with a leaning toward goodness or badness. We know, for instance, that some children are born with a strong predilection for trouble. At the extreme end, we call people like this sociopaths, people who seem to have literally no concern for the well-being of others, no sense of moral obligation, and no innate grasp of the difference between right and wrong. They seem, in other words, to have no conscience. And to some degree, the opposite is true as well. At eighteen months old, many babies seem to have a natural impulse that does, in fact, contribute to what we think of as moral behavior—they appear to feel the psychological distress of other babies.

## The Root of Good Deeds

If you've ever watched two toddlers who have spent time together, perhaps in a family day-care setting or in a sandbox, you might have witnessed a version of the following scene. One of the children falls down, hurts herself, and begins sobbing. The other child, who had been busily playing nearby, hears the crying and looks over at his buddy. A worried look suffuses his face. He studies his friend's agonized sobs for a moment, gets up, marches over to her, reaches out, and offers her his own blankie. Anyone could see that he is hoping the blankie that comforts him so reliably will also help his friend feel better.

Psychologists view this as a clear indication that some toddlers feel empathy—they feel the distress of someone else and are moved to reduce that distress. Because he is still just a toddler, unable really to think about other people's thoughts, a young child will often offer his suffering friend the object that would comfort himself rather than the friend. In one classic example, a little boy saw his friend fall and dissolve into tears. Even though the crying child's mother was standing nearby, the little boy, stricken at his friend's distress, grabbed his own mother's hand and dragged her over to the other little boy.

The term *empathy* first appeared in the work of a German psychologist, Theodore Lipps, toward the end of the nineteenth century. The German word *Einfühling* literally means "feeling into another" and conveys the somewhat primitive, nonrational quality of empathy. Psychologists believe that empathy emerges before its more sophisticated cousins sympathy and perspective taking, both of which require a level of complex thinking that young children might not yet be capable of. You watch another person who has just heard terrible news, and you feel as if there is lead in *your* stomach. Your face has the same miserable pale cast that the other person's does. That's empathy. But even if you don't feel *Einfühling*, you can think through what another person is feeling. I've watched people in restaurants be high-handed and haughty with a waiter. If they paused for a moment and imagined what it would feel like to serve one hundred people in a hot, crowded room, they might see the situation differently and they just might change their tone. Even if such perspective taking doesn't occur spontaneously, people can deliberately lead themselves through such a mental exercise, although this is a different process from empathy.

To take someone's perspective and to feel concern for what you think they are feeling both require cognitive processes not available to young children. In other words, they can "feel into another person" before they can think about what someone else thinks or feels.

But as anyone with more than one child can attest, not all kids are equally empathic. Imagine the following experiment (not one you could actually carry out, of course). Put three toddlers in a playroom. Make one of those toddlers cry, and then watch the reaction of the other two. One might look very worried at the sight of her friend's tears and then come wobbling over to offer her crying friend her bottle. The other child might glance at the one who is crying, study him for a moment, and then go right back to playing. Researchers believe there are two components that contribute to a child's level of empathy: the intensity of emotion she feels in general and her ability to regulate those feelings. Children who have very intense emotional reactions but have a lot of trouble managing their feelings might actually avoid other children in distress as a way of avoiding their own discomfort. And children who don't tend to feel strong emotions might just not care that the other child is in pain.

This should come as no surprise. Adults clearly vary in their levels of empathy. Not all adults are equally upset when they see another person look sad or scared, and not all adults are equally quick to try to help the other person feel better. As with young children, some adults get very upset when they see another person hurt, but seeing the person's pain doesn't spur them to help.

In recent years, there has been a great flurry of activity aimed at increasing empathy in elementary and high school students, as a way of decreasing bullying and social exclusion. Can you teach an unempathic person to feel the pain of others? Is that a first step toward goodness?

Norma and Seymour Feshbach, psychologists at UCLA, believe so. Their approach hinges on the link they see between aggressive behavior and empathy. All of us have periodic urges to hurt or dominate another person. But if you feel empathy, you might rein in your aggressive urges, so as to avoid the pain you'd feel for having caused someone else distress.

The Feshbachs reasoned that if they could increase aggressive children's tendency to empathize with others, they might be able to teach children to be less aggressive. Their study involved more than eighty schoolchildren in the Los Angeles school system. First, they asked teachers in elementary schools to rate how helpful and kind the children in their classrooms were. Then the children were put into small work groups that met for one-hour sessions over a period of ten weeks. Each group contained some children who had been identified as highly aggressive and some who were in the normal range (from low to moderate). The children spent the "workshop" time playing various games designed to teach them how to feel what others were feeling and see the world from another's perspective. In empathy camp, the children looked at photographs of people's faces and tried to "name that feeling." In another game, the counselors described people who had been put into various situations and then asked the children to role-play. The kids drew pictures and told stories showing how the world looked from someone else's perspective. "What would the world look like to you if you were as small as a cat?" "What birthday present would make each member of your family happiest?" Over the course of the ten weeks, the tasks became increasingly abstract and complex. Instead of imagining how a friend would feel if her favorite toy was broken, the now seasoned campers were asked to imagine "What would your best friend do if he found a lost child in a department store?"

Meanwhile, the children in the control condition also participated in thirty hours of problem solving and games, but the games they engaged in were focused on learning about trees, water, and the weather. At the end of the ten weeks, teachers were asked to think over recent days and to rate their students again (without any knowledge of the groups the children had been in). The children who had participated in the empathy-training workshops were rated as kinder, more helpful, and more thoughtful toward others than those who had been learning about the natural world. Interestingly, the researchers reported that the children far preferred the nonempathy activities (those included in the control condition). As Norma Feshbach put it, "Empathy training is hard work."

Empathy is not all that different from baseball. As anyone who's watched tee-ball or mini-league can tell you, some kids are born with the ability to hit a ball. As early as age three, some kids know how to hold a bat, how to keep their eye on the ball, when to begin swinging, and how to use their bodies to send the ball flying in the right direction. For those kids, few words or lessons are needed. They don't need to be told the right batting stance or how to swing the bat—they just feel it and do it.

However, kids who lack that intuitive feeling can learn the components—they can practice watching the ball, someone can show them the right way to hold the bat, and they can learn how to adjust to different kinds of pitches and when to hold off and not swing at all. With good instruction and practice, those components can come together and enable a Little-Leaguer to do well at the game. That kind of kid might never have the feel for the game that naturally talented kids have, but he can still play baseball.

The Feshbachs' research suggests that those children who don't seem naturally to feel the pain of others can learn to recognize the feelings of others, imagine what they are going through, and identify with their circumstances. With practice and instruction, they can become empathic and, perhaps more important, less aggressive.

If Bernie Madoff had participated in an empathy workshop, it might have helped—but it wouldn't have been enough. If a toddler feels sad when her friend cries, that doesn't automatically mean that she will grow up to be an especially kind and ethical person, particularly when doing right comes at her own expense. Empathy might be a powerful building block for doing the right thing, but there is more to it than that. The proclivity to help others at one's own expense, otherwise known as altruism, is also a key component of what we think of as moral behavior.

## Selfish Genes Cause Kindness

My stepfather was a man with a complicated moral code. A farmer, he would risk his life for a stranger drowning in the ocean and happily give away hundreds of dollars to someone down on his luck. But he would lie without batting an eyelid to keep others from interfering with his plans. He used to say, "Nice guys finish last." He'd wait a beat and then, to make sure we understood his cynical philosophy, add, "Survival of the fittest!" with a knowing nod. He assumed that this proclamation would remind us that the tougher, more ruthless person would always do the best. He was sure, as many people are, that Darwin's great discovery was that looking out for number one is the surest way to survive. If this were true, what on earth would make any of us go out on a limb for another person? Why would our kids acquire an impulse to put other people's needs first?

Psychologists and philosophers used to believe that altruism was a highly sophisticated behavior based on an exalted sense of the common good. It represented the triumph of human rational thought over our basic instincts. Yet some evolutionary psychologists have shown that monkeys, whales, and bats, among other species, regularly put the well-being of others ahead of their own needs.

What would make an animal put its own survival at risk for the good of another creature? Take a moment to consider how any behaviors (rather than a physical characteristic) might evolve. People prefer sweets because the ones who liked bitter food died eating poisons, while the ones with a sweet tooth gravitated toward high-calorie items. The ones drawn to high-calorie foods lived long enough to have babies who inherited their preference for sweet things. People with the cognitive capacity to invent and use tools were more likely to live in shelters and make weapons, which helped them survive animal attacks and bad weather. The tool users were much more likely to survive long enough to pass on their particular kind of cognition. The ones whose mental processes kept them from figuring out how to build a shelter or a weapon probably died before they had a chance to pass on their non-tool-use way of thinking.

But what possible advantage could there be in dying for the sake of another? Why would altruism give any organism, human or not, a leg up in survival? The answer, according to Richard Dawkins, is that it is our genes, not our individual selves, that need to survive. If helping another creature helps a species survive, the next generation of that species will contain more individuals who help. People with genes that cause them to help others live longer. Those who live longer have more opportunities to have babies and therefore pass on those helping genes. Selfish genes might cause unselfish behavior. This is why scientists have found that both people and animals are more likely to help out another when that other is closely related to them.

When Harald Euler and Barbara Weitzel asked adults to think back about their childhood and report how they were treated by their grandparents, they found that most people remembered kinder, more protective treatment from their maternal grandmothers than from their other grandparents. What does this have to do with the evolution of altruism? The more certain people are that their grandchildren are genetically related to them, the more likely they are to have an instinct to protect them. Your mother's mother had a lot of certainty that you were related to her, hence her great interest in your well-being (and the survival of her genetic material). Your father's father, on the other hand, could never be absolutely sure that you were genetically related to him (two different opportunities for a mixup). In one startling experiment, identical twins were much more cooperative to each other than were same-sex fraternal twins. In other words, two same-age brothers help each other a lot more when, by doing so, they are supporting the survival of 100 percent of their genes. Same-age brothers who share only 50 percent of their genes (fraternal twins) don't have as much incentive to help each other.

## Selfishness Rears Its Ubiquitous Head

Although the urge to help others might be part of the equipment we come with, so, too, is the impulse to put oneself first, even when it hurts others. And if there are signs that babies have the seeds of goodness in them, it is even clearer that in our first years, selfishness runs rampant. Some of the most important developmental psychologists have described infants as solipsistic, autistic, and egocentric. In fact, Anna Freud famously claimed that if you put a toddler on a street corner in Cambridge, by the time she made her way to Harvard Square, she would have committed every crime known to mankind. We assume that babies are born heedless of the rights of others, consumed with the impulse to please themselves at all costs.

In a videotape I made years ago in a day-care center, a little boy named Daniel, with a huge mop of very dark brown hair, is rocking away with great energy on a small wooden rocking boat. Another little boy, Max, who is about two and a half years old and has a wide freckled face and inscrutable blue eyes, is playing nearby with some blocks. Suddenly, the rocking boat catches Max's attention. He drops the blocks and walks over to Daniel, who continues to rock away in the boat. Without saying a word, Max tries to knock Daniel out of the boat so that he can get in. Outraged, Daniel shouts, "Maaaxxxx! I'm rocking!" But Max doesn't seem to register Daniel's dismay. Max quietly and insistently pulls at Daniel until he's pushed him off balance and dragged him out of the boat. While Daniel marches over in tears to complain to a teacher, Max complacently climbs into the boat and begins to enjoy the ride.

Psychologists call Max's behavior, common in toddlers and preschoolers, instrumental aggression. Max isn't being mean in order to hurt someone or dominate others. He simply wants what he wants, and he won't hesitate to knock over anyone who comes between him and his object of desire. While young children do care about other people—offering them blankies or gently stroking a sibling who has been hurt—the dominating force that energizes them is the drive to fulfill their own needs and desires.

Sigmund Freud argued that throughout life, the drive to please oneself guides and explains much behavior, but that over time, one learns to temper it in order to live with others. He also argued that we develop a conscience by internalizing the mores of our parents—becoming like them is safer than trying to defy them. While the specifics of Freud's explanation have not held up to scrutiny, research has amply documented the enormous power of people's urge to satisfy their desires. When your young child seems driven by a selfish demon within, it does not mean he is doomed to a life of heartlessness or greed. It means he is not yet able to wrestle his impulses to the ground. Human development takes time and, with any luck, involves the guidance of moral parents.

When Max knocked the little boy off the rocking toy, Daniel, grief-stricken, stomped over to the teacher to protest the injustice. Then the teacher did what adults from time immemorial have done when children displayed their raw need to run roughshod over others in order to please themselves. She chastised Max. "That wasn't nice, Max. Daniel was riding the boat. What do you say when you've hurt someone?" The urge that most adults feel to chastise is just as natural as the urge the child feels to get what he wants at all costs.

Children grow up in a world of others and usually find early on that they are not allowed simply to take or do whatever they want. If they are especially attuned to the expectations of adults—if they are eager to please others and win approval—they quickly come face-to-face with a dilemma: how can they get what they want without displeasing those around them?

That was certainly the bind Annie found herself in. By the time Annie was six years old, her attraction to surreptitious adventures had expanded. She climbed out the window of her bedroom, under the guidance of a nine-year-old friend, so that they could sneak off to the park across the street. A year later, her mother discovered her hiding in her parents' closet, phone book and telephone in hand, making prank calls to unsuspecting strangers. Again, her older friend was there with her, offering suggestions. Upon getting caught, Annie again insisted that they had done nothing wrong. She seemed instinctively to know the strategy so many adults have used when caught in the wrong: "That's my story, and I'm sticking to it."

"Annie doesn't care how she makes other people feel," her father lamented. "Where does that come from?"

What made her behavior more baffling was that it was certainly not a family trait. Hal, three years younger than Annie, had red hair and a pale, narrow face. Although he was often exuberant, he had a voice that could express woe like nobody's business. Hal seemed to have been born concerned about the feelings of others. When he was two, he insisted that Annie couldn't join him on a special trip to the store their mother had invited him on. Annie was crestfallen. For once, he had outdone her. But when he got into the car, his long narrow mouth turned down like Charlie Brown's. "I don't like what I just said to Annie," he said. He made his mother turn around and pick Annie up so she could go, too.

When Annie was six and Hal was three, they learned the rhyme "Sticks and stones can break my bones, but words will never hurt me." Annie leaned her head to one side and said, "That's true. Words don't hurt me." She gazed at her mother with her light blue eyes, calm and inscrutable. She looked as pretty as a picture and impermeable.

But Hal's eyes widened. "Words can hurt *me!*"

His sensitivity, his compassion for others, and his eagerness to help didn't rub off on Annie. Instead, Hal's thoughtfulness seemed, in the family constellation, to make up for Annie's lack of empathy.

Then came the clincher. Annie, now seven, was sharing a bedroom with Hal, now four, and their eighteen-month-old brother, Nate. Their parents had hatched this sleeping arrangement because none of the kids was a good sleeper. Perhaps, they thought, if the children had one another's company, they'd stay out of their parents' room. Hal's room became the sleeping room. Annie's room became the playroom for all. The plan seemed to be working wonders. All three kids were sleeping better than they ever had. But suddenly, three months into the new arrangement, the baby started waking in the middle of the night, crying loudly. When their mom, Jodie, went in to see what was wrong, she found the baby agitated and Annie wide awake, wanting conversation and comfort. Jodie worried that the baby was waking Annie up. Maybe she should change things around. Then, after a few weeks of this, when Jodie was at her wits' end, Annie leaned in toward her mother and confided, "I've been waking up Nate. I knew that if he cried, you'd come in. I wanted to see you."

That morning, Jodie called her older sister, desperate, and announced on the phone, "Annie is selfish. And she's sneaky. What am I going to do? I've already tried stars, checks, losing TV rights for sneakiness, and offering a trip to the ice cream store for acts of unselfishness."

Her sister, a schoolteacher, reminded her, "Discipline isn't a form of control. It's a process of education."

Way back, after the stolen jewelry incident, Jodie had been on the lookout for opportunities to instill a stronger conscience in her slightly ruthless little girl. Jodie seemed to know intuitively that Annie needed lots of what psychologist Martin Hoffman calls parenting by induction, the process by which parents help children think about how their actions make other people feel. When parents are encouraged to use this approach with children, they often get it slightly wrong. Once, after speaking to a group of parents about this, I overheard one of the dads say to his son, "If you don't share your bike, the other kids won't want to play with you." This is not what Hoffman had in mind, since the parent was simply reminding the child to think about his own interests. Encouraging thoughtful behavior works better when you say, "Think how it feels to your friend when he doesn't get a turn," thereby directing your child's attention to the feelings of others.

There are so many things developmental psychologists don't yet know, but one thing the research has shown quite clearly is that when it comes to raising children who are thoughtful, the way a parent disciplines the child has a huge impact.

One day, Annie and her mother went to see a pottery exhibit by a cousin who attended college nearby. In her typically exuberant manner, which sometimes seemed heedless of the things and people around her, Annie began twirling around the gallery. In a flash, she had knocked into one of the pedestals, sending it crashing to the floor, along with the large ceramic jug that had been placed on it. She had broken a college senior's thesis project, smashing it into a million little pieces. Annie collapsed onto the floor in alarmed tears and shame. Used to mishaps like this from her lively and somewhat unconstrained little girl, Jodie knelt down to console Annie and enlist her help in cleaning up. But Jodie took it one step farther. She and Annie wrote a note for the student, expressing their apologies and regrets about the broken jug.

A number of studies have shown that when you criticize a child for hurting another or take away a privilege or a valued item when the child has been unkind, it does no good. When your child grabs a toy from another kid at the playground, giving her a time-out will not help her learn to share. Punishment doesn't work.

Yet not all rewards work equally well, either. In one study, toddlers were put in a room with an adult who was engaged in other tasks. At some point, the adult dropped a pen or a piece of paper and then reached for it, making it clear that he was having trouble reaching it. The idea was to see if the toddler would come over and help the grown-up reach the object or do nothing. Toddlers who helped the adult moved on to the second phase of the study. In this phase, they were once again placed in a room with a grown-up who needed help. But a third of the children received praise for their help: "That's really nice." Another third received a small cube, part of a larger toy they had previously found very appealing. The final third received no reward. Instead, the adult merely took the fallen object the toddler had helped reach and went back to the original activity. During a subsequent series of play sessions, each child went through five versions of this, always with the same kind of feedback. Which type of response led to the most helping over the long run? You might think that the children who received a toy would be the most likely to continue helping adults. Not so. The children who received praise were much more likely to continue helping the adult than the children who received rewards. Perhaps more surprising, the children who received no feedback were almost twice as likely to continue as the ones who received a prize. In other words, rewards can undermine intrinsic motivation. The findings of this study remind us that, like many complex characteristics, goodness cannot simply be trained into a person.

But this issue has more layers than an onion. While it's clear that praise works better than prizes, not all praise is the same. The difference is seemingly subtle. Telling a child that it was good that he shared his cookies might get him to share more of his cookies right then and there. But it won't have as powerful an effect as letting the child know you believe his actions reveal that he is a good person.

In one study, a group of seven- and eight-year-olds were brought to a trailer set up outside their school in Toronto. The first time they came to the trailer, they were told that the experimenter wanted their opinion on a new toy, a bowling game. They were told that when they had scored seventy to eighty points, they could take two marbles from a bowl of marbles, which would be traded for a prize at the end of the game. The children were also told that they could put one of their marbles into a bowl for poor children (a bowl was on the table with a picture of two "indigent-looking children" and a sign that said, "Help Poor Children") so that the poor children could have toys as well.

While the children played the game, the experimenter stood slightly off to the side to prompt a child if he or she didn't spontaneously give a marble to the donation bowl. If the child didn't donate, the experimenter would say something like, "Remember, you can give one of your marbles to the poor children if you want to." When they were done with the game, the experimenter made one of three comments to each child. The first attributed goodness to the child: "Gee, you shared quite a bit. I guess you're the kind of person who likes to help others whenever you can. Yes, you are a very nice and helpful person." Other children were offered old-fashioned reinforcement for their good deed: "Gee, you shared quite a bit. It was good that you gave some of your marbles to those poor children. Yes, that was a nice and helpful thing to do." And finally, as in all good experiments, some children served as the control condition and received a comparatively neutral comment: "Gee, you shared quite a bit." After the statement, the children were left alone to play another game while the experimenter watched through a one-way mirror to see how much each child donated.

After the second game, each child chose a prize and was given twelve colored pencils as an additional prize for participating. They were told that they could donate some pencils for children in the school who had not gotten to participate. At that point in the experiment, the children who had received both forms of praise donated more pencils than the children who had simply been told, "Gee, you shared quite a bit." If the experiment had stopped there, the researchers could easily have thought that praise encourages good deeds and that it doesn't matter what form the praise takes. But the experiment didn't stop there.

One week later, the children returned to the trailer and participated in a task involving folding cardboard cards so they could be used as roofs for toy houses. The experimenter remained present while the children folded four cards each. Again, children heard one of three comments: "Thanks for folding the cards. You know, you are certainly a nice person. I bet you're someone who is helpful whenever possible." Or "Thanks for folding the cards. You know, that was certainly a nice thing to do. It was good that you helped me with my work here today." Or the bland "Thanks for folding the cards." The experimenter then gave each child a Viewmaster toy and said that he or she could either play with the toy or fold cards for the next five minutes while the experimenter made a phone call.

Two weeks later, the experimenter came to visit the children in their classrooms. She announced that she was collecting drawings and craft materials for sick children in the hospital. Children were given paper for drawing and asked to put their artwork in a bag to be collected in two days. The children who had been given the sense that their previous actions reflected a truly good inner self were far more likely to draw pictures for the sick children.

The moral of the story: When children are encouraged to believe they are good, they are more likely to be good. Taken together, this study and the study in which children were praised or not praised for helping an adult remind us that goodness is not a surface behavior that can easily be trained into or out of a child. Children who have the impulse to help do so because of that impulse, not because of any feedback they get. Moreover, appealing to the child's inner sense of her core goodness affects her more than more transitory pleasures such as simple praise for a specific good deed.

But not all good deeds begin in the gut or the heart. Some begin in the head. When asked to talk about their moral impulses, some people say that they don't feel empathy—they don't feel a twinge in the gut or a lump in the throat hearing the plights of others. They're guided instead by what they think is right, a moral code that leads them to do the right thing—help others, be honest, and contribute to the common good. Seeing another child crying and offering him your bottle is just the beginning. The kinds of morality we judge others by in adulthood often involve far more deliberative rational acts than that. Bernie Madoff carried out his scam over more than a twenty-year period. People who join the Peace Corps think about it for a while before they do it.

What did Madoff talk about at the dinner table when he was young? And was it different from what Warren Buffett talked about at his dinner table? Buffett provides an interesting contrast to Madoff. One of the richest men in the world, Buffett has given away a huge amount of his money. He regularly admits his mistakes and has frequently urged the government to impose higher taxes on people like himself. In 2006, he gave a vast amount of money to Bill Gates's foundation, eschewing the glamour and stature of having a foundation in his own name. Either Madoff or Buffett might or might not step off a curb to pull an old lady out of the way of a speeding cab, but when it comes to their moral thinking, they obviously differ. Did that difference start during their childhood?

How would you suss out a person's way of thinking about moral issues? Lawrence Kohlberg, considered the godfather of research on moral development, constructed stories that embodied moral dilemmas. He told the stories to children of different ages and asked for their response. He argued that their answers revealed their developmental level of moral reasoning. Children (and adults) find the stories he used intriguing and often not easy to respond to in a simple way. That is what makes them so useful in eliciting a person's train of moral thought. Kohlberg used many stories, but this is his most famous, the "Heinz Dilemma."

> In Europe, a woman was near death from cancer. One drug might save her, a form of radium that a druggist in the same town had recently discovered. The druggist was charging $2,000, ten times what the drug cost him to make. The sick woman's husband, Heinz, went to everyone he knew to borrow the money, but he could get together only about half of what it cost. He told the druggist that his wife was dying and asked him to sell it cheaper or let him pay later. But the druggist said no. The husband got desperate and broke into the man's store to steal the drug for his wife. Should the husband have done that? Why?

The answers children gave to Kohlberg's moral dilemmas led him to argue that all children developed in a particular sequence. Toddlers respond only to reward and punishment. They'll do anything and everything they want, as long as they can get away with it. The preschooler, though, begins to monitor her own behavior, eager to gain approval. She tries not to do the things that elicit a frown or her mother's disapproval. She is eager to help when she thinks this will earn a smile from her father or kind words from the teacher. As children enter elementary school and are capable of more complex abstract thought, Kohlberg argued that they begin to use a set of rules to guide their behavior, rules that reflect the conventions of their community. The schoolchild's morals are defined, then, by what is acceptable to others rather than any abstract set of principles. By the time teenagers are capable of abstract reasoning, Kohlberg argued, they are also capable of knowing the right thing to do, even when that means breaking the rules within a given institution or community. Stealing medicine to help a sick person who has no money might be illegal, but it might be the right thing to do. From Kohlberg's perspective, the more able one is to reflect and deliberate using abstract principles, the more sophisticated one's moral sense will be.

But in the years since Kohlberg devised his famous scenarios, it's become clear that what people say is the right thing to do doesn't always match up to their actions.

Psychologist Eugene Subbotsky told young children in Russia a story about a little boy who was asked to move some balls from a pail to a jar without using his hands. But once the grown-up left the room, the little boy had trouble, so he used his hands. Subbotsky asked the children in his study, "Was the little boy wrong to do that? Why?"

Almost all of the children thought it was wrong for the little boy to break the rules. But then Subbotsky put the children in the same situation as the boy in the story. He brought them into a little playroom and asked them to use a shovel to put some balls into a jar. The first time they did it, everything went smoothly. They could all accomplish the short, simple task. But the second time they had to do it, they were handed a convex shovel that made it nearly impossible to lift the balls. To succeed at their assignment, they would have to use their hands. About a third of the children lied afterward, pretending they hadn't used their hands. In other words, for some children, it is actually quite easy to pry apart their moral reasoning from their moral actions.

Adults are not all that different. Many of us spout off at the dinner table about what the right thing to do is, only to turn around and do the selfish, sneaky thing at the grocery store or in our office. Harvard's Joshua Greene believes that some scenarios hit our emotional hot spots more than others and that this might provide a clue about why we sometimes find it hard to do the right thing.

Greene and his colleagues use functional magnetic resonance imaging (fMRI) equipment to try to figure out what role emotion plays in people's moral reasoning. Greene's interest stems from an intriguing phenomenon. Consider the following dilemma. A runaway train is headed for five people who will be killed if it proceeds on its present course. The only way to save them is to hit a switch that will turn the train onto another set of tracks where it will kill one person instead of five. Should you turn the train onto the other track in order to save the five people at the expense of the one person? Most people say yes.

But then Greene considers a slightly different version of the dilemma. Again, a train threatens to kill five people. You are standing next to a large stranger on a footbridge that spans the tracks, between the oncoming train and the five people. In this scenario, the only way to save the five people is to push the stranger off the bridge onto the tracks below. He will die if you do this, but his body will stop the train from reaching the other five. Should you save the five others at the expense of one? Most people say no.

Greene presents these two versions of the dilemma to experimental subjects hooked up to fMRIs. It turns out that when people hear the second version, the parts of the brain associated with emotion light up more than when they hear the first version. In other words, our moral reasoning is influenced by how "hot" or emotional a situation is. What we think is right depends a bit on how involved our feelings are.

If hot issues push a different moral button from cold ones, what good does it do to talk with children about what is right and wrong? The answer is that it helps a lot. Children who are more able to attain Kohlberg's higher levels of moral reasoning are, in fact, more likely to be helpful, to donate money, and to engage in volunteer work. In addition, children who are more able to think about the perspective of another person (which is not the same thing as feeling what another person is feeling) are more benevolent than others.

Paul Harris and Karen Hussar wanted to explore how children think about the moral choices they make. They interviewed children who had chosen to become vegetarians although the rest of their families ate meat. What Harris and Hussar learned was intriguing and suggestive. Kids who have chosen not to eat meat seem to think about the pain animals endure when they are butchered more than do meat eaters (or those who grow up in vegetarian families). It seems that a vivid imagination is part of the mental equipment that supports moral choices, at least the kind of moral choice, such as vegetarianism, that unfolds over time and requires sustained consideration.

Harris and Hussar learned another thing as well. All of the children they studied condemned people who chose vegetarianism and then ate meat more than they disapproved of nonvegetarians. In other words, children seem to understand the idea of moral commitment. Helping children think about goodness makes a difference, not just because there is a logic underlying our moral principles, as Kohlberg suggested, but also because imagining the plights of others (whether they are people or animals), though considered an intellectual activity, might lead us to think and act differently in everyday life. Doing right is complex, and fairly young children seem to know it.

In one study, researchers told six- and seven-year-old children stories about a boy who took something from another child. Then they asked their young subjects two different questions: "Was it right?" "How would you feel if you were that character?" Many of the children said that although the act was wrong, the boy was happy that he got what he wanted. Researchers call this the "happy victimizer" phenomenon. It seems that even first-graders know that there are some things you might do that would make you feel lousy afterward and some acts that are morally wrong but might feel good. For children who don't feel bad when they hurt others or see others in pain, helping them to understand the principle of the matter makes a big difference.

Several months after Annie admitted to waking her brother in the night, Jodie called her sister again. "Did I tell you about Annie's career in drug dealing?" she asked.

At a weekly get-together with other families at the park, the kids played, the parents talked, and eventually, they all went to one family's house for pizza. They had been doing this since Annie was five. This time, Annie, now almost eight, and her buddies disappeared almost instantly. The parents figured they were off playing soccer on the open field at the park. But they had been gone a long time. When one of the mothers went to look for them, she found them huddled around Annie in the park shed. When she looked into the huddle, she saw that they were munching on sweets, a furtive yet glazed look on their faces. All of the children were forbidden by their parents to eat sweets. Annie had brought some of her money from home to the park. She knew that if she offered the other children candy, it would make her queen for the day. As she later admitted, she knew she shouldn't do it. But that didn't stop her. She slipped away on her own and went to spend the money at the park canteen buying her goodies. Then, when the parents weren't paying attention, she beckoned to the other kids, who gathered around her where the parents couldn't see. She doled out the candy, enjoying the hands reaching out to her, basking in her peers' admiration of her feat, happily enjoying her plan's success. When she was caught, she didn't seem at all sorry.

Jodie said to her sister, "Why is she such a sneak? Is she always going to be this way?"

Was Jodie right? Could a seven-year-old be sneaky? Was Annie already destined to grow up doing whatever she needed to satisfy her own desires?

The answer lay in the other pieces of Annie's story. When she was only a year old, Annie had developed a quirky habit. When she was very excited by something (a story, something she saw, a conversation), she would hold her two hands up and wave her fingers in the air, her upper lip extended and trembling as if she were channeling the tension in her mind right down into her mouth. Her godmother referred to the finger waving as "twizzling," perfectly capturing what it looked like and why she seemed to do it. Although her wide face, sprinkled with freckles, so often looked angelic, when she twizzled, she looked a little odd. Her parents periodically wondered if the uncontrollable finger waving might indicate some mild form of autism. Yet as Annie passed the two-year mark, it was clear that she connected to other people better than most. Because she was so precocious with language, she engaged family members and neighbors in all kinds of conversation and seemed to come to life with visitors. Once, during a community softball game in the park, she chose to sit with all the moms and gossip while the other children played. But on most days in the park, she was right in the midst of a gang of girls and boys. She had absolutely no trace of the characteristics associated with autism. On the contrary, she was extraordinarily endowed with intellect, gregariousness, coordination, humor, and good looks. What she also had, however, was a huge amount of drive. Annie liked excitement and was easily excited. Sneaking was just one of the many things that seemed to excite her.

Annie learned to read with ease. She loved to get the right answer at school and loved to be the one who followed the rules. She often stayed near the teacher, once offering to be her first-grade teacher's assistant. Each day when Annie got home from school, she happily pulled out the worksheets from her backpack and settled down to fill them in with energy and confidence.

By seven, she knew the pleasure of getting lost in a chapter book for hours. She gobbled up Nancy Drew mysteries and loved to discuss the small details that suggested a solution to the crime that Nancy was investigating.

When she and her aunt were on a trip to a museum of natural history, they encountered a huge dinosaur with a tiny head. A museum guide began to explain the connection between brain size and intelligence. Annie began to twizzle. She was as charged up by information as she was by sneaking.

In elementary school, some of Annie's great energy for shenanigans began to get funneled into doing well at school. She loved mastery, and, just as significant, she cared about pleasing adults, especially her teacher. Although she liked the feeling of being sneaky, she also liked to shine in the eyes of others. These forces began to shape and whittle her imperviousness to the feelings of others.

In a perfect world, your toddler would show strong signs of empathy. She would look worried when friends got hurt, help someone reach a fallen object, and in other ways exhibit her fledgling sense of caring. But she would also show you that she had the ability to manage or regulate her own emotions, so that rather than running away from other people's upsets, she would be motivated to help them. By the time she was in elementary school, she would have the intellectual capacity to think about what things looked like and sounded like from another person's perspective. And she would have benefited from your efforts to "induct" her into thinking about how her actions affected other people. There's one more thing the perfect world would provide her with: parents who themselves behave morally.

How often have you seen a parent yell at a child to be nice? You might even have done it yourself. It certainly won't surprise many readers to hear that their young children are heavily influenced by how their parents behave, but it's an easy thing to forget in the hurly-burly of everyday life with children. This explains why so many parents insist that their children share toys at the park and then rant at the dinner table about why they shouldn't have to take a pay cut just so Dick down the street can keep his job. I know a very wealthy family whose three daughters spent their childhood with every luxury. At the end of a weekend of swimming and sunbathing, the girls could simply step onto the family plane, barefoot in their bathing suits, to go back to their townhouse in New York City. They had a driver and private lessons in whatever interested them—surfing, figure skating, jazz dancing. They were surrounded by paid help. The children never saw their parents prepare a single meal. The parents were known for their ruthless dealings with the employees of the large, very successful business they owned. By the time the girls were teens, the eldest daughter seemed spoiled and high-handed with others. She expected others to work harder than she did, she wasn't all that kind to her friends, and she showed little concern for the larger world. Her parents were shocked and dismayed. But what had they expected?

When children see their parents putting other people first, they are much more likely to do so themselves. When they hear their parents mulling over how to balance their own needs with the needs of others or how to do what is morally right even when it comes at a personal cost, they internalize those arguments and actions and are much more likely to follow suit. In a society where many people believe they are supposed to knock over others to get to the first spot in line, it's easier said than done to set a moral example for your child. And as Stanford psychologist Bill Damon points out, these examples emerge in both large and small ways every single day: "What parents can do, and what they need to do, is set a moral compass. I don't mean lecturing them about what is right and wrong, or anything that direct, but being able to react and respond to whatever they observe in the child's behavior with a moral voice. It doesn't have to be heavy-handed or moralistic. What really makes a difference is when they are setting their goals in life, if they think whatever means will get me to this end, status and other self-oriented goals, if they really think anything goes, they really are at risk for bending the goals and standards—a lot of those kids will get into trouble.

"Making sure kids don't think the ends justify the means. I am convinced that Bernie Madoff did not get the kind of influence in his childhood that how you do things is more important than whether you succeed. I'll bet no one said to him, 'It's important to me that you are honest and compassionate and fair.' There are a million ways to communicate this to your kids."

When asked about their childhood, non-Jewish Germans who helped Jews during the Holocaust recalled having parents who had been deeply engaged in their communities, often risking personal comfort for larger principles. Not all of us are cut out to be heroes. But anyone who wants their children to grow up thinking and doing the right thing must provide a good example.

## When Your Child Isn't Oliver

Jodie can't make Annie less headstrong, nor would she want to. And she cannot necessarily make Annie a more docile child with less va-va-voom. She can't give Annie a deeply felt, spontaneous sense of compassion. That's not what Annie came with. But Jodie can keep her own moral compass out on display, where Annie is reminded of it all the time. Jodie can stoke the fire of their strong emotional connection, so that Annie will want to please a mother who values kindness and altruism. That strong bond will also lead Annie to want to emulate her mother's good deeds and expressions of compassion.

Annie is smart, and Jodie can make the most of her daughter's intellect by reminding her to think and imagine what she might not feel when left to her own devices. She can help Annie develop habits and inclinations that offset her heedlessness or her lack of sympathy, such as the habit of cleaning up her messes (literally and figuratively), of apologizing, and of righting the wrongs she has done.

When Annie was nine, she went to the zoo with her aunt, the same one from whom she had stolen the jewelry seven years before. Annie went running up to the pen with the animals children could feed and then went running back to her aunt, fist out: "I need quarters. Quarters. Give me quarters." She was still bossy and ready to push for what she wanted. Her aunt handed her several quarters and sat down to watch.

Annie rushed back to the little dispenser where kids were dropping in coins for handfuls of corn. A little boy, perhaps four years old, with pudgy little legs and a slightly bewildered look on his face, was standing at the dispenser, trying to figure out how it worked. His fingers were short and fat, and he was taking a long time trying to get the dial to turn. Annie's hands twitched with impatience. She wanted to use her quarters; she wanted to feed those animals. She began to push forward in the line, shoulder-to-shoulder with the little boy.

Her aunt slid closer to the edge of the bench. Annie put her hand on the little boy. Her aunt leaned forward, ready to call out to stop Annie from pushing the little boy aside, ready to remind her that he deserved a turn and that Annie would have to wait. But then she heard what her niece was saying to the little boy: "Here. Want me to help? You turn the dial like this. Yeah, that's it. Now, let the corn fall into your hand. Yay. You did it. Now you can feed the goat! Take another turn if you want."

Misdeeds are red herrings. All kids misbehave. Testing authority, satisfying one's own needs, seeking pleasure, and putting oneself ahead of others are all natural and healthy characteristics of early childhood. As Freud so eloquently pointed out, growing up is, at heart, the task of learning to redirect your passions so that you can satisfy your needs while being part of a group. On the other hand, some young children, like Annie, begin to show a pattern that suggests that they are no Oliver Twist. They are less empathic than others, more determined to satisfy their own needs at any cost, less willing to be guided by an internal sense of right and wrong. If a child is over the age of five and still behaving this way, it might be a red flag.

Luckily, morality comes from outside as well as from within. You can set a good example by doing good in obvious ways (giving away money, volunteering, speaking out against injustice, standing up for others). But you also need to set an example in subtler ways, thinking out loud about how others feel and sacrificing your own pleasure for someone else's. You can pull a somewhat selfish child toward goodness.

There is a flip side to this. Children who already feel empathic—who tend to think about moral principles and act on them—don't need to be pushed farther in that direction. Nor do they need endless praise for doing what comes naturally to them. Good children usually stay that way. Less good children can become more so.

# 4

# Success: Who Wants to Be a Millionaire?

One mom's triumph is another mom's disappointment. By the time my friend's first son, Ian, was twelve months old, he already loved toys that had doors and levers. He could spend more than an hour at a time sitting on the floor, carefully opening and closing each little panel on his favorite painted wooden activity board.

One day, his grandmother looked on smiling and said, "Look at him play with that thing. He's going to be an engineer!"

His mother laughed and countered, "Yeah, or a doorman."

By the time a child is old enough actually to do things (open doors, draw, dribble a basketball, read the letters on traffic signs, or put together Legos), most parents find themselves daydreaming about the child's future triumphs or perhaps wondering whether the child will have any future triumphs at all.

When I meet with groups of parents who have children in elementary school, I often begin by asking them what they want for their children in the long run. Middle-class parents almost always begin the same way: "I want my child to be happy." Sometimes they will say they want their children to "love learning." But eventually, those wishes and the easygoing, tender looks with which they are expressed give way to a wish parents are more reluctant to articulate: they want their children to be successful. They never say this straight out; instead, they talk about grades, skills, a competitive edge, or college admissions. But most of these specific goals represent a more general notion of success.

One forty-two-year-old father meeting with other parents at a suburban school captured the contrast in just a few sentences: "I want Tess to be happy. You know, I mean, I just want whatever she wants. As for school, the main thing is to like learning. I mean, I hated school when I was a kid. I want Tess to like coming to school. I mean, sure, she needs to get those skills down. I want her to have choices. What if it turns out she wants to be a nuclear scientist? She's gonna need to know her math to make that choice. I mean, I don't care so much what grades she gets, but if she gets to high school and she can't ace the test, where's that gonna leave her?"

We love to hear that success is unpredictable. Most of these same parents rush to read the article that recounts how even though Bill Gates didn't finish college, he is one of the richest men in the world or that Albert Einstein did badly in his elementary-school math class. We find it reassuring to think that great success might emerge late in life and appear to spring from nowhere. However, those extreme examples don't shed much light on anything. The kind of success most of us wish for our kids cannot be defined by those who become so famous we all know about them. While parents might secretly dream that their child will be a millionaire or a genius, deep in our hearts, we know it's not likely. Most of us have more modest hopes—that our children will do well at something, win the good opinion of others, and earn money, influence, or power through their accomplishments. It's not clear that those uncommon stories of outstanding ability have much to say that will help us understand the more common kinds of success our kids might actually achieve.

Several years ago, I took a small charter plane from my hometown in western Massachusetts to the eastern end of Long Island. I am a terrified airplane passenger, dependent on antianxiety drugs such as Xanax and lots of reassurance. To my worried eyes, the pilot who greeted me in the tiny terminal was just the right age. In his early forties, he seemed old enough to have done a lot of flying but young enough so I could count on his fast reflexes and the low probability that he would have a heart attack in flight. In order to distract myself and to forge a bond with the man on whom my life depended for the next forty-five minutes, I began asking him about himself. Lo and behold, he had been a student at Wesleyan, where my own son would soon be attending college. Even then, in my preflight daze, it seemed a bit incongruous to me that a Wesleyan grad would be a pilot for a tiny rural airport. Wesleyan, home to maverick filmmakers, caustic art critics, and bold left-wing activists—a charter pilot?

I asked him how he had gotten from Wesleyan to the cockpit. He said that everyone from his neighborhood was thrilled when he was accepted at Wesleyan. He came from a rural farm family, and everyone thought Wesleyan was a step up, a passport into a world of greater wealth, broader horizons, and bigger challenges. Everyone assumed that he would use this great opportunity to launch himself into business, medicine, or law.

"I tried to do what I thought everyone wanted me to do. I took two premed classes. I attended a special seminar for students interested in becoming lawyers." He knew those were the proper uses of a Wesleyan education. "But," he said with a shrug, "they just weren't for me. I just couldn't muster the interest. I didn't want to be a doctor or a lawyer. I wanted to fly. That's what I had always wanted to do."

Soon after college, he began flight school. And what started as a part-time hobby quickly became his life's work.

"I always figured," he told me calmly as he checked his flight instruments and began to navigate the plane onto the runway, "that if you work hard, you should be able to make a living doing whatever it is you love, no matter how unusual it is."

Thirty thousand feet above land, the roar of the plane engine muting his words, I felt a flash of clarity. I thought, if my child can make a living doing something he loves, I will surely feel he is a success. But what does it take for a child to become an adult who will make money doing something he loves?

If you walk into the St. Paul's preschool in Stockbridge, Massachusetts, the low hum of four-year-old boys and girls, deep in the work of childhood, envelops you. Once you settle in and begin to watch, individual children come into focus, and you realize they are not all doing the same thing. In 1990, I spent several weeks observing and filming the teachers and children at St. Paul's. I was there to collect data for a study of children's play, but I found myself keeping a kind of video journal of two of the children. I wasn't looking to keep track of those kids, nor did I seek them out because of any judgments I had made about them. Filming them didn't have anything to do with the study that had brought me there. I simply found my camera's eye wandering to certain children again and again.

One little boy, Raymond, sported thick, unruly brown hair covering a head that looked just a little large for his slender body, and his voice was unusually gravelly for a four-year-old. He walked into the preschool every day with a warm grin and a slightly quizzical expression on his face. He stepped into the swarm of activity with good cheer, as if he was hoping to hear something funny or interesting. He clearly liked the adults and would often talk enthusiastically with one of his teachers for a few moments, offering vivid descriptions of something that had happened at home. It was easy to see that the adults found him delightful, interesting, articulate, warm, and enthusiastic.

But within moments of chatting, while other kids launched themselves into making airports with wood blocks or setting up elaborate scenarios of households and hospitals in the dress-up corner, Raymond would thread his way through the small groups, heading purposefully for the painting area. When he got to the easel, he rarely hesitated but took up a brush and immediately began dipping it into one of the jars of paint. He never seemed uncertain about where to put the first mark. He didn't pause or glance away lost in thought. He simply began dipping his brush into the paint and applying the colors in unhesitant brush strokes to the white surface. With each application of paint, his tongue would move furiously in and out of his mouth, as if it were the engine powering his actions. While he painted, he seemed quite oblivious to the raucous sounds around him. Once in a while, his face would become suffused with frustration. He would rip the piece of paper off the easel, crunch it up angrily, and toss it into the wastepaper basket. What happened then was the most interesting part of the sequence. Teary-eyed and red-faced, Raymond would begin painting again, more intently and energetically than ever.

I visited St. Paul's on and off for that whole year. From September through June, Raymond would begin his day dipping a brush into red, yellow, green, and purple tempera, pulling the brush across the paper, absorbed in the lines he created on the page. But he wasn't equally absorbed during other parts of the day. One of the teachers told me that she had noted in Raymond's half-year narrative evaluation that he had trouble paying attention during circle time. I watched him when the group was gathered on the rug for their daily meeting. He did often get up and quietly wander away when the teacher was talking about the calendar, the weather, or the letter of the week. He would silently fiddle with objects that were shelved nearby or pass his hand lightly over various books that seemed to catch his eye. Sometimes he'd just look out the window. He wasn't obstreperous, just, it seemed to me, uninterested.

When Raymond was a bit older, his intensity about art was sometimes a problem for him and for his family. In fourth grade, Raymond came home and announced that he was supposed to make a project that involved research on a topic of his choice. He had decided, he told his mother, that he would make a pop-up book about the life cycle of a maple tree. His parents had no idea where this idea came from, but they didn't pay much attention, figuring that he would use the box of paper, crayons, scissors, and glue that they kept in their kitchen for anyone in the family to use. His mother assumed, she told me later, that he would bring home a book about maple trees and then create the pages he wanted for his book. She was all set to buy whatever extra material he might need—some rings to hold the pages together or perhaps some special paper. After he first mentioned it, he didn't talk about it again, and she forgot about it.

Two days before the assignment was due, Raymond had finally finished his research and was ready, he declared, to begin making the book. He began to lay out the pages as he had envisioned them, each more elaborate and ambitious than the one before. Raymond wanted one page to be a disk the reader could rotate, revealing a different limb of the tree for each season. Several pages involved shapes that sprang up in three dimensions. On another page, the reader was to pull a string and make the tree grow tall, beyond the edge of the paper. This was no ordinary book. Bringing Raymond's plans to fruition involved various unusual kinds of paper, nothing his family had at home. He wanted to find bark that could be glued onto the tree trunk and glue that would cement the seeds he planned to paste on, but that wouldn't show under the seed. He needed to invent new methods to attach things to a page that would make the figures move and shift as planned and still look smooth and pretty.

A nice project turned into a heated, tempestuous marathon of gluing and cutting. Each page required several failed attempts. Eventually he was in tears, yelling at his mother, who, she says, was yelling back. "His nose was running, his finger was bleeding, there was ripped paper everywhere, and drips from a glue gun drying on every surface. I screamed at him that I just wasn't going back to town for more paper one more time. I swore at him. I was so impatient. His plans seemed way too ambitious to me. Why couldn't he just draw a nice picture like the other kids?"

Raymond's mother thought they would kill each other before the day was over. But they didn't, and Raymond's book was outstanding. The teacher told Raymond and his mother that she had never seen anything like it. Not all children have such perseverance.

Cody's arrival at St. Paul's each morning was quite different from Raymond's. Cody had inky black hair that was so shiny it practically glistened and beautiful large brown eyes. His small frame was tighter and more muscular than Raymond's. He entered the classroom with a jaunty gait and a calm sense of self-assurance. But his route around the main room at St. Paul's told a different story. Cody's eyes would instantly scan the different clusters of kids. Several boys and girls would often call out greetings to him. He was popular, the kind of kid others wanted to include in their play. He rarely spoke much to the teachers, more interested in jumping into the goings-on at the sand table, the Matchbox car races, or the group effort to make a really tall skyscraper. Activities didn't draw Cody in—other children did.

When the children were asked to decide where to spend their "work" period, Cody would sometimes have difficulty making a decision. He'd often begin at the carpentry table, where he'd pick up a hammer and begin pounding in a nail. But within a few moments, his enthusiasm would pale. His eyes would begin wandering, looking to see where his friend Alec was. He'd lay down the hammer (or the paintbrush, the book, or the puzzle piece) and leave to see if another area of the room would offer more appeal.

Cody was bright as a whip—that showed through when stories were read aloud and he asked sharp questions or at circle time when he told his own stories. He could add numbers accurately and swiftly, and he learned to read with ease. When the children were introduced to a new activity or worked with small pieces (Legos, gadgets, magnifying glasses), Cody was always among the first to figure things out. But nothing really kept his interest for long.

Every September, Cody was excited about school. He missed his friends during the summertime. But as eager as he was to see the other kids at school, around October, he began to feel bored and disenchanted. School sucked. There was nothing to do. The assignments were too easy, and they were dull.

When he was nine, his parents moved him from the public school to a private school, certain that in a more enriched atmosphere, he'd begin to discover what topics he cared about. At first, he was thrilled. He made friends immediately, teachers found him appealing, and he seemed enthusiastic about his classes. But by the spring of that year, he began to feel that school was just no good. In seventh grade, he switched schools again, and then again in ninth grade. He slid through high school, passing but not excelling at anything.

Cody and his parents often spoke of his love for sports. He had a lithe, athletic build and took to soccer, basketball, and baseball easily. In preschool, he was always out in the yard, eager to be a part of any game. He signed up for Little League, soccer team, and the community basketball program. He loved to buy the right shoes for each activity and had lots of pairs. When he was ten years old, the other kids started outpacing him. Some of them were bigger, some came from families with dads who coached, and many practiced for hours every day after school. He became more and more frustrated with each team he was on. He and his parents felt that they had bad luck when it came to the coaches. He never seemed to get enough time on the field to show how good he was. The coach often favored some other kid. By the time he was a freshman in high school, he had quit team sports.

During the last two years of high school, Cody really just went through the motions. He liked his friends, he started dating a girl, and he loved to hang out. He got into a small college in his home state that didn't require good grades or extracurricular accomplishments. But he soon found it boring—he felt he had already moved beyond what college could offer. He dropped out after two years, deciding instead to wait tables and live independently. Attractive, with friends, and good at his job, he was fine. But he still hadn't become the master of anything.

There is no question that practice and hard work lead to success. But even among those who work hard, one or two always go farther and do more than the others. Imagine a group of twenty people who all do the same kind of work, whether it be basketball, farming, music, or mathematics. Assume that these twenty people grew up in the same community, come from the same social class, and were born within a few years of one another (in other words, they are part of the same cohort). Now, imagine that they all had the same basic educational opportunities and all worked equally hard, whether because they shared the same cultural values about work or because these twenty kids were the ones who particularly loved basketball (or farming or mathematics or music). Even with all of those shared circumstances, some of the twenty will do better than others. Examples of this abound. One basketball player makes more shots, dominates other players, and sees the whole court better than the other players, even if all of them make two hundred baskets a day, lift weights year-round, and practice re-bounding daily for two hours. One farmer gauges the first frost more reliably than another, gets more milk from his cows, loses fewer animals to infection, and produces a bigger crop. What explains that kind of difference between individuals? We often look to talent to explain why one person rises to the top. It is easy to look at the stars in any field (Derek Jeter, the Beatles, Freeman Dyson) for some sense of what makes a person stand out in his or her chosen field. But outstanding talent is all too rare and therefore can't explain the kind of individual differences in success that abound among the average population. Something else accounts for the distance between those who get by and those who flourish.

## The Urge to Do Well

When my son Will was four years old, he already loved to play basketball, although we were mystified about where this interest came from. He'd stay out on our blacktop for hours dribbling the ball. His older brother Jake would wander by, sometimes taking a shot, sometimes lounging on the porch, reading a book and watching his brother's relentless activity. One day, I heard Will talking in his high, earnest voice to his big brother. I could tell from the stream of sound that he was dribbling the ball as he spoke and following Jake, who was walking toward the hammock with a book.

"Jake, Jake, do you wanna know something, Jake? Wanna know something? Wanna know how you get good at something? There's only one way. You have to practice and practice and never take a break, and that's the only way to get good at something."

Several months later, I found myself sitting near Will while he practiced his four-year-old version of long jumps on our lawn. He was already very athletic but had the short, solid legs of a pre-schooler. He had found two branches and was using one to mark a starting line and the other as his target. He took several leaps from the starting line to the target. When he had successfully landed just past the target stick three or four times, he moved the target stick about six inches farther away and tried again. When he had conquered this as well, he moved the stick a good two feet farther along. He stood for a moment at the starting line, bending his legs a few times, as if to prepare his body for the leap.

Suddenly, he paused and called out to me, "Mom! Mom! Do you think I can get from here to there? Do you think I can make it?"

I took a quick glance at the distance between the two sticks and responded emphatically, "Whew, that's a long distance. Nope, I don't think you'll get that far."

My small, dark-eyed, chubby-cheeked son gave me a withering glance and said in his most disapproving tone, "You're just saying that so that you can be excited when I do it." After shooting me one more glowering look, he walked over and pushed the target another two feet away.

Somehow, even as a four-year-old, Will had a great desire to improve. Motivation, long understood to be one of the corner stones of success, has presented teachers, parents, and researchers with a tantalizing mystery for years.

Step inside almost any classroom in this country, and you will hear and see teachers trying to motivate their students. In some classes, children earn a star every time they answer all of the questions on a quiz correctly. Some teachers offer elaborate reward systems—for instance, awarding children a piece of candy if they earn a certain number of checks on a chart. As students get older, teachers are likely to use good grades as a motivator. In college, many professors feel that the promise of a good test score will motivate their students to read the books they assign. The powerful intuition underlying these common acts is that rewards are a good motivator. And in one sense, this is true. You can get some children to work hard for a star, a candy, or a grade. But being motivated for a particular task and being a motivated person are not the same thing. The logic behind offering stars and candy flies in the face of the process by which children develop an internal drive to do well.

To see why, consider the following experiment conducted years ago by Richard Nesbitt and his colleagues at Stanford. The experimenters brought markers (a kind the children had not seen before) and paper to groups of children in a local nursery school. In one group, children were told that if they used the markers to make pictures, they would get a certificate with a star and a ribbon on it. Another group of children were not told this, but when they were finished, they unexpectedly received the ribbon and star awards. A third group of children were offered the drawing materials, but no mention was made of possible awards, and none were received.

Most kids like to draw, so you might expect that the kids who also received a reward for their drawings would be twice as interested in making more pictures. And yet the opposite was true. A couple of weeks later, when the researchers returned to the nursery school, they found that the children who had expected a reward for their first pictures had spent much less time drawing in the subsequent weeks. The researchers also asked adults who had not been part of the research team to rate the children's artwork. The drawings of those who had worked toward a reward were deemed to be of lower quality than those of the children in the other two groups. The lesson psychologists drew from this study is that extrinsic motivation lessens a person's intrinsic interest in an activity. This might be particularly true when the activity holds some natural appeal. In other words, if children naturally like doing something, offering stars or candies might actually cause them to like the activity less.

And yet, as Raymond discovered at St. Paul's while making his paintings, even the most appealing activities can be frustrating and discouraging. The more you care about the thing you are doing, the more upset you might be when it doesn't go well. Anyone who has seen a child try unsuccessfully to make a skyscraper with blocks knows that even though something is pleasurable, that doesn't mean every minute of the process is fun.

But why do some children persist when the going gets tough, while others do not? Psychologist Carol Dweck has made it part of her life's work to find out. She believes that some children feel helpless, while others feel sure that they can get better at things: "Helpless and mastery-oriented children are pursuing different goals in achievement situations, with helpless children seeking to document their ability, but failing to do so, and mastery-oriented children seeking to increase their ability, and looking for information that will help them do so."

When four-year-old Will rejected my cheesy ploy to let him impress me, he exemplified the mastery-oriented kind of motivation Dweck has identified: he preferred to try something genuinely difficult rather than merely appear to succeed. Of course, he wanted to impress me—but only if he did something that was actually difficult. In a series of elegant studies, Dweck has shown that children can be sorted into two groups: those who focus on their performance and those who seem more interested in achievement.

In one line of experiments, Dweck offered children the choice between an easy and a difficult version of a task. Children who were focused on performing were likely to choose the easier task, whereas children who focused on achievement preferred the harder task because the "stretch" felt so good for such kids. In the long run, needless to say, children who are achievement-oriented will do better than children who are performance-oriented. Even though picking the easier task might ensure "shining" during some pivotal moment (for example, during an interview for college or work or in a tryout for a team), children who are drawn to challenge make more progress in school and in life.

But the problem, as Dweck sees it, is more layered than this, because it's not self-evident why some children are focused on mastery and others on performance. Watch a child begin to work on a mildly demanding task (such as solving all of the math problems on a worksheet, building a small machine, or crossing a bridge made of ropes), and you might overhear her mumble, whisper, or moan, "I'm not good at this," "This is too hard for me," or simply, "I can't." On the other hand, some children respond in another way altogether: "It's a little easier this time," or, "I'm just gonna make it halfway this time, all the way next time." It seems that underlying the two kinds of motivation are two different ideas children have about what might explain their abilities. Those offhand comments reflect two very different implicit theories of ability. The first Dweck calls the "entity" theory of ability. Some children seem to believe that you either have an ability or you don't, as if it were an entity within you. Such kids often assume that if you have the ability, you were born with it. Other children have what Dweck calls an "incremental" theory of ability. They assume that they can get better at a given skill or activity, bit by bit. Children with an entity theory are much more vulnerable to a performance orientation.

Imagine, for a moment, a seven-year-old girl who sits down to solve some addition problems assigned by her second-grade teacher. If she has an entity theory of ability and she's good at math, she's likely to feel confident but won't necessarily push herself when she gets to more difficult problems. She might figure that she's good enough to get by, and that's enough. However, if she's struggled with addition in the past and believes that ability is an all-or-nothing capacity, she's not likely to spend a lot of time trying to do well on the problems or get extra practice. She might figure that won't get her anywhere. She'd rather take the easier problems and do well on them than take the harder problems and show how bad she is at math.

On the other hand, if your child believes that people can get better at things bit by bit, the challenge is worthwhile. By reaching a little beyond what she can already do, she might well get better. The seven-year-old with an incremental theory of ability is less focused on how easy math has been in the past and more interested in how much better she can get if she keeps trying. This individual difference shows up in all kinds of settings—school, playground, gym, even within the family context.

If you listen in on parents and teachers talking to young children, you can hear these two different approaches in action. A little boy brings home a spelling test from school. Eight words are spelled correctly, and four are wrong. One parent says, "Look at that. Good job. You are a great speller." This comment expresses and encourages an entity theory of ability. The parent is drawing her child's attention to his ability as if it were a steady talent. Another parent says, "Look at that. Good job. You got two more right than last time. All that practicing paid off." This parent is drawing the child's attention to the progress you can achieve with effort, encouraging his child to use an incremental theory of ability.

Dweck has shown that a child's theory of his ability can be influenced. In one experiment, Dweck and her colleagues recruited low-performing seventh-grade students from a New York City public school. Each child participated in one of two eight-week motivational workshops that met once a week for twenty-five minutes. All of the children were taught something about learning and the brain. But the children in the experimental group received four sessions that focused on the message that intelligence is malleable, that connections in the brain are made from learning, and that students are in charge of making those connections happen. To balance this "extra" experience, the subjects in the control group instead received lessons and discussion regarding memory. After the workshops, the researchers asked the students' teachers to report on any students showing change in motivation in math class. Children who had learned that practicing can change the brain seemed more motivated, more interested in trying, and more engaged in their lessons. Just as telling, the math grades of the students who had learned that abilities can change began to climb.

Researchers are not the only ones who can influence a child's theory of ability. Parents can influence their children's motivation through things as low-key as comments that highlight the value of progress and the benefit of effort. On the other hand, families that talk all the time about talent are likely to encourage their children to form an entity theory.

This difference manifests itself at a national level as well. In a classic study comparing educational patterns in the United States with those in China and Japan, Harold Stevenson and his colleague Shin-Ying Li interviewed parents about their children's education experience. It became apparent to Stevenson and Li that one of the clearest differences between China and the United States concerned the relative emphasis parents put on ability and effort. Asian parents tended to underemphasize their children's "natural" gifts and put great faith in the power of effort. They felt that success in school depended almost completely on diligence rather than talent. United States parents, on the other hand, tended to overestimate their children's academic talents and underestimate the value of effort. American parents, and teachers as well, were much less sure about the value of homework, for instance, whereas Asian parents and teachers thought homework was very important and contributed to children's academic success. Unsurprisingly, Asian children reported liking homework more than U.S. children. It is clear that some cultures encourage children to believe that trying pays off. The United States has not been one of those cultures. And yet within the United States, there are many kids with a powerful drive to do well.

Melissa was one of them.

Melissa remembers only one consuming interest from her childhood: getting good grades. Her family expected all four of their children to do well. Melissa attended a good public school in suburban New York, where she got the highest grades in her class and was the valedictorian. When she was waiting to hear from the colleges to which she had applied, she'd bike past the mailboxes of the other top students, peering into their mailboxes to see if they had received thick or thin envelopes. When she learned she had been deferred for early admission to Harvard, she was devastated. Then, in April, she was accepted at Stanford and Yale, as well as at Harvard. She remembers Harvard as one long marathon of studying, with regular breaks for primping with the other girls, drinking just enough to flirt with men, and working her way into and out of one romantic soap opera after another. She worked hard. But she doesn't remember being consumed by the topics she was studying or the professors whose lectures she attended. Yet she graduated summa cum laude and gained admission to one of the most selective graduate programs in the country for her academic field, chemistry. From there, her trajectory continued exactly as it had begun. She got the best postdoctoral position after graduate school and went straight into a tenure-track position at one of the most selective colleges in the country, where she got early tenure. Sure, she was smart. But she had something else as well.

Odd as it may seem, most psychologists are reluctant to make any broad generalizations about the nature of human development. Cautious and precise, researchers typically offer sixteen qualifications for any general statement about human behavior. Asked if it is true that younger siblings are more easygoing than older siblings, they will list all of the situations in which that is not the case. Presented with the proposition that boys and girls differ in certain cognitive tests, they will provide you with ten circumstances that nullify that difference. Yet if you listen closely enough, you can detect a few psychological patterns that psychologists always come back to.

If you sit down to lunch with a group of psychologists and listen to them talk casually, as they gossip about colleagues and friends, they will invariably, however unwittingly, mention a person's neuroticism or introversion or how easy he or she is to work with. When they use these terms, they are drawing on a concept that emerged almost one hundred years ago—the idea that everyone has certain personality traits that cause him or her to act in particular ways again and again and that explain his or her behavior across a wide range of situations. And if you pay attention to the specific qualities psychologists use in their own casual talk, you will begin to realize that they are invoking the explanatory power of five traits in particular: openness, conscientiousness, extroversion, agreeability, and neuroticism. These traits are so prevalent in the field of psychology that there is even an acronym for them: OCEAN. Thousands of experiments done over the span of a hundred years across the globe have shown that these five dimensions are easy to detect and surprisingly useful in forecasting a person's future.

Among the sturdiest of these is the one Melissa possessed so much of: conscientiousness. This all-important quality is not hard to measure, either. Typically, when researchers want to assess the conscientiousness of adult subjects, they simply ask individuals to rate, on a scale of one to five, how true various statements are about themselves:

- I am always prepared.
- I am exacting in my work.
- I follow a schedule.
- I get chores done right away.
- I like order.
- I pay attention to details.
- I leave my belongings around.
- I make a mess of things.
- I often forget to put things back in their proper place.
- I shirk my duties.

Interestingly, people seem to get this right about themselves. People who feel that the first six statements fit them closely but that the second four are off the mark tend to do well at school and at work. In contrast, subjects who say that the first six statements do not capture them well at all and that the last four describe them accurately tend to struggle professionally. They procrastinate, they have trouble following through on projects, and they waste time.

It's harder to imagine the five-year-old who could, or would, give you reliable answers to those same questions. And yet psychologists have been sure for a long time that very young children do show early signs of conscientiousness. So, how do you get an accurate assessment of a child's conscientiousness? You ask the people around her.

Jens Asendorpf and Marcel Van Akenwere followed 151 schoolchildren in Munich from the time they were four until they were twelve years old. They wanted to know whether it was possible to measure conscientiousness in preschoolers and whether young children who seemed very low or high in this dimension remained that way as they got older. When the children were four, their teachers were asked to rate each of them on the following dimensions:

- Is persistent in activities.
- Doesn't give up easily.
- Has high standards of performance for self.
- Is attentive and able to concentrate.
- Is planful, thinks ahead.
- Can be trusted, is dependable.
- Is competent, skillful.

Six years later, the children's parents were asked to rate them on those same dimensions. Another two years later, the researchers sought out friends of their young subjects and asked them for ratings. Asendorpf and Van Akenwere found that a child who was rated by his teachers as persistent, attentive, and trustworthy at four was likely to be rated the very same way by his parents when he was ten. He was also likely to be rated that same way by his friends when he was twelve years old. Perhaps more important, those children who were seen as conscientious by their teachers, parents, and friends were also likely to do better in school.

In every study, even where there are strong, clear patterns, some shifting around occurs. A few of the kids who were rated as highly conscientious in Asendorpf and Van Akenwere's data didn't do so well in school later on. A few of the kids who teachers thought were not conscientious were rated as highly conscientious by their parents. Good researchers pay as much attention to those jagged lines as they do to the straight ones. When Asendorpf and Van Akenwere looked closely at the discrepancies, they found that when the teachers' ratings of the younger children didn't agree with the parental ratings, it was the teachers' ratings that predicted later school success. One way of interpreting this is that teachers are better judges of a child than his parents are. But it also suggests that the signs of school success are just as easy to see in a four-year-old as they are in a ten-year-old (remember, the teachers first rated the children when they were four, and the parents first rated the children when they were ten). The child who is able to focus on a task and keep a clear sense of her priorities, who is able to delay fun in order to fulfill her obligations for school, and who wants to meet the expectations of the adult world tends to be headed for school success, and children exhibit these qualities when they are four years old.

While it's not all that surprising that the child who plans and pays attention is likely to get good grades, it is somewhat more surprising to see that this quality might have a bigger effect than other important indicators, such as a child's intellect, her family's commitment to education, and the particular teachers she is assigned to. Think of it this way: if you went into a preschool classroom and could choose only one quality to use as a way of predicting who would thrive in high school, your best bet would be conscientiousness.

Another child might have had Melissa's particular aptitudes and a lot of ability, but without Melissa's patience, focus, and eagerness to meet the expectations of adults, another child would not have ended up where Melissa did. Sean certainly didn't.

There are lots of good stories from Sean's childhood. His family called him Gosling because of his white-blond crew-cut and cherubic cheeks. When he was eight, he won a state prize for one of his short stories. When his baby sister fell and got a deep gash across her chin, it was Sean, age ten, who held and comforted her, bleeding and crying, all the way to the hospital. By the time he was twelve, he had organized a community soccer game on the town green. When he was fourteen years old, a sophisticated, beautiful older girl from the neighborhood fell madly in love with him. When he was sixteen, he put together a literary magazine of young voices from the L.A. ghetto. As Sean grew up, these anecdotes seemed to his family to create a map indicating where his life was headed. Sunny, vibrant, smart, warm, and reliable, he seemed to be on a path headed directly toward success.

Other stories, less flattering, were barely remembered or quickly dismissed. He took a quarter off his father's bureau when he was six, refusing to admit it afterward. He used someone else's credit card to make long-distance phone calls in high school, and he failed French, even though his aptitude scores were the highest in his class. One of the discarded stories goes like this: when Sean was three years old, his mother, Joan, took him along with her to visit her old friend Alice, who happened to be a child therapist. Holding his mother's hand, Sean bounced happily into Alice's office, plunking himself down in the corner, where Alice kept toys for her young patients. Sean played contentedly while his mother and her friend chatted.

As they said good-bye, Alice pulled Joan aside and said, "I am not sure if you noticed, but while we were talking, Sean pocketed one of the small toys from the play area."

Joan shrugged and laughed, thinking to herself, *Alice is a psychiatrist. Doesn't she of all people know that three-year-olds don't follow all the grown-up rules? It means nothing.*

Joan all but forgot this passing moment, a tiny bit of driftwood in the ocean of experiences that made up family life. The stories of Sean's appeal and ability seemed more salient and seemed to go together, until many years later, when Joan began racking her brain to understand what had gone wrong. By the time Sean was in his early thirties, he had been fired from every job he had been hired for. In constant financial crisis, he was addicted to both gambling and drugs. He lied and stole. Sean probably would have rated low in conscientiousness. But there were other hints that Sean might be not only low in conscientiousness but also high in a characteristic that can cause a lot of trouble.

As I described in chapter 2, Jerome Kagan's research has showed that even when they are babies, we can identify those who will be easygoing later on and those who will react too strongly to new experiences.

The big story Kagan told concerned the strength and stability of shyness (a.k.a. inhibition). But there is another chapter to the story of that research. While most of the children who were classified as uninhibited turned out to be garden-variety kids—comfortable joining a new classroom, trying a new activity, or meeting new people—some of those easygoing kids were *extremely* uninhibited. And *those* children turned out to have a different kind of problem when they got older. Children who had "high temperamental exuberance" as toddlers had low impulse control as teenagers, leading to problems such as drinking, gambling, and lying. And high exuberance turns out to be even more stable over time than inhibition.

Even as a little boy, Sean had been bursting with outgoing energy. But he also kept secrets. He smiled, he pleased, and then he did something he shouldn't while no one was looking. What seemed like vitality was in fact the first sign of impulsivity. In Sean's case, glimmers of impulsivity and the sneakiness it led to were overshadowed by his many appealing strengths. No one really saw that episodes such as the toy pocketing formed a pattern of red flags marking out a path toward future trouble.

These two dimensions, conscientiousness and impulsivity, mark a continuum of sorts, and they seem to provide a startlingly good lens through which to see a child's future ability to get and keep a good job. And yet that's not always enough.

All through Melissa's steady and impressive climb toward the golden ring of her academic career—tenure at an excellent college—she looked at those around her with envy. Why didn't she love what she was doing the way they did? She felt like a fraud. After each major accomplishment, she felt empty, not sure what to set as her next goal. She did excellent research, which got published in all of the best scientific journals. But within weeks of publication of each article, she would forget what the results of her study were. In fact, often just after she collected the data, when some other avid scientist would stay in his or her office until midnight just to go over the results, Melissa would put the data in a drawer and not look at it for weeks. She could never quite lose herself in the work itself. Her parents were proud of her. She had a good salary and the prestige of an excellent job. She was invited to conferences and put on committees at her college. She had intelligence, drive, and diligence. So, from one perspective, she had great success—she embodied the power of childhood conscientiousness to put a child on the path to achievement. And yet something was missing.

"I don't wake up thinking about my research," she said. "I stop thinking about this stuff the moment I leave the office. I never can remember the results of my old research. My brother, who is an economist, thinks it's just weird."

Soon after she got tenure, she felt flat. What would motivate her now? By the time she was thirty-eight, she dreamed of what she would do when she retired. She had lots of conscientiousness but not quite enough of something else. And that something else turns out to be critically important. She claimed she didn't have a passionate interest in the work itself. Remarkably, this vital component of success has only recently begun to attract the attention of researchers.

Developmental psychologist Judy Deloache became interested in what she calls young children's "extremely intense interests" (EII) when her own children were small. She describes the origins of this new work as follows:

> First, I had a little boy who had a fascination with vehicles. One of his earliest words was "cu," (short u, as in duck), which meant car. A little later came "cuck," meaning truck. Whenever we were driving around, he would invest lots of attention in other vehicles—lots of "cu" and "cuck" alerts. His fascination started to ebb after his second birthday, and there wasn't much evidence of it by age three.
>
> Equally interesting were two children of some of my best friends many years ago. Both are college students now. One had an intense interest—balls. This is one of the most common EIIs among boys. Everywhere he went, he was always on the lookout for anything spherical—gum balls in a machine, light fixtures, actual balls, etc. His parents acceded to his passion and purchased many, many balls for him. They were always underfoot in their house when we went over for our weekly dinner with them.
>
> The other child had a much less common EII—brushes. The first evidence of his passionate interest in brushes was his recurrent desire to sweep—to use a broom. This gen-

eralized to brushes of all kinds. His parents bought a huge number of brushes for him; at one point he had toothbrushes in every room of the house so he was never without one.

Knowing these two children with these Extremely Intense Interests at the same time made a lasting impression on me. I did an initial very preliminary study that convinced me that there was something of general interest to be investigated. However, not until a few years ago did I initiate a formal study into it.

It has taken researchers and educators a strangely long time to realize that when a child is interested in something, he learns it better. This inexplicable gap in our inquiries into learning has persisted, despite the fact that researcher Daniel Berlyne demonstrated almost fifty years ago that people remember an item more easily if they learn it in order to satisfy their curiosity. More recently, two psychologists, K. Ann Renninger and Suzanne Hidi, have been slowly but surely trying to pin down the role interest might have in a child's emerging academic competence.

Parents who take time to watch their baby and toddler play will notice that some toys, or groups of toys, are more alluring than others. One child is excited every time he sees a toy car or truck, and another spends hour after hour with small action figures. But does it really matter whether a child has a chance to play with the toys he likes best? It seems so. As described in chapter one, when Renninger and her colleagues offered a baby a toy in which he had shown prior interest, the baby spent longer exploring the toy and used a wider range of actions on the toy. In other words, he stretched his cognitive repertoire when he was interested in the toy. In another experiment, psychologists divided fourth graders into two kinds of study groups. Some of the children were asked to work collaboratively in small groups, learning the material harmoniously. The other children were also put into small groups, but they were encouraged to focus on controversial aspects of the material and argue with one another, debating the topic. At the end of several days the children were tested for their knowledge of the material. Children who had been encouraged to get really invested and discuss aspects that had grabbed their interest not only learned more, they were also much more likely to give up a recess period to watch a film on the topic. This seems so obvious as to be laughable. Don't we all know it's easier to learn stuff we want to learn? Yet we have continued to ignore this fact when thinking about schools and learning. However, it is not simply that interest leads to learning. Interest might be the very component that leads someone from doing what is required to going beyond what is required.

Stefi always had friends. It seemed that from the time she was three until she was fifteen years old, all she cared about were her friends and decorating herself. She always did her work. Her mother, Robin, said, "You never needed to check on Stefi. She'd come home from school, go to her room, sit down at her desk, and do each assignment one after another. And each morning, she went to school with everything she needed to hand in. She has always gotten a B plus or A minus in every class. But you'd never know anything was happening in those classes. Not one night did she come home and say, 'We read the most amazing story,' or 'The teacher said the funniest thing today.' I didn't know what she cared about, except for friends, clothes, and her hairdo. She matured early. Once in eighth grade, she walked in for breakfast wearing this tight, low-cut blouse with her bosom just flowing over the top. I said, 'Stef, I don't think you should wear that to school. You'll be sitting in math class, and the math teacher will be staring at your boobs instead of the math problems, and all the boys in the class will be watching your boobs instead of thinking about math. I just don't think that's right.' Stef stared at me for a second, a totally blank look on her face, and said, 'I don't have math today.'

For the longest time, I really had no idea who was in there. Then, when she was fourteen, she went for the summer to an island off the coast of Canada to work with a group of teenagers running a summer program for young children. I felt she came back from that experience a different person. Suddenly, she could talk about ideas, and she understood abstract concepts. I felt like her brain had literally changed. This past summer, she started making purses using pieces of felt, beads, and feathers. Wherever she carried one of her purses, people asked her about them. She started to sell them. She has a thriving small business now. Then, in the fall, she found out about a course uptown on custom-designed pocketbooks. She signed up, and every Saturday, she gets herself up there first thing, to take the class. People keep asking to buy her bags and purses. I really thought for the longest time that Stef was going to end up working in an accessories store. But suddenly, it seems as if she is a serious person with a lot of interests. And she's a real entrepreneur."

Robin thinks that Stef changed in some wonderful, dramatic way as she entered adolescence. That's how it must have felt to watch Stef morph from a child who seemed concerned only with her next party and her next purchase to a young woman who had direction, energy for work, and an eagerness to plunge in. As Stef was growing up, fashion and friends seemed like warning signs. To Robin, they signaled superficiality, an absence of real interest. Instead, they *were* the real interest. Stefi had initiative, just not for school or books. It was for friends and accessories. Once she had developed a more goal-oriented frame of mind (something that often only kicks in when children enter early adolescence), she put her interest to work. Actually, Stefi's mom was right about her all along. She did care more than anything else about decorating girls. She might well end up working in a shop. It will probably be a luxury women's boutique, and she will probably own it. The accessories and hairdos weren't a red flag. They were a signpost.

One of the most important accomplishments of adulthood is to love one's work. Loving what you do for a living is different from getting (and keeping) a job with a high salary or lots of status. Where does such love come from? A clue to this comes from a somewhat unexpected source: a complex study of the lives of adolescents.

In the early eighties, psychologist Mihaly Csikszentmihalyi set out to learn what no one had figured out: What is it teenagers are doing, thinking, and feeling as they go about their everyday lives? He recruited his young subjects from Chicago public schools. Each teen was given a beeper (this was before the age of BlackBerrys and iPhones) and a packet of forms. For one week, he or she would be beeped at random times throughout the day. Each time the teenager got beeped, he or she was supposed to fill out a few pages answering questions such as "What are you doing right now?" "Who are you with?" "On a scale of 1 to 10, how good do you feel?" "Draw a picture describing your state of mind," and "How focused do you feel?" The data provided a vivid and detailed picture of the highs and lows of teenage life.

Csikszentmihalyi was particularly interested in trying to figure out what might explain why some teenagers in certain situations reported feeling so energized and involved and at other times so aimless and disconnected, while other teenagers never reported feeling energized and involved. He focused on one particular phenomenon, which he termed "negentropy," a state of total engagement and focus on something that is socially meaningful and productive. When a person experiences negentropy, he is so involved with what he is doing that he loses any self-consciousness, feels at one with the activity, and becomes unaware of the passing of time. Csikszentmihalyi argued that students who regularly experienced negentropy were more likely to be well-adjusted, happy teenagers who made a smooth transition to adulthood. Kids who played the violin, did a sport they loved, or were involved in a chess club were the kinds of kids who regularly experienced negentropy. Key to their experience was the chance to devote themselves to something they really loved and were good at.

Some kids, often the ones who stand out, seem to have a kind of zest for life, an enthusiasm that lifts their skills and interests to a new level. Rebecca Shiner calls this "surgency." She and her colleagues studied a group of 205 children between the ages of eight and twelve, assessing not only their conscientiousness and motivational orientation but also what she thought were the four components of surgency: dominance, expressiveness, attentiveness, and self-reliance. The researchers returned to these same kids twenty years later and asked them to describe themselves and their daily lives. They found that children who had been motivated to gain mastery became adults who took pleasure in daily activities and worked hard to accomplish goals. Children who had high levels of surgency became adults who were persuasive, forceful, socially potent, and likely to derive pleasure from hard work.

Shiner found something else as well. Just as other researchers have shown, kids who are conscientious do well in school, and kids who do well in school are more likely to get good jobs and keep them. One of the reasons conscientious children do well in school and at work is that they tend to be very rule-abiding. And along with their tendency to follow rules, it turns out that they are likely to be highly self-controlled and tend to avoid risks. A conscientious child might be very successful in school, which is a good route to getting a job that has good status and good pay. Those are the kids who are likely to be good at their work later on. But they might also avoid taking the kinds of risks that lead to great accomplishment. This might explain why the Melissas of the world do very well in conventional terms but might not often break new ground in a given domain.

Do you want your child to earn a lot of money? Do you want her to have influence over others? Do you want her to do work that has an impact on people's lives? Do you want her to be really good at something? Do you want her to gain recognition from others? Probably the answer to all of these is yes. For most children, becoming Bill Gates or Michael Jordan is not likely. Short of that, however, there are big and important differences in the kinds of work-related success people find in adult life. Some people cannot seem to hold a job, others have steady work but never find the satisfaction and recognition they yearn for, and some eschew earning power but love what they do so much that it buffers them from other disappointments.

What are the behaviors that indicate a child is headed for success? Early ability, of course, is a good sign. But ability without motivation and conscientiousness rarely takes a child far. Children who seem eager to do well and are able to do well are on their way to success. When that is coupled with a great capacity for loving work—whether it's collecting dinosaurs, making tree houses, pitching a baseball, or solving mathematical puzzles—parents should relax. Such a child has the essential components of success.

What are the red flags? A child who finds it hard to persist, even at the things she enjoys, might find it harder to find work she likes and to do well at work she likes. Usually, this shows itself in small moments—the comments she makes while she attempts something challenging, her tendency to choose an easier rather than a harder goal, and her attention to her own talents rather than the progress she has made. And although children seem to come ready-made with a lot or a little of this quality, it is something that can, to some extent, be changed. You can help a child become more oriented toward improvement and less oriented toward instant (and easy) attainment. Even if you live in a culture such as ours that elevates talent and minimizes effort, your own comments and approach to daily life will influence the way a child views her efforts. When she struggles with something, commend her effort and remark on her improvement, rather than whether she is good at it or not. Stress the role of effort in your own work, and talk about the satisfaction you take in your progress rather than your victories.

What are the red herrings? Ironically enough, the easiest mistake parents can make in this regard is to be disappointed or alarmed if their child doesn't always win the prize, earn the best grade, or get chosen for the most elite team. Those early victories are great if you get them. But not getting them isn't a predictor of a lackluster or dismal future. And it actually tells you nothing about your child's tendency to thrive as she gets older. Prizes, outstanding accomplishments, and big wins in grade school do not predict success in adulthood. And the lack of those early victories does not predict failure.

Children who are encouraged to work hard at things they love are likely to find success, if not fame and fortune, when they are adults. Making sure that your child has a chance to work hard at things she loves is the best tool you can give her for carving future success.

# 5

# Romance: The Origins of Love

This chapter begins in a funeral home. The funeral is for a man who has died at fifty-eight from a massive stroke. I am there because the dead man was the husband of someone with whom I work. An interim pastor is presiding over the funeral. The funeral home is in a small, depressed town in western Massachusetts, Adams. It used to have thriving mills and a lively main street. Now it has little that thrives. There is a tiny, ramshackle diner that has offered the same menu for fifty years. There is a large-chain grocery store, the Big Y, some empty factory buildings, several old dark-brick school buildings, a five-and-dime, and a motley assortment of other drab storefronts.

The people at the funeral are like the people in any small rural town—the men and women work in factories and local stores or at trades such as carpentry, plumbing, and masonry.

The pastor looks like a thousand other ministers—short white hair, a receding hairline, a white beard, and kind eyes set in pink, weathered skin. He is low-key and admits he doesn't know the family well. His sermon is simple and banal. It would be easy to tune out. But then, out of nowhere, in his ordinary homespun way, he mentions an idea that rests at the core of what we know about human love.

He says, "In the shepherd's prayer, the baby lamb asks what we all want to know. How can the shepherd who brought me into this world, who cared for me and looked over me, who brought me food and protected me from wolves and other predators, take me away? He will surely take my life away when he butchers me or offers me up for religious sacrifice. How can the one who gives me life take life away? This is what we all want to know." Then the pastor adds, "When young men and women come to me to seek my blessing because they want to marry, I always say to them, 'If you don't want to suffer, don't do this.' But of course, they have no choice. It's always too late. They already love each other. And every baby is already in love with its parents the day it is born."

The pastor has that dead right. But he has made one small yet crucial mistake. When babies are born, it's actually only their mother they are in love with. And that love turns out to be the starting gate for all future romance.

## The First Romance

I often tell my introductory psychology students the story of Frederick II of Prussia. He wanted to find out which language was the original language of mankind. He commandeered a whole cohort of babies and decreed that they be raised by nurses who took care of every physical need but remained totally silent. That way, he figured, he would find out which language the children spontaneously spoke when they were free of adult influence. He was a clever experimentalist but obviously not very nice. The story goes that he never got the answer to his question, because all of the babies died. Silent wet nurses, it turned out, weren't enough for the babies. They needed something more. It took a couple of hundred more years for researchers to begin to understand just what it was those babies had been missing.

During World War II, a British doctor, John Bowlby, made the same discovery under somewhat different circumstances. Bowlby visited orphanages in London to check on the health and welfare of the babies orphaned because of German bombing. Strange as it now seems to us, Bowlby was stunned by the malaise of the babies, who were for the most part well cared for in basic medical and physical terms. They had been well fed, given safe, comfortable cribs, kept clean, and given decent medical care. Nevertheless, the babies were withdrawn, developmentally delayed, and small for their age. They suffered from what came to be known as failure to thrive. Bowlby realized that the babies were suffering from the absence of a mother figure, someone who loved them and could be loved by them, someone whose physical presence provided them with a sense of well-being. From his experiences in those orphanages came Bowlby's seminal trilogy: attachment, separation, and loss. He described the essential bond that forms between a child and his mother and the terrible toll it takes on a child to have that bond broken.

But it was Harry Harlow who used experiments to demonstrate vividly what happens when an infant cannot be close to a parent. He couldn't experiment with humans, of course. Instead, he isolated baby monkeys from their mothers. When these little motherless monkeys became juveniles, they couldn't get along with other monkeys. While monkeys raised with a mother would play, share food, and peacefully coexist in a small space, the motherless monkeys would alternate between huddling by themselves in a corner, rejecting any overtures from other monkeys, and attacking those who approached. We take it as a given now that Harlow's research demonstrated how essential it is for primates (including humans) to get something other than food and safety when they are born. But understanding that the bond is essential is only the first step.

It might not be enough simply to have an adult around a lot of the time. In a second famous experiment, Harlow placed baby monkeys in a cage with two parent surrogates. One was made of wire, but it offered nutrition—a bottle of milk attached to the wire. The other surrogate, placed in a different part of the cage, had no bottle but was covered in soft terrycloth. Harlow found that the babies would hurry over to the wire mother to drink milk and as quickly as possible, hurry back over to the terrycloth mother, where they would spend the bulk of their time trying to cozy up to the soft fabric-covered figure. The implication was obvious: babies crave comfort. But Harlow's monkeys faced a stark choice: soft terrycloth or wire. Even the soft surrogate offered a pale facsimile of emotional nurturing. Isn't there something more complex to the bond between mother and child than the emotional gratification gained from snuggling? Surely not all babies who grow up with their mothers are alike.

Mightn't there be better and worse mother-child relationships? Imagine any playgroup where a parent brings his or her child to play each week or any playground where parents bring their babies and toddlers. If you watch for a while, subtle differences will begin to take shape before your eyes. One mother seems to know what her baby's reaching gesture means—this time she wants the ball, this time she wants her bottle, this time she just wants a smile. Another mother keeps scanning her baby's face anxiously, looking for clues while the baby fusses and fusses, unable to make himself clear. One toddler rushes off to fling herself into the sandbox. Her father sits nearby talking with his friend. Every ten minutes or so, the little girl looks up. Her father meets her gaze and nods, and she happily returns to her work with trucks. Not all of those pairs are bonding in the same way. This is what Bowlby's disciple Mary Ainsworth wanted to know more about.

Her method for assessing the relationship between a mother and her child remains one of the most ingenious in psychological research. Figuring that not all mother-child pairs would be the same, she set out to examine differences in their emotional connections. Watching parents and their children in everyday situations is good for getting a sense of the variety of parent-child bonds. But it wouldn't provide an objective and reliable way of categorizing such pairs or of testing the stability of such differences over the course of childhood. You'd see one mother in a grocery store ignoring her baby while searching the aisles for cereal. How would you compare that to a mother who worked most of the day but spent twenty minutes totally focused on her child at bath time? And what if the day you watched a mother play with her child, siblings were in the room, diluting the relationship between your target baby and his mother?

Ainsworth's genius was to create a situation that would be the same for all of the mothers and babies she observed. But bringing a mother and a baby into a room to play for a few moments would not necessarily reveal the nature of their attachment. It would be hard to know what you were comparing. Which slice of interaction would you focus on? The moment they snuggled? Perhaps, as Tolstoy implied, all snuggles look pretty much the same. Would you watch them as they concentrated on playing a game? Maybe their level of education or intelligence would explain more about what went on than the quality of their relationship. If one pair spent the time cooing at each other, and the other spent the time looking at a book together, how would you evaluate their differences or similarities? And here is where Ainsworth was most inventive.

A close reader of her mentor, Bowlby, Ainsworth realized that a good attachment shows up best in the very moment it is threatened, when a mother leaves her baby. She reasoned that babies would differ in the way they reacted when their mothers left the room. She also figured that the second most revealing moment would come when the mother was reunited with her baby. Again, her hunch was that not all babies would deal with this in the same way and that the differences would show something about the kind of attachment each mother had with her child. And this is how the "strange situation paradigm" was born.

Each baby (ranging from nine to eighteen months) and mother participating in Ainsworth's research were brought into a room set up to look like a living room, with comfortable chairs, toys, and, in some versions of the study, an unfamiliar adult sitting in the room. After a few minutes, the mother got up and left the room. Ainsworth and her colleagues watched through a one-way mirror to see what would happen when the mother left. Most babies cried. Some cried inconsolably, while others cried for a few moments and then began to explore the toys near them. A few seemed not to notice or watched their mothers leave with little expression on their faces.

And here's a crucial point that flies in the face of much Western folk wisdom about child rearing. Contrary to popular opinion, it was not a good sign when a baby seemed calm or oblivious to her mother's departure. As much as we all admire the baby who easily goes to a stranger, from the perspective of Ainsworth, this suggests that the baby doesn't have an adequate connection to her mother. In other words, crying can be a good thing.

But not all unhappy babies are the same. After the mother had been out of the room for a few moments, she came back in. Ainsworth watched to see what happened then. The babies who had seemed not to care when their mothers left seemed equally unaffected when they came back in. These babies are not, as some might think, the calm, well-adjusted babies who are independent and comfortable with strangers. They were, in Ainsworth's worldview, lacking an essential bond with their mothers. Most of the babies were overjoyed when reunited with their mothers. They would crawl or walk right over to them, burying their faces in the mothers' necks or bosoms. But the love story doesn't end there. After just a few moments of cuddling, many babies would clamber off their mothers' laps and happily toddle off to play with the toys.

However, some babies who were distraught when their mothers left and delighted when they returned seemed unable to regain their equilibrium. These more riled-up babies would rush over and nuzzle their moms when they came back into the room. But the reunion lacked both the joy and the brevity of those other babies. They seemed conflicted. Some of them hugged their mothers but then, as if remembering their sadness, would pummel them. Some pinched their mothers. Some began whimpering, as if they still hadn't gotten over the upset of being left in the first place. These babies would crawl back over to the toys but keep turning to watch their mothers, as if to make sure they didn't leave again. They seemed to have trouble regaining their composure. These babies might return to playing with the toys, but they seemed distracted by the possibility that their mothers might leave again. And because they kept their eye on their mothers, they never really got reabsorbed in their play.

This ambivalent behavior on the part of some babies led to one of the pillars of attachment theory. The nature of a child's bond with his mother has consequences for the way that baby interacts with the world.

But Ainsworth observed a third kind of attachment as well. Some babies didn't care at all when their mothers left the room in the first place and seemed equally uninterested when they returned. Although it can be a relief to a young mother if her baby doesn't mind when she leaves for work, to developmental psychologists, that calm obliviousness reads as detachment. And detachment can spell trouble on the road to adulthood.

Even the best relationship between a baby and her mother is

not simple. The powerful love a well-attached baby feels from and for her parents bubbles with shifting feelings. No matter how close a baby and a mother are, they have conflicts; they yearn for each other and feel sick of each other. This first relationship forms the basis for all others, and inevitably it carries with it a mother lode of complex dynamics.

When my sister's daughter Maddie was four, she was angry at my sister for something. Maddie and my sister were sitting on a chair together, locked in a battle of wills. Finally, my sister said in a quiet but exasperated voice, "Maddie, that's it. You cannot go out to play right now with Erin. We're leaving soon to go grocery shopping, and there is no time. We're not discussing it anymore."

Maddie's face looked like a small storm—her mouth turned down, her eyebrows bunched together, and her eyelids were red from crying. Holding her mother's shirt with her little fists, she kicked her foot into her mother's back, nudging her mother off the chair, moaning tearfully, "Go away. I need you."

## Mothers vs. Fathers

When Lenore was born, she was supposed to fix her parents' marriage. Aida and Sol had been unhappy together long before their wedding. But they were serious, thoughtful people, both from strong, middle-class, Jewish immigrant families, and they intended to make their family work. So first they had a daughter, and then they had two sons. In between, they each had a few affairs, as well as fairly sustained stints of psychotherapy. They fought about money. They fought about sex. They fought about the children. Sol wanted them to go to public school, and Aida wanted them in a more open environment. Aida wanted the children to play after school, and Sol thought they should have chores. Sol didn't like the way Aida flirted with other men. Aida didn't like the way Sol hovered over her with his constant air of superiority. These differences simmered under the surface. If you had met their family, you would have seen an intelligent, attractive, well-educated brood, a family that rode bikes together in the park, took weekend trips to the shore, and had long dinners with friends, filled with conversation about books and politics.

But underneath the veneer of urbane control, anger and discord rumbled. Sol loved his kids, but he didn't really like being with them. Aida loved her kids, but she liked her freedom, too. A closer look at the interactions within their lovely home would have shown that not all of the relationships were what they seemed to be. However, Aida and Sol didn't believe in angry displays in front of the children. Their tension lay deeper than that and took form only in the privacy of their respective therapy sessions or the bedroom, where they talked and talked and talked about their troubles.

When Aida's third child, Adam, was three, she had an affair with someone she met at a dinner party. But it was over within months, and Aida realized that she desperately wanted her family life to be happy. Maybe she should have one more child, a baby to cuddle and love, someone to cement their life together as a family. She and Sol had problems, but they shared a commitment to the life they had built. A child would refresh that and give them a new start.

When Lenore was born, tawny, with large brown eyes and a sunny temperament, Aida was sure this would set things right. Aida took a three-month leave from her job as an occupational therapist to care for her little Lenore. And what a delicious baby. Lenore would gaze up joyfully from her baby carriage as Aida happily strolled with her in the park and met friends to chat, sunbathe, and enjoy the silky-skinned new baby. Lenore was just the right baby for Aida, at just the right time. When Lenore cried, Aida's gentle, firm touch calmed her right down. When Aida spoke to Lenore, the baby gazed up happily at her mother's face. Aida felt she was looking down into a wonderful reflection of herself—the same deep brown hair and eyes, the same tilted nose. She was such an easy baby—easy to feed, easy to hold, and so ready to laugh. It was like looking down at herself, only better, because she was looking down at a baby who adored her.

Sol was another story. By the time Lenore was born, he was completely disaffected by family life and spent little time at home. And from the day she was born, Lenore was so clearly Aida's baby. Sol, on the other hand, adored their eldest child, a black-haired, blue-eyed girl named Miranda. Miranda and he were two peas in a pod, and from the time Miranda was a baby, she and her father understood each other. Miranda was the apple of Sol's eye. Not Lenore.

By the time Lenore was four years old, Sol and Aida were too unhappy to stay married. Aida and the children went to live in another part of Westchester, and Sol moved into a small apartment in New Jersey.

Lenore spent every Saturday night with her father. He was kind and attentive. They did nice things together—he read aloud to her, and they took walks through the park, went to puppet shows, and made visits to Aida's favorite cupcake store. Even so, she missed her mom. Her dad's small apartment was sterile and gloomy. The neighborhood seemed lonely to her. She never felt totally herself when she stayed with her father. He was somewhat formal with her, using big words when he spoke. "He wanted to discuss things. I wanted to play," is how Lenore recalls it. They just didn't click. But her time with her mom was the opposite. They liked the same food, they thought the same things were funny, and they made each other feel better. They were in sync.

In the years since Ainsworth set up the "strange situation paradigm," researchers have unearthed some powerful mechanisms that push mothers and their babies toward each other. Ainsworth couldn't have known how overdetermined that first love affair really is.

Babies come into the world equipped to like people. If you show a baby pictures of lines and dots in a random design and pictures that form the barest outlines of a facial configuration (squiggles and dots where eyes, nose, and mouth would be), the newborn will look longer at the pattern suggesting a face. Babies also prefer a symmetrical pattern to a nonsymmetrical one. They are hard-wired to like indications that they are looking at a person. All of this means that from the moment they are born, they are tuned toward others—no one more so than their mothers.

When researchers play the sound of a baby's mother on one side of her head and the sound of another female voice on the other side of her head, the baby will turn in the direction of her own mother's voice. Remarkably, a newborn baby seems to recognize her mother's smell. Within a few hours of life, she will turn toward clothing her mother has been wearing, rather than toward an object worn by someone else. Babies are wired to prefer their mothers above all others. And vice versa.

Mothers are wired to prefer their babies. When women give birth, they release a hormone called oxytocin. In recent years, neuroscientists have learned that the release of oxytocin triggers feelings of love and attachment. This seems to explain, in part, why women tend to feel that they love the man with whom they just experienced an orgasm (another cause of oxytocin release). The mother who has just given birth and is floating in an internal bath of oxytocin feels a wave of love looking at the newborn placed on her chest. This isn't all in her head. It's all through her body. The role of oxytocin in triggering maternal affection explains why the route to attachment is somewhat different for babies who are separated from their mothers at birth, raised by a father, or adopted. It is not that these other kinds of parent-child pairs don't bond, but it is true that they don't have the same natural boost of hormones. However, that initial burst of hormonally triggered attachment is only the first step.

Although the bond between mother and baby is hard-wired, sometime during those early months, what begins as an automatic preference evolves into a textured relationship, replete with fulfillment, unrequited love, and the kinds of subtle corrections that go into any romance.

For one mother, those early exchanges with her baby feel just right. She loves the fact that when he cries, she knows just what to do—she takes his legs and pushes them up against his tummy. He feels better and quiets down. She feels like a good mom. Another mother might find that, as euphoric as she felt in the hours after her little girl's birth, in the days that follow, her baby seems like an inscrutable stranger to her. She peers into her little girl's face, cooing and singing. She longs to see a smile in return. But the baby turns away. These sequences form a kind of dance.

When parent and baby click, it reflects what psychiatrist Daniel Stern called attunement. And some pairs are more attuned than others. In his early research on attunement, Stern and his colleagues filmed mothers interacting with their babies, who were seated in inclined infant seats so that they could "talk" to their parents. Viewing a split screen of the filmed data, showing the mother on the left and the baby on the right, Stern could measure just how closely each parent-child pair mirrored each other's sounds, gestures, and facial expressions. He found that most mothers and their babies are extraordinarily well coordinated. But he also found that some mothers were out of tune with their babies. For instance, a mother might keep looking at her baby and making sounds, while the baby turns his face away, avoiding more interaction. Some babies cannot tolerate the level of interaction the mother yearns for. In some cases, the tables are turned. The baby makes all kinds of sounds, with his eyes glued intently on his mother's face, clearly eager for a response. But the mother, perhaps lost in her own thoughts or finding it difficult to respond with the same animation as her baby, just gazes off in the middle distance.

Stern's camera work and microanalysis revealed very subtle hits and misses in the nonverbal conversations mothers and babies constantly engage in. His method allowed clinicians to identify mothers who displayed a lack of synchrony with their babies. They were certain that such a mismatch would cause difficulties in the vital bond between mother and baby. Stern and his colleagues worked with the pairs who had the most trouble. Their goal was to help mothers learn to match their own gestures, gaze, and vocalizations to those of their babies—sort of like teaching someone who wants to dance the tango how to follow the steps of her partner.

Years after Stern first identified this intricate pattern, researchers began to see that the quality of that dance had consequences they hadn't realized. For instance, researchers have found that babies who engage in lots of back-and-forth with their moms do better on a variety of cognitive tests when they first go to school. It seems that experience at such finely tuned back-and-forth exchanges leads to skills essential for talking, solving problems, and learning from others. When researchers have followed depressed mothers and their children from infancy, they notice that it can be hard for a mother who is depressed to pick up on her child's subtle invitations to "talk." She often misses the sound or expression the child uses to start conversations. Lacking a rich exchange with his mother turns out to limit the baby's own emotional repertoire as he grows. What might begin as an emotional problem for the mother can lead the child to have a long-lasting problem with relationships as he grows up.

If you've watched a baby gaze at her mother's face, you can easily spot the signs of true love. And although most scientists, as well as the general public, have all too happily rejected much of what Sigmund Freud told us, a few of his ideas have gained strength with time and better scientific methods. One of his strongest ideas had to do with the roots of love.

Freud told us that the roots of love are found in a mother's arms. Specifically, we first fulfill our need for pleasure at our mother's breast. As Freud and others noted, a baby who has just nursed has the sated, relaxed look of someone who has just had sex. And surely, the slightly suspended breath and rapt gaze of a baby whose mother is trying to win a smile from her evokes the passion of romantic infatuation, a feeling she might not have again until she's in her late teens.

When my first son was three, I became pregnant with our second child. I bought a book called *How Babies Are Made*. My son loved hearing me read that book aloud to him. We read it again and again, even after his little brother was born. One day, he picked it out of a pile, climbed onto the couch where I was sitting, and asked me to read it one more time. The new little baby was lying next to us, sleeping peacefully in his basket. When I got to the page that said, "When a man and a woman love each other very much, they lie close together, and the man puts his penis in the woman's vagina," and prepared to turn the page, my son rolled over from his seat next to me on the couch so that he was lying on my torso, and with his face very close to mine, he looked straight into my eyes and said, "Let's try it right now." After a split second of astonished confusion, I said, "Oh, well, little boys don't do that with their mommies. But when you grow up, you might meet someone you like very much, and you'll probably want to try it with that person." He flipped back to his seat on the couch next to me, shrugged airily, and said, "OK. I'll try it with Courtney tomorrow." Courtney was a four-year-old classmate in his preschool.

By the time he was four years old, he had a favorite game to play with me. "You be Guinevere, and I'll be the White Knight. I'll save you." I'm not sure what I did to "be Guinevere" or what it entailed to have him save me. As is so often the case, four-year-olds get as much out of planning and narrating their play as they do enacting it. Designating our respective roles—his as a powerful knight in shining armor and mine as the beautiful damsel in distress who would love him for his strength and daring—seemed very satisfying to him. That same year, soon after his little brother was born, he had a great idea for Halloween: "I'll be a king, and Will can be a little pig." I tell these stories when I teach college students, in order to bring to life what Freud was talking about when he said that every child goes through his or her own Oedipal drama. It's often less subtle or abstract than people might think. But although little girls might want to marry their daddies and little boys court their mothers, those romances do not predict much about how a particular child's love life will unfold.

When Lenore was thirteen, she still looked eleven. She hadn't gotten her period yet, and she was thin and flat-chested. Although she looked like a child, she had the daydreams of a teenager. She and her friends talked endlessly about boyfriends. She had the most vivid imagination among them and would describe the boy of her dreams in detail—what they would do on the first date, the note he would write to her the day after the first date, and how he would behave in the weeks to follow. She could envision her first romance in novelistic detail. But she still hadn't even held hands with a boy.

Meanwhile, her older sister, Miranda, was deep in the throes of a love affair, and her mother, newly separated from her stepfather, was spending a lot of time with the new man in her life. Lenore could see what love looked like, even if she hadn't come anywhere near it herself. She studied Miranda's romance, as if it provided her with a blueprint for her own future.

Lenore excelled easily at her suburban public school. Actually, the work was too easy—it didn't come close to tapping her enormous reserve of energy. Instead, that energy went into imagining life as she yearned to live it. She recalls, "I saw every movie that came to town. I read every new romance novel that I could get my hands on. I told long, elaborate stories to my friends about the love affairs I would someday have. The stories were so detailed and so vivid that half of the time, I convinced my friends that the men were real people I had already met. Meanwhile, here's what was actually happening. I came home from school each day at three, did my homework, ate dinner with my family, watched one hour of sitcoms, and went to bed. My mental life and my actual life had nothing to do with each other. The emptier my days, the fuller my daydreams of handsome men with exotic names."

But while other girls in her neighborhood were tasting their first kiss, letting boys feel their breasts, and considering going steady, Lenore hadn't even been to the movies with a boy.

When Lenore was eighteen, she went with her brothers to a party at the lake near their home. And that's where her dream came true. Ryan was twenty-three and very handsome. He had broad shoulders, thick blond hair, and an infectious laugh. She could tell he was used to flirting. She had been waiting all this time to charm and be charmed by a boy like this. This was it. It was happening! For three weeks, they met at nearby parties, swam at the lake, and lay in the hammock together. They also had sex. She felt she had been ready for this since she was nine. Lenore was in love. But it was now August and time for her to leave for college. They spoke on the phone three times each of her first seven days at college. Then she suddenly woke up on the eighth day and felt as if a fever had just broken.

"I still can't explain it," she told me. "During those three weeks, it was as if I was on a drug. When I was away from Ryan, I couldn't breathe. When I was with him, I couldn't really hear or see any-one else. The first night at college, I told my new roommate that I thought about him every second. I wrote him a passionate love letter. Then, a week later, boom. It was over. I didn't miss him. I didn't want to talk to him. I suddenly felt slightly disgusted by the whole thing." Lenore shook her head ruefully and said, "What a brat I was. I didn't write to him. I didn't call him. When he called,

I let the machine pick up. It's obvious to me now that even though I thought I was so grown up, I wasn't anywhere near ready to be in love or even have a boyfriend."

It wasn't that she had met someone else. She didn't want a real boyfriend. She preferred to lie in bed in her dorm at night, telling her roommate all about her current mad crush (one week the drama professor, another the varsity baseball player or the day student enrolled in her biology class). She preferred those late-night conversations about love to a living, breathing boy.

## The Second Romance

In the middle of the twentieth century, Harry Stack Sullivan constructed a theory that explained how friendships might pave the way to romance. He argued that preadolescents formed what he called "chumships," close, intense friendships that allowed children to practice the intimacy of adult love. It didn't matter that most friendships during the preteens are between children of the same sex. Sullivan reassured parents that with "normal development," children would transfer the patterns and behaviors they had practiced with their chums to members of the opposite sex. Sullivan rarely mentioned that he himself was gay.

Almost all of the literature on adolescent love suggests that young teens unwittingly use their buddies to practice love. They spend time together, they fight and make up, they listen to one another, they reveal intimate thoughts and feelings, and they feel at times as if no one can understand them as well as their best friend. A close scrutiny of memoirs shows that wherever you see close friends in late childhood, there is a strong whiff of Eros. Even kids who don't remember talking about love, masturbating together, or practicing kissing one another remember a sense of connection to a best friend that had the same intensity we usually classify as passion.

Some psychologists have even argued that the love young children feel is basically the same as the passionate love of adulthood. To compare feelings of children with those of older adolescents and adults, Elaine Hatfield and her colleagues recruited 236 Hawaiian boys and girls ages four to eighteen. First, the researchers made sure that each child understood the concept of boyfriend/girlfriend. Then they asked each child to select one boyfriend or girlfriend to answer questions about. Each young subject was asked to complete what is called the Juvenile Love Scale, a list of questions adapted from a similar survey used to evaluate the feelings of adults describing their romantic partners. The children were asked to rate the truth of each statement—1 was very untrue, and 10 was very true.

1. I feel like things would always be sad and gloomy if I had to live without _____ forever.
2. I have kept thinking about _____ when I wanted to stop and couldn't.
3. I feel happy when I am doing something to make _____ happy.
4. I would rather be with _____ than anybody else.
5. I'd feel bad if I thought _____ liked somebody else better than me.
6. I want to know all I can about _____.
7. I'd like _____ to belong to me in every way.
8. I'd like it a lot if _____ played with me all the time.
9. If I could, when I grow up, I'd like to marry (live with) _____.
10. When _____ hugs me, my body feels warm all over.
11. I am always thinking about _____.
12. I want _____ to know me, what I am thinking, what scares me, what I am wishing for.
13. I look at _____ a lot to see if he (she) likes me.

14. When _____ is around, I really want to touch him (her) and be touched.

15. When I think _____ might be mad at me, I feel really sad.

In order to make sure that puberty itself does not cause children to begin feeling passionate love, the researchers rated each child on a puberty scale. They found that the scores of young children did not differ dramatically from scores of older children and that children of all ages demonstrated passionate love quite similar to the kinds of feelings adults have for someone with whom they are in love, regardless of whether they had facial hair or were menstruating. According to what these children said about their own feelings, they experienced passion pretty much the way adults do. For most kids, though, that passion does not pass straight from their mom to their lover but takes an important detour into the world of friends.

Bernie had lots of friends and a rotten home life. If you had met him when he was eleven, you would have made two completely opposite bets on his future love life, depending on the situation in which you saw him.

If you had seem him on a basketball court or cutting up with his buddies after school, you would have seen exactly the kind of chumship Sullivan was talking about. He loved his pals. They played sports together, they went swimming together, they stayed out past their curfew together, and they got into trouble together. He candidly recalled the "circle jerks," which seemed to be such a sordid but compelling element of boyhood friendships. He and his friends liked girls, but only for a few hours at a time. What they really liked was the bond they felt with one another. And Bernie was particularly popular. He had a flair for telling entertaining stories, he was funny, and he had endless energy for a good time.

"I was this real outgoing, talkative, gregarious little kid," he said. "There's a story everyone in the family loved to tell about me. Our family's place in upstate New York was on a lake, and the whole social life took place around boats. Lots of cousins and aunts and uncles own property. Each night, a different family member cooked dinner. We're talking thirty to fifty people. You'd get from one house to another by boat. The story they tell is that I was sitting out on the end of the dock greeting everybody as they arrived. This two-year-old saying, 'I'm Bernie. This is my grandmother's house.'" When he thinks about his teen years, all of the good memories are of the time he spent with his friends.

But if you had seen him at home, you would have seen a different picture. Bernie's early years seemed to come right out of a picture book (smart, successful dad, pretty devoted mother, and two younger sisters, living in a beautiful suburb of Philadelphia), but by the time he was eleven, everything had fallen apart. His parents had divorced. His mother, completely undone by the change in her circumstances, had become deeply involved in a religious cult. And Bernie's cozy life as a privileged and talented member of the middle class had been thrown out the window. Bernie had to go to work after school to help his mother pay the bills. Meanwhile, he felt increasingly estranged from her. He often had to run interference for his younger sister, who fought so much with their mom that she finally left the house to live with their father.

"When I was little, it was Utopia," he said. "My mom was very loving, very attentive, always there. She started a nursery school in our house. My mom was always having birthdays and parties for us—other kids were always at our house. But later, after they got divorced, everything changed. She couldn't handle three kids, and the divorce had broken her. That's the whole time the Jesus shit started to happen, and she became a necessary evil to me. She woke up every day wondering what the Lord would have her do that day. But she also became totally disengaged. She wouldn't consider seeing a movie or reading a book. She didn't know anything about music. She just didn't care about anything. I stopped being able to count on her at all. She couldn't cook anymore. And she didn't approve of how I was living my life because of her religious beliefs. But here's the sick part. Even though we had almost nothing in common, and even though I felt so angry at her, I made my mom proud. And that was our sick, twisted relationship. She felt that people admired her because of my achievements or successes. And I think that when I was little and my parents were still married, she felt I was the link that would tie her to her husband.

"But by the time I was twelve, she was the 'often person,' not the 'intimate person' in my life. By the time I was twenty-five, it became impossible to be around her at all. She wanted the 'picture' version of our relationship, not the real version. She was so out of touch she didn't even realize it had become a fraud. Actually, it was worse than that. She didn't even care that it was a fraud. She didn't care that I only came to church with her to meet girls. If I was sitting next to her in that pew, everything was good."

If an intimate relationship with a mother is so important to later love, things didn't look good for Bernie. Not only had his attachment to his mother become a sham, but his way of interacting with girls wasn't so promising, either. He'd spend hours courting a pretty girl (he recalled, "My favorite thing was getting a girl to change her mind"), only to grow quickly tired of her, yearning to hang out with his buddies from the basketball team or the golf club where he earned money in the summer. When he got to college, he had many conquests but no relationships. Not with girls, anyway. Girls were for sex. Boys were forever.

Then, when he was twenty-five, he met Edith at a business meeting. She was beautiful, as most of his girlfriends were. She was funny, too, and, like him, she was athletic and smart. Success had come easily to both of them. They both stood out in a crowd. And they stood out to each other. Bernie recalled feeling instantly smitten. His office mate remembers him coming home from the meeting and saying, "I gotta marry that girl."

Edith was taken with him immediately though reluctantly. She already had a boyfriend. Bernie was kind of brash. He watched sports on TV and used expressions like "Ma'am" and "Sure thing." She read edgy fiction and hated sentiment. Nevertheless, Bernie didn't let up, and she gave in to his relentless pursuit and her deep attraction.

They had one other thing going for them. It is not simply that Bernie and Edith felt a connection, a sense of similarity at a deep level. Chance was also on their side.

## Finding the Time and Place for Love

George Burns and Gracie Allen were married for thirty-eight years, and the world got to see just how much they loved one another. Someone once asked Burns what the secret to such a long happy marriage was. Burns answered instantly, "Marry Gracie." But psychologists think something else is just as important as finding the right person. It's finding him or her at the right time in the right circumstances.

In 1974, psychologists Arthur Aron and Donald Dutton set out to test the hypothesis that people get confused between anxiety and arousal. How to test it? Ask people to cross a bridge! Aron and Dutton brought young single men (between the ages of eighteen and thirty-five) to cross over a wobbly suspension bridge with low cable handrails, which hung over a 230-foot drop. Another group of men were invited to cross a solid, wider bridge with handrails ten feet off the ground. After each young man had crossed his bridge but was still standing on the edge of the bridge, a female interviewer approached and asked him to complete a questionnaire with six irrelevant questions and then look at a drawing and tell a story about it. After each man had finished his questionnaire and drawing, the female experimenter gave him a phone number and told him to call if he wanted to know more about the study (to test the effect of having a woman interviewer, half of the wobbly high bridge subjects and half of the sturdy low bridge subjects were interviewed by a male experimenter). The stories written by the men were scored for sexual imagery on a scale of 1 to 5. Men on the wobbly bridge received an average score of 2.47, while those in the control group received just over a 1.41. With the male interviewer, the wobbly bridge group received a .80 score, and the control group received a .61. In addition, half of the eighteen men who had accepted the interviewer's phone number followed up with a phone call, whereas only two of sixteen in the control group did so. With the male interviewer, fewer men accepted the phone number, and only two of seven wobbly bridge men and one of six control bridge men called. The men aroused by crossing the scary bridge were much more likely to think about sex and to respond flirtatiously to the woman interviewer. When men (and possibly women) are in arousing situations, the arousal spreads—a feeling of anxiety or fear either sets off a feeling of desire or, more likely, is interpreted as being sexual arousal. Years later, Aron wrote articles urging long-married couples to try new and somewhat scary things together. He is still sure that when people are a little nervous, they get a big fat side benefit: they think they are excited romantically by the next person they see.

Bernie and Edith met during a high-stakes meeting between their two companies. Both were at a pivotal point in their very pressured high-climbing careers. The adrenaline might have been prompted by work, but it spread a rosy glow over the fledgling couple. However, that kind of fortuitous timing is only short-term. There is a longer-term kind of timing that might also affect the chances that a person will fall in love. Psychologist James Pennebaker and his colleagues named this phenomenon after an old country song, "The Girls Look Prettier at Closing Time," and set out to prove that the singer was correct.

The subjects for the study were fifty-two males and fifty-one females selected from three bars close to the campus of a university in the South. Experimenters entered the bars at 9:00 P.M., 10:30 P.M., and 12:00 midnight, which was half an hour before closing time. Experimenters asked people in the bar to rate members of the opposite sex who were also there, on a scale of 1 to 10. The closer it was to closing time, the higher the ratings were. The moral of that story: As you feel your time for getting a partner wanes, your available choices look better and better.

Bernie and Edith had good timing. They met when they were twenty-five—in our culture, that's just when people feel compelled to settle down with someone. Perhaps Bernie felt the bar was closing, which made Edith look not only beautiful but as if she was "the one" to him. But as we all know, there is a 50 percent divorce rate in this country. Bernie had a bad track record with women. The longest relationship he had had before Edith was six months. Would they last? John Gottman could have told them.

Gottman and his colleagues have been able to predict a couple's longevity from just a few moments of taped interaction. Couples who will weather the storm of daily married life seem to talk to each other differently from couples who won't make it.

In one study, Gottman and his colleagues recruited fifty-six married couples and asked them to talk about how satisfied they were with their marriages. They were also asked to describe how they met, courted, and decided to get married and how the marriage had changed. After three years, the researchers contacted the couples to find out how their marriages were going and examined the original interviews of the couples who had divorced. What they learned was quite startling. The men in marriages that did not last had shown low levels of fondness when they talked about their marriages but also when they talked to their wives. The husbands and wives in these couples rarely talked in terms of "we" and didn't express much feeling during the interviews. They were often negative and articulated their marital disappointments.

Gottman has used these and other data to argue that you can predict whether a couple will last based on the way they talk about their marriage and the way they talk to each other. Bernie and Edith argued a lot. They both often swore at each other. They freely mocked, challenged, and snapped at each other. Bernie flared up, looking like a fire-breathing dragon. Edith would roll her eyes, suck in her breath, and become distant. But when they talked with friends, their conversations were laced with things they had done together, funny stories about each other, and common references. They laughed at each other's jokes, were profoundly interested in each other, and looked at each other often. Their talk was filled with signs of marital stability, and the signs of conflict indicated nothing much at all.

When Bernie tells the story of his upbringing, it's surprising that he came out of it intact. He even feels that it is something of a miracle that he ended up in such a loving marriage. But buried in his narrative, amid all the dysfunction, is a slender thread connecting the stable love he experienced early on with his mother to his friendships that paved the way for courting Edith.

Meanwhile, Lenore seemed to be dying on the vine. Midway through Lenore's nineteenth year, she realized that all of her friends were dating. She had a worried feeling that something was wrong with her. She knew she was pretty. She recalled, "My mother always told me how pretty I was. And I looked like her. And everyone talked about how pretty she was, even her. But somehow I didn't attract boys the way my friends did. The pizzazz I had with girls, with adults, with children, with teachers, I just didn't have it when I was talking to guys. I felt flat, the same way I felt when I talked to my dad. I began to feel I'd never have a real boyfriend."

It has long been the case that psychologists tend to study the phenomena that lend themselves to good experiments, rather than what we find most important or fascinating to understand about human behavior. So it's no shock that the science of love has wavered and faltered. Perhaps surprisingly, a prominent expert in intelligence, Robert Sternberg, turned his attention for a period of time to the equally important matter of love. He has argued that love consists of three parts: intimacy, passion, and commitment.

In the best of all possible worlds, two people in a long-term relationship (say, marriage) feel connected on all three levels. They confide in each other, they feel known by each other, and they feel close. That's intimacy. They also desire each other, feel jealous when their partner appears to desire another, and feel excited by the presence of each other (at least some of the time). That's passion. Finally, they both feel they are in it for the long haul. This sense of loyalty—a plan to stay together—helps them weather the times they don't feel passion or intimacy. That's commitment. The question is, what leads one person to create this kind of loving bond and renders another incapable of the full package?

The answer, according to those who are interested in how people develop, is that love is just a grown-up form of attachment. A child's experience of first relationships paves the way for her adult love life.

However, it's not so easy to prove that there is a direct line leading from the way you felt in your mother's lap to the way you feel at age twenty-seven with the person you plan to marry. Ask anyone to talk about his or her love life and in the same breath to recall his or her earliest relationships, and you are just asking for rewritten histories, ones that create a continuous narrative whether there is one or not. People will recount stories of a distant, unloving mommy to help explain a crumbling marriage or a powerful, overwhelming father to explain why they could never meet the right guy. Those kinds of tales are usually just-so stories. Although these homespun stories might often be baseless, there is a connection between one's early relationships and grown-up love. The trick is identifying the real thread.

Phillip Shaver and his colleagues have chipped away at this elusive challenge from a number of angles. When they ask people to describe their earliest memories of their parents and their early life at home, the answers can be sorted into the three attachment styles first described by Ainsworth. And remarkably, the number of people falling into each of the three styles almost perfectly mirrors the breakdown of attachment styles found in the original research with toddlers. This suggests that though psychologists often think that self-reports are unreliable, in this case, people's accounts are accurate and quite revealing. When the same subjects described their adult relationships, a clear pattern emerged. Those whose earliest memories captured an anxious, ambivalent attachment were the same ones who described a nagging sense that their partners didn't love them enough and felt constantly distracted by the worry that their mates might be cheating on them. These were the adults who constantly hankered for more reassurance from their romantic partners. Sadly, people who have ambivalent attachments as babies often seek out mates who suffer from the same kinds of ambivalence. It's not hard to imagine that such couples are in for a tough time. The same is true for those who experience what Ainsworth termed "avoidant attachments." The baby who watches impassively as his mother leaves the room and barely acknowledges her return might well turn out to be the man who has difficulty creating intimacy with a lover, who has trouble forming a long-term attachment, and who avoids the kinds of closeness so important to long-lasting love.

Shaver's work only shows that there seems to be some stability between how a person recalls early relationships and how he or she experiences current romantic relationships. It doesn't prove that early stability guarantees happiness in later love life. But taken together, the data on early parent-child interaction and the little we have gleaned about what goes into successful adult love suggest that developing a capacity for closeness in early life has a huge impact on the closeness you can find in your love life. As psychologist Susan Golombok has pointed out in her book on parenting (*Parenting: What Really Counts*), it is not the structure of family life that seems to matter as much as the quality of family life.

Growing up with a single parent might tell you little about your chances of a happy marriage. The quality of the relationship you had with that parent says a lot more. When you experience intimacy as a young child, you are good at it, and, just as important, you seek it in your grown-up love life.

Vera and Matthew met in their late twenties. They both had been briefly married to other people. They were smart, hardworking, and deeply immersed in their shared life working on educational films. All of their friends worked in film, and they loved nothing better than to gather with editors, cameramen, screenwriters, and set designers to talk shop and gossip. They both came from stable, strong families, and of course, they wanted to have children. They had a lot of trouble conceiving, but with medical intervention, they finally had a son, whom they named Alex. Alex was adorable, bright, and full of pep. Vera had waited a long time to have a child. The photographs of her with her little boy show her beaming with delight. But people are who they are. And Vera was cool and crisp. She found it hard to confide the details of her personal life, even to her closest friends. She wouldn't have considered changing her clothes in front of anyone, not her mother, her sister, or her friends. She thought it odd when friends kissed one another hello. There were huge gaps of information between members of the family. They didn't like to pry.

Vera was not one of those moms who took naps or baths with their babies. She had trouble nursing and put Alex on a bottle when he was three weeks old. She couldn't understand why other people had difficulty getting their babies to sleep. She had no trouble giving Alex a quick kiss and resolutely closing the door behind her. By three months, Alex slept through the night. As Alex and her friends' children got older, she found it strange that other little boys told their mothers all about what they did with their buddies, what their conversations at school were like, and what they were feeling. She thought it was better for children to have some distance from their parents, someone who could be an authority. When Alex was a teen, she commented to a friend that it was good to make rules that Alex didn't like—how else could he rebel and therefore grow up? She took him to the park, read books to him, and played games with him. However, if you watched them together when Alex was little, you could see that although she was loving and attentive, she was distant, and Alex seemed slightly oblivious to her comings and goings. It was hard to catch them absorbed in each other. He didn't flop against her when he was tired, and she didn't nuzzle his stomach with her head. When she mentioned her concerns about him, she might have been talking about an acquaintance or a character in a book, rather than her flesh and blood. The very slight reserve they had with each other was subtle, not easy to catch at first glance. As child psychiatrist Susanne King says, "What begins as a pretty basic kind of attachment needs a chance to grow into something more. Children need a chance to experience giving emotionally as well as getting."

When Alex was in high school, Vera and Matthew kept waiting for him to find a girlfriend. Although they had a sense that he had crushes, Vera didn't like to ask. She felt that was intrusive. And they had less and less sense of what his social life was like. When Alex went off to college, they were sure he'd find a sweetheart. He had roommates he seemed to like, he enjoyed his class work, and he did well. But no romances. After college, Alex moved to Boston. He got a job working in a bookstore and began to take graduate courses in English, which had been his major in college. But he didn't seem to have many friends. He met a girl in one of his classes, and he dated her for a few weeks. Matthew and Vera were relieved. But then, mysteriously, the relationship evaporated. Even Alex seemed uncertain what had gone wrong. At twenty-nine, he still hadn't had a close relationship that had lasted more than three months.

Meanwhile, Lenore was miserable. At twenty, she was the swan who had become an ugly duckling. Why didn't boys ask her out? Why wasn't she sexy? At eleven, her mind had been dancing with future lovers. Except for her truncated whirlwind romance with Ryan, she lived like a nun. No one approached her. How could a young woman already be an old maid? A therapist suggested that her trouble finding love had to do with the uneasy rapport she had with her father, maybe because her parents had divorced, maybe because her mother had been too competitive with her. Maybe maybe maybe.

When my eldest son was a toddler, I spent a lot of time in a New York City park with other young moms and their children. I remember one mother in particular who seemed to be perpetually angry, controlling her little boy's every move. She called him "Pudge." I confided to some of the other moms that I predicted he would not feel attractive as he grew up. She constantly reminded him what he should and shouldn't do in the playground: "Pudge, stop that right now. I told you we wouldn't stay if you kept grabbing other children's trucks. Pudge, take that out of your mouth. That's revolting." Watching this mother and her young son, I heard a small warning bell go off. With such constant criticism, how could this kid ever feel autonomous and confident when he was older? So much of their interaction was suffused with conflict. I wasn't the only one who didn't like what I saw. "Oh," the mothers on the bench said, "this doesn't bode well for Pudge's love life. He's doomed to marry the same kind of heckling micro-manager he's got now. Everyone marries his mother."

There was another mom in the park who walked in each day

holding her son's hand. They often skipped together as they neared the gate. He'd give her a kiss before running off to the swings. Sometimes he'd leave the play area and come back over to his mother sitting nearby on a bench. She always seemed to know ahead of time what he was coming for. The thermos of juice, the cookie, the other toy truck, or the mittens would be ready by the time he got there, as if she could read his mind. He'd give her another big wet kiss before heading back off to the swing sets. The other mothers would shake their heads at this pair: "Oh, boy. I feel sorry for his girlfriends. They're gonna be out on a date at a nice restaurant, and he's gonna want to get up to make a call to his mother, just to say hello. No one will ever measure up to Angel Mommy."

The first prediction is probably not true. People don't marry their mothers (or their fathers, for that matter). There isn't one shred of evidence for that old nut. And there isn't one theory that even makes sense of such a prediction. The second prediction is probably not true, either. A good relationship with a parent doesn't get in the way of love—it paves the way for love.

I read novels. So it's hard not to think of love in terms of the great love stories, which offer vivid pictures of the different kinds of love we might wish for our children. When we gaze adoringly and anxiously into our babies' eyes, we might not all have our hopes pinned on the same romantic future. Do you want your son to know the all-encompassing passion Heathcliff felt for Cathy? Do you want your daughter to feel the gentle, steady devotion that Jane Eyre felt for Mr. Rochester? Would you prefer she elicit the feelings Mildred drew from Philip in *Of Human Bondage*?

In our society, the majority of people end up finding a mate. That doesn't mean, however, that they have found love. And a passionate romance doesn't guarantee that your child will form a lasting, supportive, committed relationship, either. The road to love is filled with happenstance, good and bad luck, and the influence of outside forces.

But children who experience emotional closeness when they are young are much more likely to seek intimacy in adulthood and to be able to share themselves with others. If your child finds you to be emotionally reliable and consistent when she is little, if you and she like being with each other, if what begins as a bond becomes rapport, her romantic future is off to a good start. In fact, a loving reciprocal relationship with a primary parent is as close to a love potion as you can get.

When Lenore was twenty-three, she married Paul. During the years that followed, they faced plenty of tough times. Paul suffered untold stress when he was diagnosed with diabetes, and he became seriously depressed. After about ten years together, when Lenore changed jobs and Paul started a new business, they were so broke they almost lost their house. They fought and once came close to divorce. But they also raised four children and recently celebrated their thirty-fourth wedding anniversary. When asked if they are in love, Lenore smiles wryly. "We were in love. Absolutely. I totally remember those days. I think he does, too. And now we'd rather be together than apart. We still like to wake up in the same bed. We're good."

# 6

# Happiness: The Path to Contentment

"For Sale: Baby shoes, never worn." If his suicide didn't make the point, his supposed one line memoir shows Ernest Hemingway's dim view of life. On the other hand, Elizabeth, the young heroine from Thomas Hardy's novel *The Mayor of Casterbridge*, seemed to earn the good fortune that a fundamentally happy child carves out for herself: "Her strong sense that neither she nor any human being deserved less than was given, did not blind her to the fact that there were others receiving less who had deserved much more. And in being forced to class herself among the fortunate she did not cease to wonder at the persistence of the unforeseen, when the one to whom such unbroken tranquility had been accorded in the adult stage was she whose youth had seemed to teach that happiness was but the occasional episode in a general drama of pain."

Why is one person happy with so little and another, talented and fortunate, miserable anyway? When you gaze at your baby and watch her play, can you tell whether she will grow up happy?

Even as a two-month-old, Lily liked peace and quiet. Her mother quickly realized that although she herself was naturally drawn to a slightly more rough-and-tumble style of parenting, it wouldn't work for her tiny girl. Lily liked to be lifted gently and lowered into her crib gently. She liked soft voices and a gentle up-and-down rocking motion. She was calm, happy to be held by anyone as long as they weren't loud. Gorgeous from the day she was born, she had a heart-shaped face, with gray eyes that ended in a small tilt and a lush, wide mouth. From the moment she could smile, adults and older children wanted to make her smile again. When something pleased her, a slow glow rose from her face, illuminating those around her.

Yet babies are not simpler than adults, and Lily was filled with seeming contradictions. Although she craved quiet and order, she was also zany. At three, she liked to dress in wild costumes—pants on her head, brightly striped knee socks, large leather shoes for bike riding, her uncle's yellow fishing gators for suppertime. She liked to make crazy faces and say raucously funny things in a crowd. There are photographs of her looking like a cross between the Artful Dodger and Tinkerbell. As soft and dreamy as she could appear, she was as tough as nails. She learned to swim, in a freezing-cold murky pond, before she was two, and she could navigate the rocks in a waterfall before she was four. No dog, however big, scared her. She liked sour foods and, with a belly laugh, would crunch into her favorite snack, a dill pickle.

When Lily learned to talk, she became even more entrancing to those around her. She added new syllables to the phrases she liked best—her uncle's dog Slash became "Slasher," and at noon, she often called out boisterously for "Lunchialia!" She had lots of easy charm, which she seemed to bestow effortlessly on the objects and people around her.

If you had met Lily when she was a toddler, you would have seen an easy, calm baby, full of smiles, equanimity, and an infectious sense of humor. And things seemed to go so well for her you would have bet money that she was a child destined for a cheery, happy life.

But no baby is an island. Every baby's temperament unfolds in a world of people and events. Lily came into the world a younger sister. Hazel, six years older, had been tempestuous from day one. She was full of life, but she was also full of vinegar. She hadn't been an easy baby, gassy and unsettled from the first. As Hazel grew older, she continued to demand a lot of attention, good and bad, from the adults around her. So, from the day Lily was born, she was the angelic foil to her high-strung sister.

Other aspects of Lily's life impinged on her as well. Don't they for everyone? When Lily was two years old, her family moved from San Francisco to a suburb a few hours away. Her mother gave up her full-time job in a community arts agency to work as a freelance graphic designer. Her father, a musician, took on a full-time job teaching music in a high school. Her older sister, Hazel, was ecstatic and loved their new house by a lake. Lily's parents were thrilled—this would be the first time they had actually owned a home, and they were exhausted from working and raising children in an expensive and noisy city.

But the transition was harder for Lily. At three, she was particularly vulnerable to change, and research shows that a move of homes and neighborhoods is one of the biggest adjustments a child can face. Lily had thrived on calm and routine and found the move disruptive and deeply disconcerting. She began to protest when her mother left her at day care. Those separations, so easy and unimportant when she was younger, suddenly seemed filled with anguish. As her mother kissed her good-bye at the door of the preschool, Lily's soft, wide mouth would turn down, and her eyes would turn a dark, murky gray. She'd complain huskily, "Why do you have to go? Why do you have to leave me?" Her mother, torn and unsettled, would leave her at day care, fretting all the while at how hard it was for her usually sunny child to handle this small routine.

Lily's protests rattled her mother. What had been a harmonious, flowing connection between Lily and her mother now seemed rife with small upsets. A cloud began to accumulate over their relationship and over Lily herself. If you met Lily when she was eight, you would never have been able to guess that her start in life had been so sunny.

Lily's teacher shook his head about her and said, "Lily comes into school as if she were carrying the weight of the world on her shoulders." Although she was beautiful, athletic, and good at her schoolwork, she often scowled or shrugged when family members asked her how school was. She complained about her teachers ("He's boring," "She's mean," "She never calls on me"). She was frequently aggrieved by her friends. The things that lit her up were few and far between. She developed a habit of shrugging diffidently when asked almost any kind of question. Her soft, low voice, which seemed when she was little to beckon, now deflected, sounding muted rather than husky. What had happened to her?

Happiness is the magic elixir of life. If you have lots of it, you can weather all kinds of terrible disappointment and even misfortune. If you don't have it, even the luckiest life feels gray. While academics endlessly debate the precise elements of happiness, most people know it when they feel it and often know it when they see it in others. You don't need to be a research psychologist to see that some people have a zest for life, a pervasive sense of well-being that lifts them above the general population, gives them a bounce in their step, and makes them really attractive to others. Franklin Delano Roosevelt was one of those people.

In a *New York Times* article about happy presidents, Lou Cannon described FDR's irrepressible good mood in the face of tremendous pressures: "In a little-remembered book, 'F.D.R., My Boss,' Mr. Roosevelt's secretary Grace Tully affectionately described how he cheerfully added to his stamp collection, dabbled in architecture, played cards and 'made a ritual of the cocktail hour' where serious talk was avoided during the depths of the Great Depression and World War II. Happiness was part of F.D.R.'s makeup. 'From the bottom of his heart he wants [people] to be as happy as he is,' wrote his adviser Raymond Moley."

Roosevelt had a lot of good fortune. He was rich. He was hugely successful. But he also was paralyzed from the waist down. He presided over one of the modern world's most devastating wars. He was responsible for the well-being of a society thrown into the worst economic depression ever recorded. His marriage was not happy, and he was unable to live with the woman he really loved. Nevertheless, he felt good. To paraphrase the Cowardly Lion, "What does he got that we don't got?"

The roots of his happiness can be traced all the way back to his childhood in Hyde Park, New York, on the Hudson, where he lived with his mother and father. In her biography of FDR, Jean Smith quotes him: " 'In thinking back to my earliest days,' he said many years later, 'I am impressed by the peacefulness and regularity of things both in respect to places and people. Up to the age of seven, Hyde Park was the center of my world.'" Smith writes, "America's confidence in FDR depended on Roosevelt's incredible confidence in himself, and that traced in large measure to the comfort and security of his childhood."

Stability and a pleasant home environment gave FDR a boost, and these factors are generally an antidote to life's ills. Children who come from stable, warm families have an advantage when it comes to their long-term prospects for happiness. But FDR had another weapon in his happiness arsenal: he made it easy for people to make him happy. Both his mother and his father recalled him being a delightful son, one they took great pride in but also enjoyed. "We never subjected the boy to a lot of don'ts," Mrs. Roosevelt wrote. "While certain rules established for his well-being had to be rigidly observed, we were never strict merely for the sake of being strict. In fact, we took a secret pride in the fact that Franklin instinctively never seemed to require that kind of handling." When he got to boarding school at Groton, he made friends easily, and the teachers liked him. But he had something else as well. Even as a little boy, he was enthusiastic about his interests, having begun stamp collecting by the age of ten. He had a gift for pleasure.

Several summers ago, I was visiting my childhood home on the eastern end of Long Island. My parents' house is on a small country lane with only three houses next to it and lots of open potato fields. Usually, it's very quiet there. But one morning, as I sat on a chair in my second-floor bedroom, high above the lawn, listening to the stillness of a sultry August day, I slowly became aware of an odd sound floating through the air into my window. It took me a few seconds to figure out what I was hearing. It was the voice of a little girl, maybe five years old. She was singing a tuneless little song, over and over again. I couldn't hear any words, just a little girl's singsong lilt and a five-sound phrase, repeated again and again with exactly the same cadence each time. "Da de DA de dah. Da de DA de dah. Da de DA de dah." The first two "da's" went up the scale, the third was the loud high point, and then came the final "de dah," which took her back down the scale. She was singing the way you do when no one is listening, when you are singing just for your own pleasure. Sometimes her voice would fade until I could barely hear her, and then it would rise again in volume, brimming with renewed enthusiasm and energy. As I strained to listen, I realized the young chanter wasn't just sitting under a tree—she was doing something. So I peered out the window to find out what. Through the bushes, I caught a view of the young singer. She was a slight girl of about five, with pale thin legs and arms. She was wearing faded shorts and a hot-pink T-shirt. Her brown hair fell to just below her chin and flopped when she jumped. She was leaping, with a kind of calm sobriety, between two tall trees. Each time she landed under one of the trees, she reached up and swatted at one of the low-hanging leaves, then turned to make her leap back to the other tree. That was the game. It must have been really fun. I sat there, listening to her leap and chant, for a good fifteen minutes. When I finally pulled myself away from the hypnotic allure of the little girl's game and went downstairs to join my family, she was still at it.

Her absorption in that small sequence captures the remarkable capacity young children possess for delighting in the smallest slices of life. Just recall the universal game of peekaboo with a nine-month-old. Imagine the baby's nervous and expectant excitement while she waits for your hands to come off your eyes as you say, for the thirty-fourth time, "Peekaboo!" Her surprised laughter contains an intensity that adults typically reserve for very special occasions.

But a child doesn't need to be playing a game to be thrilled by life. Seemingly mundane activities can be equally absorbing. Watch just about any toddler sip water from a cup. She grabs the cup with two fists, focused on her task. She brings the cup up to her mouth, widening her eyes as she peers at the liquid within. You can just imagine how inviting that small amount of water looks to her. She puts her lips around the edge of the cup, readying herself to taste. Each infinitesimal gesture, the ones that become so automatic we'll never give them another thought unless we are deprived of them because of illness or hardship, is carried out by the toddler in a deliberate way. She notices what she is doing. She marvels at the texture of cool liquid slipping into her mouth. You can see how she relishes the sensation of filling her mouth with the wet substance, and you can almost see her decide just how quickly to let it slide to the back of her mouth so that she can swallow it. The gulp looks almost as wonderful as the first taste. But the pleasure of sipping water does not lead to laughs and smiles. Children often take very seriously the things that make them most happy. For the young child, such pleasures are not giddy punctuations that contrast with the more serious or dull routines of everyday life—the routines contain a multitude of opportunities for the young child's delight.

What FDR, the little girl on the lawn, and any toddler sipping from a cup have in common might well be the quality we most yearn for later in life: the young child's ability to immerse herself in the pleasure of small things. Many of us, no matter what our childhood circumstances, can recall a kind of exquisite joy in ordinary moments that seems harder to come by as we age. The young child's capacity for intense pleasure is a seedling, something to be built on and nurtured rather than cast away. Yet by the age of four, the capacity to get a kick out of life has, for some, faded. Some preschoolers seem sadder than others. Lily did, for sure. Is a sad child doomed to a sad life? Can a glum child become happy?

Martin Seligman thinks so. While psychology has traditionally concerned itself with people's problems—depression, anxiety, shyness, and anger, just to name a few—Seligman, a research psychologist at the University of Pennsylvania, has spent recent years trying to understand why and how people feel good.

The science of happiness, however, poses an unusual research problem. While psychologists usually depend on surreptitious methods to find out what people really feel (by tricking their subjects into revealing thoughts and emotions thought to be inaccessible to consciousness), it's hard to imagine being happy and not knowing it. So, positive psychologists (the way Seligman prefers to describe psychologists who want to understand people's strengths) just ask their subjects how happy they are.

Seligman typically uses something called the Authentic Happiness Inventory. He invites subjects to sit down at a desk and answer a list of twenty-seven questions about their outlook on life. The score provides researchers with a measure of a person's overall sense of well-being. Participants in Seligman's studies are usually simply asked to rate themselves on a long list of questions that are designed to tap into a person's sense of self. A subject might answer the following kinds of questions:

(1)

    A. I feel like a failure.

    B. I do not feel like a winner.

    C. I feel like I have succeeded more than most people.

    D. As I look back on my life, all I see are victories.

    E. I feel I am extraordinarily successful.

(2)

    A. I am usually in a bad mood.

    B. I am usually in a neutral mood.

    C. I am usually in a good mood.

    D. I am usually in a great mood.

    E. I am usually in an unbelievably great mood.

(3)

    A. When I am working, I pay more attention to what is going on around me than to what I am doing.

    B. When I am working, I pay as much attention to what is going on around me as to what I am doing.

    C. When I am working, I pay more attention to what I am doing than to what is going on around me.

    D. When I am working, I rarely notice what is going on around me.

    E. When I am working, I pay so much attention to what I am doing that the outside world practically ceases to exist.

Sure enough, the way a person scores on Seligman's questionnaires matches up pretty well with other indices of a person's well-being—

people who get a high happiness score tend to be viewed by others as quite happy. They also tend to make fewer visits to doctors, suffer less frequently from depression, do better at work, and report greater marital satisfaction. The results of those questionnaires, given to hundreds of people across the country, have provided researchers with some clues about the essential components of happiness.

Data from these studies have led Seligman and others to believe that how happy we feel stems in large part from how we think—a startling concept emerging after almost fifty years of behaviorism and psychoanalytic theory. In the 1960s and '70s, behaviorists and psychoanalysts dominated the way we understood people's emotions. Behaviorists thought sadness was a learned response and that if you could learn to act happy, you would come to feel happy. Psychoanalysts believed that depression was anger turned inward. The anger was presumed to have its origins in an earlier emotional loss of some sort. Freudian psychoanalysts thought depressed patients were overly dependent on love and approval from others and unable to deal with small disappointments.

In this climate, psychologists Aaron Beck began his research by trying to find empirical support for the psychoanalytic model of depression. He studied dream content in an attempt to prove the existence of internalized anger in depression. If such a construct existed, he expected depressed people to report higher degrees of hostility and anger in their dreams. His results showed that depressed and nondepressed people did not differ in the frequency with which they had angry dreams. Instead, he found that depressed people tended to have more dreams in which they are victims of rejection, disappointment, or criticism.

He also noticed that depressed patients were more negative and pessimistic about themselves and their performance than nondepressed patients. As Beck wrote, "the studies led to the conclusion that certain cognitive patterns could be responsible for the patients' tendency to make negatively biased judgments."

In addition, during his treatment of patients, Beck became aware that people experienced what he called "negative automatic thoughts," a second stream of thinking of which they were unaware. Beck had been with one patient who was telling him how angry he was with him. While exploring these feelings in the therapy session, the patient noted that he was also having self-critical thoughts about expressing the same feelings. Through therapeutic encounters like this, Beck came to the conclusion that patients were communicating with themselves at an automatic level all the time. These thoughts tended to be fleeting, specific, spontaneous, and consistent in theme and almost always involved a distortion of reality. Beck maintained that negative thinking was not merely a symptom of depression but its cause. He argued that depressed thinking is characterized by the "cognitive triad," a negative view of oneself, one's future, and the world. If a person sees the world in negative terms, he will constantly be confirming his own worst fears: *I'm bad, no one likes me, there's nothing I can do to make things better.* Beck argued that depressed people couldn't simply be retrained to act in happier ways; they needed to learn how to reinterpret the world.

Seligman, influenced by Beck, turned his attention to children who were depressed. He wanted to show that children who are gloomy, like depressed adults, explain the world differently from children who feel good. And he wanted to show that this explanatory style could be changed.

When asked to explain various imaginary scenarios, children reveal two clearly distinct patterns. Some explain good events in terms of global stable qualities about themselves. For instance, this kind of child thinks he got an A on a test because he is smart. Other children, however, assume that good events are mere chance, nothing to be counted on. When this kind of kid earns an A on a test, he's sure he just got lucky or that the particular test was unusually easy.

But the same child who sees good events in terms of stable, underlying strengths typically explains bad events in more specific and temporary terms. A child with a positive outlook might think she didn't get a part in the play because so many older kids tried out that year, while a downbeat child figures it's because she's no good at acting. Happy children explain life's events one way, and glummer children explain things in the opposite way.

Psychologists have developed a questionnaire that elicits these two patterns of explaining life's events. The most standard version of this assessment is called the Children's Attributional Style Questionnaire. The questionnaire contains forty-eight items. Each presents the child with a hypothetical situation, followed by two statements about why the event happened. For instance, the young subject might read, "You run in a race at school and lose," and choose from the two explanations, "I'm not athletic" or "I just didn't give it my all that day." The array of questions is carefully designed to reveal three different dimensions of a child's explanatory style.

Psychologists believe that both optimistic and pessimistic outlooks rest on three kinds of explanations children use to understand their own successes and disappointments: how responsible they feel for what has happened ("It was my fault"), how stable they think the cause of the event is ("I'm never good at that"), and how likely it is that the cause of the event will occur in other situations ("I'll never do well at that"). Optimistic children draw on the mirror image of those three kinds of explanations: they think they caused positive events to happen ("I did a great job"), that good things have stable causes ("I'm good at that"), and that the cause is likely to generalize to other situations ("I'll do well every time I do that").

Each of the forty-eight items on the questionnaire focuses on one of these three kinds of explanations, posing either a good or a bad event. For instance, one of the questions might be: "You break a glass in the kitchen. Choose a or b to explain what happened: (a) I am not careful enough. (b) Sometimes I am not careful enough." This choice identifies whether children think bad events are caused by permanent stable characteristics or by temporary characteristics. Another item on the questionnaire says: "You try out for a sports team and do not make it. Choose an explanation: (a) I am not good at sports. (b) The other kids who tried out are very good at sports." In this case, the child who answers, "I am not good at sports," attributes a bad event to herself, while the more optimistic child assumes that it was caused by factors outside herself. The questionnaire also gives children a chance to show how they interpret good events. For instance, one of the items says: "You make a new friend. Choose an explanation: (a) I am a nice person. (b) The people I meet are nice." The optimistic child who might well have assumed that bad events were caused by external factors might attribute this nice incident to her own good attributes, while the more pessimistic child, likely to think he caused his own bad luck, might well think making a new friend happened because of other people, not because of him. Children's answers to the forty-eight questions tend to be pretty consistent, hence the designation of a pessimistic or optimistic child.

Lily never completed the Children's Attributional Style Questionnaire, so we don't know how she would have scored. But when the painting she spent three weeks on in third grade wasn't chosen for the school exhibition, she shrugged. "I knew it wouldn't get in. I can't paint." When her father canceled the trip they were supposed to take together to Washington, D.C., when she was in fifth grade, her mouth turned down. But she didn't protest. She said softly, "It's OK. I knew we probably wouldn't go." She felt burdened by schoolwork, oppressed by the demands of teachers and the daily ebb and flow of social life. At home, she became a somewhat withdrawn observer of the louder, more vibrant exchanges between her older sister and her parents.

It's not obvious why Lily had developed such a negative outlook. She was born, like most children, with the ability to derive huge satisfaction in everyday life. But that was not all. She was also born with some of the other elements that predict happiness. Early on, she had a sunny disposition, good looks, humor, and what's known as low neuroticism. She didn't ruminate, she didn't dwell on grievances, and she didn't seem in her early years to be beset by the kind of indecision and ambivalence that plague neurotic people. Yet even so, as she entered elementary school, her sunny self became overshadowed by a vague sense of discontent with people and experiences. She seemed to draw less and less satisfaction from her work, whether it was writing, reading, soccer, or knitting. Nothing seemed to draw her in deeply. The less engaged she got, the gloomier she seemed. By the time she was twelve, it was a joke among her friends that if they asked Lily to make a decision about where to go for lunch, what dress to buy, or what movie they should see, she'd shrug and say in a low voice, "I don't mind."

Seligman is certain that kids like Lily can learn to think differently and that when they do, they begin to feel happier. Using Beck's framework for treating adult depression, Seligman set out to show that you could also shift a child's view of herself, her future, and her world—that you could teach unhappy children to have happy thoughts and that such thoughts would make them feel happier.

In his original study on the topic, Seligman and his colleagues enrolled a group of two hundred eleven- and twelve-year-old children from Philadelphia in a six-week after-school program. Children were chosen to participate because in questionnaires they filled out at their school, they reported feeling depressed and/or were experiencing problems at home, such as that their parents were fighting. Half of the students participated in small groups who spent the twelve weeks learning "coping skills." The goal was to teach the children how to identify their own negative beliefs and pessimistic explanations and come up with more positive accounts for the things that happened to them at home and at school.

Researchers have found that children who have a negative explanatory style are also more likely to feel that they have little effect on situations—they feel helpless. Happier children seem to feel more confident that they can change a situation, that they can determine their own level of success, and that they can come up with solutions to problems. Psychologists refer to this as a sense of self-efficacy. A description of the Dalai Lama by the journalist Pico Iyer provides a vivid portrait of just the things Seligman has been looking at all this time.

"Dream—nothing!" is one of the many things I've heard the Dalai Lama say to large audiences that seem to startle the unprepared. Just before I began an onstage conversation with him at New York Town Hall this spring, he told me, "If I had magical powers, I'd never need an operation!" and broke into guffaws as he thought of the three-hour gallbladder operation he'd been through, weeks after being in the hospital for another ailment. For a Buddhist, after all, our power lies nowhere but in ourselves.

We can't change the world except insofar as we change the way we look at the world, and, in fact, any one of us can make that change, in any direction, at any moment. The point of life, in the view of the Dalai Lama, is happiness, and that lies within our grasp, our untapped potential, with every breath.

Easy for him to say, you might scoff. He's a monk, he meditates for four hours as soon as he wakes up, and he's believed by his flock to be an incarnation of a god. Yet when you think back on his circumstances, you recall that he was made ruler of a large and fractious nation when he was only four years old. He was facing a civil war of sorts in Lhasa when he was just eleven, and when he was fifteen, he was made full political leader and had to start protecting his country against Mao Zedong and Zhou Enlai, leaders of the world's largest (and sometimes least tractable) nation.

This spring marked the completion of half a century for him in exile, trying to guide and serve 6 million Tibetans he hasn't seen in fifty years and to rally 150,000 exiled Tibetans who have in most cases never seen Tibet. This isn't an obvious recipe for producing a vividly contagious optimism.

Yet in thirty-five years of talking to the Dalai Lama and covering him everywhere from Zurich to Hiroshima, as a non-Buddhist, skeptical journalist, I've found him to be as deeply confident, and therefore sunny, as anyone I've met. And I've begun to think that his almost visible glow does not come from any mysterious or unique source. Indeed, mysteries and rumors of his own uniqueness are two of the things that cause him most instantly to erupt into warm laughter. The Dalai Lama I've seen is a realist (which is what makes his optimism more impressive and persuasive). And he's as practical as the man he calls his "boss."

The Buddha generally presented himself as more physician than metaphysician. "If an arrow is sticking out of your side," he famously said, "don't argue about where it came from or who made it; just pull it out. You make your way to happiness not by fretting about it or trafficking in New Age affirmations but simply by finding the cause of your suffering and then attending to it, as any doctor (of mind or body) might do."

Who knows where the Dalai Lama got his sense of self-efficacy? But Seligman believes this, too, can be taught to ordinary kids. The children in Seligman's study were also taught how to take more control of their own actions—to think about goals and consider alternative solutions to the problems that might come up each day. Finally, the workshop leaders taught them relaxation techniques and showed them how to be more assertive.

The experimenter worked hard to make the sessions fun and un-school-like. They used comic strips, role-playing, games, and videos to teach each core concept in their program. They created two characters, Hopeful Holly and her brother, Hopeful Howard.

Holly and Howard became known throughout the twelve-week sessions as the Silvers, because they could find the silver lining in even the darkest cloud. In a range of stories and scenarios the teachers presented to the children, the Silvers had to combat Gloomy Greg and Pessimistic Penny. The researchers also created characters for the other components of their program: Say-It-Straight Samantha, Bully Brenda, and Pushover Pete. Meanwhile, the children in the control condition were told that they were on a waiting list and could participate the next year. That way, all of the kids could ultimately have a chance to learn the coping skills, but meanwhile, the researchers could compare the children who had been through the twelve weeks of small-group sessions with similar children who had not experienced the training.

When Seligman and his colleagues went back to visit these children six months later and again two years later, they found that the children who had been in the experimental condition were doing better than the children in the control condition. They reported less unhappiness, and their teachers also described them as more cheerful and optimistic. Children who did not participate in the treatment group showed worse symptoms of unhappiness two years later than they had in the first place. In other words, if a child seems to be morose and negative when she is eleven, she is likely to get more so over time if she doesn't learn a new way to deal with everyday life, and children who get some help continue to benefit from the treatment a full two years later. Seligman is very gung-ho about his approach. He has used the basic model in a wide range of school districts—urban, rural, and suburban. He has moved on from using highly trained doctoral students to training teachers and parents to show kids how to think more positively, and he reports great success. He feels certain that in a relatively short period of time, you can retrain pessimistic children to think more optimistically and thereby become happier. Lily was smart and pretty and went to a good school. But according to Seligman, her negative thinking kept her from enjoying all of her good fortune.

The irony is that some kids seem to be born with such a strong dose of optimism that they can withstand disappointments much worse than the ones Lily encountered. Colin was one of those kids.

When Colin was fifteen years old, he became haunted by the feeling that he was going to hurt someone or perhaps already had. He recalls these dark feelings first emerging when he was at boarding school as a young teen. But he kept his troubles to himself. It was only after his first semester of college at the University of North Carolina that his scary thoughts began to dominate his life. He could no longer hide his problem from the people around him. Plagued by terrifying impulses and images, he couldn't eat, he couldn't sleep, and he certainly couldn't work or be with other people—in fact, he could barely talk. "I became catatonic," he recalled. Until then, his very typical-seeming family had almost no idea what he was going through.

Colin was one of four children. He had a twin brother, a sister five years older, and a brother ten years older than he. They were well off and lived in an affluent community in Virginia. His father was an attorney and extremely well connected politically. His mother was a homemaker. They had friends and a nice house. To have encountered the family in those days, you would have thought they were just another lucky American family. They had health, wealth, education, and a large intact family. Colin, too, seemed to have plenty going for him. "I did well in school. There was nothing about me that was particularly odd. I guess I was the family clown. My parents were good parents, though they were somewhat estranged from each other." Distant with each other, they were not particularly affectionate to their children, either. Colin said, "I don't ever remember being told that we were loved or hugged. What I needed as a child and what they were able to do was slightly off. I needed more direct nurturance than they were able to give."

Colin is not the first person to have grown up feeling that his parents didn't express their affection. If you think that lackluster parenting is the cause of a child's emotional problems, then you haven't really looked at the data. Many children grow up in families where parents don't show much affection to each other or don't acknowledge anger. Colin lived in a family much like others.

In telling me about his family, Colin described his siblings. "My twin was the social one. I was the student. When we were kids, I felt my brother did the social networking for both of us. I had a sister—she was five years older. She's dead. But I'll tell you about her later. And I had a brother who was ten years older. I always felt my sister and I were the low ones on the totem pole, the way my parents saw it."

Colin went on, until finally I interrupted him. "You said your sister is dead. What happened?"

Colin's voice is low-key, with the gentlest Southern lilt to it. He is one of those people who express complex and sophisticated thoughts in unusually simple, lucid terms. Even on the telephone, his modesty and sense of humility come through. He answered my question quietly. "My sister was murdered. She was being stalked by somebody. She had been doing some modeling for an art class, and one of the students took a fancy to her. I think that is the defining experience in my mother's life."

After about a year, Colin was forced to withdraw from college. He was almost completely immobilized and suffering delusions. Although they were emotionally restrained, his parents were not negligent. When Colin asked if he could see a psychiatrist, they agreed. The psychiatrist diagnosed him with schizophrenia and prescribed a regimen of heavy medication, including an antipsychotic. But Colin didn't get better. He got worse. On the advice of the doctor, Colin's parents sent him to a highly regarded residential hospital for people with mental illness, the Austen Riggs Center in Stockbridge, Massachusetts.

At Riggs, the therapists took him off the medication he had been taking. His therapist said to him, "I think when we get beneath the surface, we're going to find that the things you are feeling are feelings that everyone has."

"When I first got there," Colin said, "I didn't want to get better. But then I began to realize people liked me and wanted to do stuff with me, and I noticed that when we hiked or swam, people were happy, so I figured that if I was doing those activities, I must be happy, too."

Colin stayed at Riggs for a year and a half and stayed in the neighborhood for another two years so that he could continue intensive therapy. But he didn't just get better. He thrived. After leaving the Riggs community, he was admitted to a good liberal arts college as a transfer student. It was there he realized that he wanted to study psychology. He went on to attend one of the best PhD programs in the country, did an internship at the Yale Child Study Clinic and his clinical residency at McLean, a renowned mental hospital in Boston. Now in his fifties, Colin is a clinical psychologist who directs a treatment program for pregnant women who are addicts. He is also the doting father of a teenage daughter, although he is now divorced from his daughter's mother.

It would be nearly impossible for Colin to know for sure whether he did suffer from schizophrenia when he was a teen, but the odds are against it. Most people who are diagnosed with schizophrenia never get cured. Their symptoms might be alleviated, they might learn to cope with it, and they might even return to a somewhat normal life with the support of continual medication, but few leave it fully behind them, as Colin has. The only medication Colin has taken as an adult was the antidepressant prescribed to him briefly in the first months after he got divorced.

What happened to Colin in his late teens might always be

something of a mystery, but it's just as much of a mystery that he weathered such a psychological hurricane and came out the other side so well. Hearing about Colin's life, one cannot help but wonder how a man who has suffered such dramatic mental illness, has felt plagued by the darkest of thoughts, and has been almost completely incapacitated by his troubles can live such a happy, full adult life. It's impressive, but not surprising, that he might have found some modicum of stability, rid himself of his most terrible fantasies, finished his schooling, and achieved success professionally. But was he happy? I asked him.

"I'm a pretty happy soul. I've had to learn my way into this. The human spirit is pretty phenomenal. I'm fortunate. Many people have the problems I've had and don't get past them. It's all kind of bonus time for me. I've been very lucky," Colin replied.

Colin said that he doesn't remember all that much of his childhood, wryly adding, "Clinically speaking, that's interesting in and of itself. I don't think any dark thing happened. I was happy in the sense that I was born seeing the humor in things. My father said that was my saving grace." Although Colin remembers being pretty cheerful and having a good time, he added, "I wasn't exuberant the way one might like to see in kids. But not every kid is exuberant.

"I've come to realize over the years that my mother has given me a wonderful legacy of hope—she's a very cheerful person. There was no room for anger in my family. I was much more emotive than anyone else in the family. I was a little high-strung. It was extremely important to my father that I did well in school.

"My mother had this very abiding faith, and her sense that everything was going to work out gave me my own sense of optimism. The first thing I did after grad school was work with adolescents. I used to tell parents that the main goal for teens is just to get through the thing, period. The second thing is to try to become self-supporting. The third thing is to be as happy as one can reasonably expect to be. That's a kind of concave way to look at it. It's not just one joyful party. Working with the population I do, happiness is just a little thin on the ground. A colleague said to me, 'Colin, you're one of the most optimistic people I've ever known. You make me sick.' Another colleague said, 'I always believe that something good might happen.' When I asked her where she got that sense, she looked at me in disbelief. 'I learned that from you.'"

Colin remembered a therapist at Austen Riggs asking him if he had ever had suicidal thoughts. "I said, 'I feel like a rock precariously balanced on the point of a plateau.' I might have fallen off the point but not the plateau. I think that plateau was my sense of hope. My hope is part of my faith. I have a particular way of thinking about religion. To me, God is our collective sense of hope in the world. That's the entirety of my religious belief. I've spent time around people who don't believe in anything outside themselves, and I don't like that. That's the reason I go to church."

As with many people who report a fair level of happiness in adult life, Colin's belief in something larger than himself (what some call faith or spirituality) seems to be an ingredient in his optimism. Research shows that people who are religious tend to live longer lives and often report higher levels of personal satisfaction than nonreligious individuals. But as Colin says, this might be simply because religion provides people with a "collective sense of hope," rather than because a belief in a deity is, per se, uplifting. That sense of hope, it turns out, is a powerful vaccine against hardship.

In 1954, Emmy Werner set out to Kauai, Hawaii, to answer a question: What happens to children who grow up with all the odds against them? Werner went to Kauai as part of a group of pediatricians, psychologists, and public-health workers to gather information on one thousand children from conception to adulthood. Kauai is the westernmost county in the United States. It was home at the time to a population of about 28,000 diverse people—not only Caucasian but also of Chinese, Korean, Japanese, Portuguese, Puerto Rican, and Filipino descent. The island was mostly agricultural, and the people were known for their friendly, laid-back approach to life.

The researchers began their time on the island by obtaining a household census. Five nurses and one social worker listed the occupants of every home, along with personal data. Women of childbearing age were asked if they were pregnant. The research team left cards with all of the women, encouraging them to mail in the cards as soon as they suspected pregnancy. The goal of the researchers was to track pregnancies from the earliest date possible. As a result of the campaign to raise awareness about the study (which included letters mailed to the women, meetings with community leaders, advertisements on milk cartons, and organized mother-and-baby care classes), the team tracked 2,203 pregnancies in 1954, 1955, and 1956. The pregnancies resulted in more than 1,963 live births, which have since been tracked into adulthood. Among those children, Werner found many to be the products of teen pregnancies. These kids almost all grew up poor, without access to education or good medicine. Many of them lived in highly stressful family situations as well.

Twenty-three years after Werner arrived in Kauai, she published the answer to her question in a book titled *The Children of Kauai*. With the publication of that book, she created a new entry in our lexicon of child development: resiliency. Her data showed that some children who grow up in the toughest circumstances seem to thrive anyway. One of the factors that seems to buffer kids from poverty, stress, and inadequate family life is an optimistic outlook: "A potent protective factor among the high-risk individuals who grew into a successful adulthood was a faith that life made sense, that the odds could be overcome."

Colin certainly had that sense of hope. But he had something else: a sense of purpose. At one point, he recalled a family member asking him if he was learning a trade at Austen Riggs. He laughed and answered, "Yeah, as a matter of fact, I did learn a trade there: psychotherapy." Listening to Colin talk about his work as a therapist, it is quickly apparent that his ability to help other people is an essential part of who he is. And that, too, is an ingredient of happiness that might begin long before a person actually gets a job. In fact, it might begin in preschool.

When the little girl outside my parents' house was leaping and chanting, she was lost in a moment of aimless pleasure. But often children's most intense moments of pleasure come when they are engaged in a different form of activity altogether.

When my son Sam was about six, he asked if he could work at my husband's toy store on the weekends. Friends knowingly smiled and commented, "What kid wouldn't want to work in a toy store? He can spend all day trying out his favorite merchandise." But they had it wrong.

My husband came home after the first Saturday of Sam's new job. I asked how Sam had spent the day, and he told me, "He had to price about twenty boxes of merchandise. It usually takes the people who work for me about two days to get that much merchandise priced correctly. Sam had it done in about three hours. He's the most enthusiastic employee I've ever had. I'd give him a task, and he'd leap to it, finish it, then come over to me and say, 'What's next?'" Sam loved working. And why not? Adults need to feel useful, and so do children.

John Dewey argued back in the early twentieth century that children were bored at school because what they were learning seemed to have so little to do with the world that really mattered to them, the world of their parents and their community. In his classic piece, *School and Society*, Dewey argued that society had made school irrelevant. He claimed that children would want to learn more if what they were learning seemed meaningful—and by meaningful, he meant activities and skills that were a part of society. It was this idea that led him to argue that children should learn through "oc-cupations," activities such as carpentry and sewing.

For the past century, educators have made a big to-do over the motivational and academic merits of Dewey's approach. Teachers who use real-world activities to teach skills (setting up stores to teach math, putting together a newspaper to teach writing, ask-ing children to enact scenes from the past to learn history) are all showing the influence of Dewey's thinking. There is consensus that children seem to like school better when they do projects that bear some resemblance to the activities they see around them in the grown-up world. Not only do they like it better, but children also seem to learn more when what they are learning has some connection to the real world. And it is true that a vast array of research has demonstrated the power of Dewey's vision. When children work on projects that seem more closely related to the ac-tivities of the real world, they are more interested in the material, they are more excited to learn, and they seem to remember what they learn better. But if you watch children build wood structures, cook food, sew quilts, and write newspapers, it becomes quickly clear that the children aren't only more motivated to learn. They are also happier. Children like to feel useful.

Any parent who has asked a preschooler to help set the table or wash the car has seen the zeal with which most young children fling themselves into the pleasure of hard work. They like effort, they like activity, and from the moment they are born, most of them yearn to be part of the world around them.

In the early 1960s, cognitive psychologist Jerome Bruner thrust himself into a raging debate about the nature of early mental development. One group argued that young children were born with all of their mental abilities—most famously, Noam Chomsky claimed that children were born with the ability to speak gram-matically. Another group argued that children needed to learn everything, mostly by being rewarded for correct actions, language, and responses. Bruner offered a third way of looking at development. He argued that what children are born with is a great desire to become part of the social world. Because of that innate desire, they learn whatever will get them "in"—they learn to talk, to engage in thinking patterns that are part of their community, to solve problems, and to participate in the rituals and routines they see around them.

Because children are wired to become part of the social world around them, they find it rewarding to contribute to daily life. And, as with so much else about young children, there is a cyclical pattern to this dynamic. When children do things that are valued by the people around them, they win the approval and appreciation of others, which only strengthens their natural urge to help out. Obviously, allowing children to contribute and feel useful has its limits. Children who are forced to do chores or schoolwork at the expense of play and time with friends are not happy and often are deprived of the very experiences they need most in order to develop. But here is where Dewey's idea has such relevance. When children do work that helps them learn and is meaningful to their community (whether it's their school community, their ethnic community, or their geographic community), they gain a kind of satisfaction and meaning from their efforts that is not possible when the work is simply a way of getting a good grade or earning the right to recess.

Lily's high school years were lackluster. And she seemed lackluster. She did okay in school, but nothing really grabbed her, and she didn't shine in any one course. When she was fourteen, she switched schools. She decided she wanted to play field hockey. But she didn't prepare for the tryouts. She didn't do exercises or run in order to get fit enough to do the routines required during the tryouts. She didn't practice the basic moves, and she didn't learn more about the game. Her parents told her she was a natural at field hockey, that it was great that she was going out for the sport, and that she was sure to do fine. They felt they were encouraging her and bolstering her self-esteem. But when it came time for the tryouts, she didn't look that good compared with the other children, even though she was easily as athletic. She *could* have been good at field hockey. But her seeming indifference had kept her from becoming good at it. Not making it onto the team made her feel worse and confirmed her interpretation of herself: she wasn't good enough, life wasn't fair, and you couldn't expect good things to happen. She explained her disappointment in global, pervasive, and stable terms, just as Seligman said. On top of that, not being on the team meant not playing field hockey every day, one less thing about which to feel good.

Lily had lots of friends. She seemed to shine with them. Buried in what had become her somewhat flat manner were little sparks of interest that offered clues about what might bring her out of her malaise. She loved to cook, and what really lit her up was to see people enjoy her homemade candy. Sensing Lily's need to be more engaged, her mother enrolled her in a candy-making class. She enjoyed it, but somehow it didn't catch fire, deepen her love of cooking, or open the door to more enthusiasm for life. She also loved to work with younger children. She enjoyed the feeling that she could take care of a baby and loved holding the hand of a toddler. She wanted others to depend on her. She babysat during the summers—she got a kick out of the money, and she liked it that the children asked their mothers to hire her rather than the other babysitters.

The summer after her sophomore year in high school, she decided that in addition to babysitting, she would scoop ice cream at a local shop. Her parents were worried that she was working too hard, that she wasn't going to have time to relax. But they had undergone a shift as well. By this time, her stormy older sister was having a really rough time. Hazel had decided that rather than going to college, she would spend a few years in Hawaii surfing and supporting herself with odd jobs. After two years, she moved back to San Francisco, feeling dissatisfied and lost. She no longer wanted to surf but had no clue how to move forward. What had seemed to Hazel and her parents to be the natural pleasures of adolescence turned out to feel more like a swamp of transitory satisfactions that kept her from actually moving forward with her life.

Once again, Lily's life was shaped in part by her sister. Her parents, not wanting to see Lily get marooned, began to insist that Lily work hard at school and encouraged her to find a few things she really loved and wanted to be good at. They began to take great pride in her hard work and her good grades. Lily longed not to relax but to throw herself into something. She wanted to feel exhausted, to feel useful, and to be good at things. The staff at the ice cream shop loved her. The customers loved her. In her senior year, Lily began singing in the school choir. Her beautiful voice was praised by all.

Lily's soft voice once again sounded content and alluring, rather than subdued. Her raucousness resurfaced. She wore a pretty diamond stud in one ear and a tiny mummy in the other. She caught people off guard and made them laugh—the angelic face and the sharp, ironic jokes were irresistible. She liked who she was. She went off to college pleased with life.

In order to appreciate how happy it makes children feel to be competent, imagine the opposite. Think for a moment of a child you've known who has struggled to read. The head hangs down, and the body sags. Each day of not being able to decipher the letters on the page brings dread. A child who cannot read feels miserable while he struggles at reading time. And many of the children who have trouble reading begin to feel sad at other times of the day as well. When reading is what every student around you is supposed to be able to do, when the world is offered up in signs, pages, and screens of words, a nonreader is reminded constantly of what he is not good at. His whole demeanor is a study in the opposite of happiness.

Like many children in kindergarten, Craig had learned to recognize common words from memory and to sound out simple words—the first steps toward reading. Most children catch on fairly easily after this, learning to use the meaning of words and sentences as a guide to greater fluency. But Craig, at nine years old and a third-grader at a school in rural Massachusetts, had never made that leap. While most children his age could read simple chapter books, he could not even read a picture book.

At the beginning of the school year, his teacher, Ms. Brennan, had paired the children and asked them to read aloud to one another. Craig would hesitate over the first words he did not recognize and then take so long to read anything that he and the partner would both give up or run out of time. Craig refused to read aloud to his teacher. He would chat and describe the picture, then spend long minutes sounding out the first few words until she provided them so he could move on.

He had been tested for vision, hearing, and reading disabilities, but none had been identified. His family was not highly educated, Ms. Brennan said, "not school people particularly, and I don't think there was lots of time at home for reading.

"He was an appealing child," she continued. "He'd come stand at the corner of my desk and chat with me about the foster kids who lived with his family. He talked a lot about his dog, something like a St. Bernard. He liked to draw. He'd walk up to my desk while I was busy with odd jobs and slip a drawing he had just made for me onto my desk. But he had a cautious, wary manner. He never acted reluctant or angry about reading time." She added that she suspected he found his difficulty in reading frustrating and that the frustration was itself part of the problem.

She developed a hunch about what was holding this child back.

First, she said, he was not getting enough practice reading, and learning to read and practicing reading are closely intertwined. Second, because he was not practicing, he was not improving, and that itself was undermining his self-confidence. He was so worried about sounding stupid in front of other people, she decided, that he clammed up. He was a strong little boy, and when he shut down, there was not much she could do. Ms. Brennan knew that not being able to read was a much bigger problem to Craig than he would admit.

In early October, Ms. Brennan announced that each day, the children would have half an hour to read alone. Choosing the place in the classroom to read was quickly as important to the pupils as choosing the book. They rushed to claim the best spots under a desk, against the radiator just under the window that looked out onto an internal quad, and the most popular place, near the teacher's small terrier, Barnaby, who came to school every day with her. During lessons and lunch, Barnaby was in his crate, but during reading time, he was out. In mid-November, Ms. Brennan realized that Craig had successfully avoided reading aloud for nine weeks of school. And so she suggested that he read near Barnaby, promising him first choice for that spot. She also suggested that rather than read just to himself, he read aloud to the dog. This proved to be the key. Every day until mid-April, the boy selected *Go Dog Go* by P. D. Eastman, settled himself near Barnaby, and recited the book to the dog while pointing to the words and looking over the pictures. By June, Craig was picking a wide range of picture books to read to Barnaby, popping out of his chair eagerly for read-aloud time. Learning to read gave Craig something important to feel genuinely happy about.

Some children seem born happy. They smile readily, they are easy to soothe, and right from the get-go, they approach life with gusto. Three qualities that contribute to a person's happiness are agreeableness, openness to experience, and low neuroticism.

These aren't qualities you can learn to have. You either have them or you don't. Although most of us don't think of our children in terms of these dimensions, it's not all that hard to get a rough sense of how your child fares with them.

Pippi Longstocking, one of the happiest people to bound across the pages of a book, certainly would have scored high on agreeableness and openness to experience and low on neuroticism. Perhaps unwittingly, writer Astrid Lindgren created a young girl who possessed the very qualities that seem to make some people prone to feel good. Although Pippi lives alone, with no parents or siblings (she never knew her mother, and she hasn't seen her father in years because he was lost at sea), she does not feel isolated. She shares her home with her pet monkey, Mr. Nillsen, and her horse. When she moves to the small Swedish village in which the story is set, she immediately makes friends with her conventional neighbors, young Tommy and Annika. But Pippi's ability to form connections goes beyond that. When burglars invade her house, she ends up dancing all night with them and making breakfast for them. She doesn't hesitate or ruminate about things and thus would get a low score on neuroticism. And although bad things have happened to her, she expects things to be good. She is optimistic.

If your child is born a Pippi, you'll know it early on. Those children, like my son Sam, seem to get a kick out of life, feel sure things will go well, and automatically interpret good things as stable and general, while seeing bad things as momentary hurdles that can be overcome. If your child is like that, you are lucky. Such a child can face a lot of disappointment and still bounce back.

But not every child is born a Pippi. Are gloomier children doomed to a life of sadness or negativity? The answer is unequivocally no. And that's because we now know that the way we think is a key ingredient of the way we feel. Positive interpretations lead to more happiness. And children can learn to think differently.

If you think your five-year-old gets less pleasure out of everyday life than other little boys and girls, and if you think she seems sad a lot of the time, one of the first things to do is get a reality check. Find out if other adults who are part of her life see her that way. Talk to a therapist who specializes in young children, and describe what she is like day in and day out. Young children who are clinically depressed should get help—it can make a big difference.

However, many children aren't clinically depressed, but they just tend to put a negative spin on things. If you yourself put a negative spin on things, you have a double job in front of you, because it's hard to get your child to see the world differently from how you do, and children learn a great deal by listening to how their parents talk. However, you can try to encourage your child to attribute disappointments to temporary, fixable, specific causes and explain good things in terms of enduring, stable causes that are likely to affect many aspects of their lives.

The other thing you can do that will help your child to be happy is to make sure that she gets to do things at which she is good. Being good at things makes kids happy.

Finally, and this might be the most important of all, accept the fact that not all children are jubilant. Happiness comes in many shades, and to some extent, we all are born with our happiness thermometers set at different points. Contentment, a sense of hope, and the ability to relish the things we do in everyday life are the components of happiness. A child could experience these components and still not seem to be bursting with joy. Lily will never be Pippi. One of the greatest gifts you can give your child is to know and accept who he or she is. If your child doesn't burst into smiles when you give her her favorite cookie or when a friend arrives to play, don't try to make her into a smiler. She might show her pleasure in subtler ways. If your child seems pensive or is often quiet, learn to recognize that as her way of experiencing life, not a lack of enthusiasm.

Sadness is a red flag. A child who doesn't seem to dive into any activity, who can't find anything she loves to do, or who seems flat about everyday life might be depressed. Children who think they are helpless to make good things happen to them or who expect bad things to happen to them are giving a clue about their general level of happiness. Listen to the way your child interprets his life. Pay attention to the way you interpret life, because that is what he is hearing as well.

While sadness is a red flag, disappointment is a red herring. If your child reacts strongly when something bad really does happen (she doesn't make it onto a team, someone she loves moves away, or she has a serious fight with a friend), that doesn't mean she is sad. Allow your child to feel bad, and trust her to get over it. Children can get through really tough times. A generally happy child can weather terrible sadness or frustration.

Being low-key is a red herring. A child doesn't have to be jubilant to be happy. She needs to feel a sense of optimism, she needs to feel that she can make things happen, she needs to feel that she is good at things, and she needs to feel connected to others. Lily began life with these qualities, and as she moved through adolescence, she regained them. So did Colin.

The good news, once again, is that a child who is basically optimistic is likely to remain that way. The other good news is that although you cannot turn Eeyore into Roo, you can help a child feel happier by helping him think differently about the world and finding things to do that he loves and is good at. And you can understand that children have different ways of showing happiness.

# Accepting Fate, Rejecting Fatalism

Soon after I began writing this book, I was invited to give a talk to parents at a public elementary school in Los Angeles. I decided to try out some of the ideas I would be writing about. For about an hour, I spoke about children's future love lives, how to read the signs that indicate whether your child is smart, and how to tell whether your child will have friends when she is older. The parents were a varied bunch—some young first-time parents, others seasoned, most middle-class, from a mixture of ethnic and racial backgrounds. It was L.A., so most of them came in casually, with the look of people who take things lightly and might at any moment make a joke about one of their children. But as I spoke, apprehension began to emanate like a vapor from my audience. I could tell what each parent was worried about, because as I began each new topic, one or another person would suddenly lean forward a little, holding his or her torso more tightly, eyes widening slightly.

Because most of the parents in that school are middle-class, they spend time, money, and energy trying to be "good parents." They read books about parenting, they attend school functions, and they talk endlessly with their friends about child rearing. Like most parents everywhere, they care a lot about their children. In recent years, such parents have been made to feel that they can and should fix anything that's not just right about their children. And here I was, telling them that there are many qualities that not only show up early in life but also remain quite steady over time. They were torn between anguish at the idea that some difficulties cannot be "solved" and relief that some things can just be left alone.

After the prepared part of the talk, I invited them to ask questions. Hands shot up all over the auditorium. A slender, nervous-looking woman with long blond hair and hip faded blue jeans said, "I had to really rethink my social life when Hannah was born. I realized a lot of my friends weren't true friends. I went to a lot of parties, got high a lot, did stupid things. I didn't want her to grow up seeing me in that crowd. I really began to see that those people didn't mean anything to me. Now I spend a lot more time alone. I don't want Hannah to waste time with false people. But I mean, it's not that I don't want her to have friends. I just want her to make the right kind of friends."

It took me a while to figure out what she was telling me and a few more moments to figure out what she was asking. She was putting into words a common phenomenon. Often, when a parent regards her child, she sees two layers: her actual little boy or girl, standing just behind a transparent hologram of herself. It can be difficult for many parents to know which is which. It was hard for this woman to watch her child navigate the world of friendships clear of the shadow thrown by her own past social life. What she wanted to know from me was whether she could influence her daughter's friendships.

I listened for a while and suggested that her behavior would influence her child and that she could create certain kinds of opportunities for her child to bond with others, but she couldn't dictate what friends her child was drawn to or how her daughter interacted in groups. And although she could make some conscious decisions about her own social life, a lot of who we are is beyond our deliberate control. In the past seven years since her daughter was born, she couldn't possibly have become a different person. I couldn't tell if my answer made her feel better or worse.

Another mother came up to me at the end of the evening. In her late forties, she looked vigorous and animated. "I know Lucia is superbright. And we're very laid-back parents. I tell her all the time, 'You're doing a great job. Don't worry about the grade.' But I am beginning to think she needs extra help with her academic work. I mean, she spends a lot of time just lying around with her cat. Reading doesn't come all that easily to her. I don't want her to fall behind."

Stalling for time, I asked, "How old is she?"

The woman answered, "She's five. It's not that I'm worried about her. I know how bright she is. But still, I don't think her performance reflects her real abilities. I just wonder what I can do to help her." Her lyrics said, *No worries.* Her tune said, *I'm worried. I'm going to fix things.*

These parents were torn between wanting to find out what they could do to help their children grow up into happy, successful, popular people and wanting to know that it was all going to be fine no matter what they did. They yearned to hear that they didn't have the burden of "doing it right."

By the time your child is born, she is already a complex assortment of characteristics. It's almost impossible for the nonscientist to sort out a child's inherited characteristics from those she will develop because of the home she lives in or the parents she lives with. Even scientists are not yet ready to do this analysis with any certainty. After all, in most cases, parents give their children both

their genes and an environment in which to grow up. The environment parents create is as much an expression of their own genes
as it is a result of their deliberate choices or a reflection of their
culture. Even when a child is raised by adoptive parents, it can be
very hard to disentangle what the child brings to life from what
she acquires through her experience. Children help create the environment that shapes them. The same environment is experienced
differently by different children. The ways in which we raise our
children are often no easier to alter than it would be to change
their genes. The way we respond to our kids, the kind of behavior
they see in us, the dynamics between parent and child, all of these
forces, which have as big an impact on a child as her genes, are
largely outside our conscious control. So, when it comes to helping
your child live a happy and good life, it doesn't really matter where
she got the qualities she got. What matters is what you can do to
help her navigate the path that will lead her to her adult self.

When you sift through the vast sea of research on child development, two important ideas stand out. First, the clues about
what kind of person your child will grow up to be are there if you
know what to look for. Much of a child's future is evident early
on, in nascent form. A child's true self is even more visible in the
five-year-old than in the twelve-year-old. Most of this book has
been about identifying what those clues look like and what they
can tell you.

But once you know what to look for and how to interpret it, you
still have to figure out what do. The research also shows that there
is only so much you can change about your child. Many qualities are set very early in life. The ones that aren't can be nudged
in ways that really matter, but you can't remake your child into a
different person.

Recently, a good friend was admitting to me that she was sometimes too hard on her eight-year-old son. "Sometimes I really
come down awfully hard on him. You'd be appalled."

"Oh," I said, "I doubt it. He knows how much you adore him."

"Yeah," she said, "but there are certain things I just can't stand. When he loses things at school, I get really upset. I do *not* want him to be scatterbrained and lose things. Ted can be a dreamer."

I broke in. "There's nothing wrong with being a dreamer, right?"

"Well, sure, but I don't want him to be a dreamer about everything."

I had just finished writing this book. I said, "You can't make him be the person you want him to be."

She gave me a crazy look—her eyes wide with fear, anxiety, anger at me for what I said, and defiance. She didn't want to give up on the thought that she could shape his dreaminess.

You can help a child who repels other kids learn how to tone it down and learn to say friendlier things to his peers. You can try to find or create situations where she is more likely to connect to another child. A child who puts a negative spin on everything can learn to see things through a rosier glass. If your child seems callous about the feelings of others, you can draw his attention to the way other people feel. But you cannot change a child's basic intelligence or make a shy child gregarious. You have to accept fate but reject fatalism.

As I have said throughout this book, knowing that many aspects of a child's character are stable is just as often good news as it is worrisome. Recently, I saw a friend for the first time in more than a year. She asked me how this book was coming along and said, "I just keep repeating to myself what you told me, 'Once smart, always smart. Once smart, always smart.'"

I tried not to laugh. Why would she be worried? She is smart, and so is her husband. Her son has given every sign that he, too, is smart. He solves problems easily, he learns and remembers information effortlessly, and he likes to think. He is growing up in a house with books, tools, and space to play in. He goes to a friendly school that's not too big, with grown-ups who like kids. Nevertheless, she needs to keep reassuring herself that he can't lose his smartness. She worries that if he is not in a challenging math class, he might lose intellectual ground. If he hangs out with jocks rather than nerds, he might somehow become duller. But what she feels is what most of us feel. Wouldn't it be great if we could just sigh and relax, secure that our child's good qualities are here to stay?

My friend's son is not going to get dumber. But he might become unmotivated or begin to feel that there's no point in trying things that are difficult. He might have the belief that if you don't succeed at first, you might as well turn to something different. And this is where my friend can have an influence. She can help her son find things he really cares about, and she can highlight the value of effort and the importance of incremental improvement. She can nudge, but she cannot remake.

Many behaviors are red herrings, things that seem alarming when you're in the thick of everyday life but don't necessarily mean much about who your child really is or where she's headed. Children tell you who they are through a million small things they do and say. The first step is to see the pattern, no matter how quirky it (and your child) may seem.

The second step is to know what you can and cannot change in your child. Keep in mind that you can guide a child in a better direction, but you cannot redesign her.

When my son Will was about seven years old, I could already see that he was moody. He was a powerful little boy—strong, athletic, and intense. In moments of joy and accomplishment, he radiated triumph and delight. But when angered or hurt, he would become enveloped by a storm cloud and often didn't know quite what to do the rage and urge for revenge that overtook him. One day, he got into a fight with his brother Jake. He began ranting and railing, and I could see he was seconds away from leaping at Jake. I took him by the hand, and we went outside, where I asked him to tell me what he was so mad about. He began explaining the hurtful, terrible thing Jake had done (I no longer remember what it was). I hadn't let go of his hand yet, and as he spoke, the grip changed, and it was he who was holding my hand. Not just holding it but squeezing it hard. When he was done telling me why he was so upset, his small hand relaxed its hold. I looked down and saw deep red marks where his fingernails had dug into my skin.

I said, "Will, you're so angry. See how angry you are?" and drew his gaze to my hand.

He looked astonished and dismayed. He had had no idea how powerful his anger was.

I remember telling my mother that I was concerned about the intensity of his rage. She scoffed at that idea, reminding me how kind he was. So I shut up, but it stayed on my radar. Not long after that incident, Will was mad again. I reminded him that it was fine to be angry but not fine to hurt people. So he started yelling at his brother, saying angry, mean, rude things. I said it was fine to be angry but not to talk that way. Then I thought to myself, *Hey, make up your mind. Which is it? Can he feel anger, or can't he? If I don't allow him to express his anger in a way that has an impact, what good is it?* I suggested that he make some really dramatic, forceful drawings of the worst words he could think of and show them to people when he was mad. I reminded him that art could be a weapon.

He paused and then smiled. He ran for the markers and set to work, making huge neon 3-D posters of the raunchiest, most offensive words he could think of, with all kinds of vivid patterns around the letters. For days afterward, he triumphantly and vigorously held his swear words up to our faces when the need arose.

It was a lesson to me. I couldn't make Will into a person with a mild temper. Would I want to? But it was up to me to help him cope with his powerful responses, learn how to handle who he was.

As a teenager, Will was thoughtful, gentle, and insightful. When a boy in his second-grade class peed in his pants, Will was the one who told the other kids it was a new look—mottled jeans, all the rage. But he hadn't become a different person. When a boy taunted his best friend with racist slurs, Will punched the boy hard in the face. I once watched him play basketball. I was sitting as close to the court as you could get. The player from the other team who was defending Will became increasingly aggressive, provoking Will with elbows and ugly words. As Will walked off the court for the halftime break, I heard him say in a guttural voice, "I'm gonna ram it down that bitch's throat."

Later I commented to him about it, amused at how riled up he had been.

He stared at me blankly and said, "I didn't say that."

Just as when he was seven, at eighteen he could be gripped by violent emotion and in those moments didn't even realize how strong his anger was.

My mother periodically brings up my earlier concern from Will's childhood. She will laugh and say, "And you were worried that he didn't know how to handle his anger. Look at him. He's the most loving, thoughtful, tactful man."

Yes, he is. Will grew into someone whose enormous personal and physical power is matched by his gentleness. But he is still someone with a lot of strong feeling, someone who can be scary when angered. As an adult, he has told me about the moments when he could easily push an adversary into the ground. "But I ask myself, is it worth it? Would it be right?" Somewhere along the way, he found out how to live with his aggression. I don't think my noticing it when he was young hurt him—it gave me a chance to provide him a helping hand.

If you think you see a worrisome pattern, you can help change your child's path. Slightly. You can offer her new ways of interpreting bad and good events. You might be able help her learn new ways to approach friends. You can get help if your relationship with her is not as solid or close as it should be. You can try to be kind, principled, and hardworking yourself. You can savor joy in everyday life and have close relationships, hoping to set a good example. But you cannot make your child into a different person. Not everyone is gregarious, sunny, filled with ambition, or highly intelligent.

You might have been hoping that these pages would offer you a list of things to watch for. But there is no list that can capture your child—or any child, for that matter. As I said at the beginning, your child's life is a story. Few behaviors are red flags, and many are red herrings. Any one characteristic or incident in your son's or daughter's life has to be understood in terms of the other things he or she does and experiences. A lonely child who has intense interests and great ability is in a different situation from a lonely child who has no interests. A weakness is less of one in the context of other strengths.

On the other hand, a weakness that might seem insignificant on its own is of greater concern if you notice that it is part of a pattern. When something is a genuine red flag, it almost always appears in a series of red flags.

And remember that there are often plenty of subtle clues that things are better than you thought—a child who doesn't get wonderful grades but whose words and gestures reveal that he is very smart, a child who isn't the most popular but clearly has strong warm relationships with a few other kids, or a child who isn't Miss Sunshine but nevertheless seems to get a quiet kick out of everyday life. The good patterns are just as important to decipher. If you see a good pattern, it will help alleviate your alarm when your child hits a bump and allow you to enjoy the person you got.

Even if your child has a lot of trouble in one part of her life, you can help by building on her strengths. If a child tends toward gloominess but has strong, close relationships with other people, that's great. It will mitigate the pain of her low moods. Give her ample time and opportunity to enjoy her friendships and connect to others. Those friendships might not make her ebullient, but they will buffer her when joy is hard to come by. If your son is very smart but not all that driven, give him chances to do the things that feed his intellect. You cannot inject him with ambition, but you can encourage him to focus on the pleasures of work that excites his mind.

Back in that school in L.A., another parent came up to speak to me. He was very tall, with sandy hair and pale gray eyes. He walked with the lope of a former athlete. He and his wife, who was with him, were the parents of three young children. He spoke with a slight drawl in his voice, as if he had lived in the South. He said, "You know, it sounds an awful lot to me like you are talking about the serenity prayer used in AA."

I was thrown. What does parenting have to do with becoming sober? Warily, I said, "Really?"

The man answered, "Yeah. The prayer goes like this: 'Please grant me the strength to change what I can, the serenity to accept what I cannot, and the wisdom to know the difference.' It seems to me that you are telling us that there are some things you can change about your kid and other things that won't change, no matter what you do. And that you're better off accepting those things and working with them rather than butting your head against a wall."

I couldn't have said it better myself.

# Selected Bibliography

Adolph, Karen E., & Robinson, Scott R. 2008. In defense of change processes. *Child Development,* Vol. 79, pp. 1648–53.

Ainsworth, Mary D. Salter, & Bell, Silvia M. 1970. Attachment, exploration, and separation: Illustrated by the behavior of one-year-olds in a strange situation. *Child Development,* Vol. 41, pp. 49–67.

Aron, Arthur, Paris, Meg, & Aron, Elaine N. 1995. Falling in love: prospective studies of self concept change. *Journal of Personality and Social Psychology,* Vol. 69, No. 6, pp. 1102–12.

Aron, Arthur, Fisher, Helen, Mashek, Debra J., Strong, Greg, Li, Haifang, & Brown, Lucy L. 2005. Reward, motivation, and emotion systems, associated with early-stage intense romantic love. *Journal of Neurophysiology,* Vol. 94, pp. 327–37.

Arsenio, William, & Lover, Anthony. Children's conceptions of sociomoral affect: Happy victimizers, mixed emotions, and other expectancies. In *Morality in Everyday Life: Developmental Perspectives*, Melanie Killen & Daniel Hart, eds. New York: Cambridge University Press, 1995.

Asendorpf, Jens B., & Van Aken, Marcel A.G. 2003. Validity of Big Five personality judgments in childhood: A 9 year longitudinal study. *European Journal of Personality*, Vol. 17, pp. 1–17.

Asher, Steven R., & Paquette, Julie A. 2003. Loneliness and peer relations in childhood. *Current Directions in Psychological Science*, Vol. 12, No. 3, p. 75.

Asher, Steven R., Paquette-MacEvoy, Julie, & McDonald, Kristina L. 2008. Children's peer relations, social competence, and school adjustment: A social tasks and social goals perspective. *Social Psychological Perspectives*, Vol. 15, pp. 357–90.

Asher, Steven R., Parker, Jeffrey G., & Walker, Diane L. Distinguishing friendship from acceptance: Implications for intervention and assessment. In *The Company They Keep: Friendship in Childhood and Adolescence*, Bukowski, W.M., A.F. Newcomb, W.W. Hartup, eds. New York: Cambridge University Press, 1996.

Bagwell, Catherine L., Bender, Sarah E., Andreassi, Cristina L., Kinoshita, Tracy L., Montarello, Staci A., & Muller, Jason G. 2005. Friendship quality and perceived relationship changes predict psychosocial adjustment in early adulthood. *Journal of Social and Personal Relationships*, Vol. 22, No. 2, pp. 235–54.

Bagwell, Catherine L., Schmidt, Michelle E., Newcomb, Andrew F., & Bukowski, William M. Friendship and peer rejection as predictors of adult adjustment. In *The Role of Friendship in Psychological Adjustment*. Nangle, Douglas W., & Cynthia A. Erdley, eds. U.S.A.:Jossey-Bass, 2001.

Beck, Aaron T., Rush, John A., Shaw, Brian F., & Emery, Gary. *Cognitive Theory of Depression*. New York: The Guilford Press, 1979.

Berscheid, Ellen, & Hatfield, Elaine. *Interpersonal Attraction*, 2nd ed. New York: Random House, 1969.

Bierman, Karen Linn. 1986. Process of change during social skills training with preadolescents and its relation to treatment outcome. *Child Development,* Vol. 57, pp. 230–40.

Blackwell, Lisa S., Trzesniewski, Kali H., & Dweck, Carol S. 2007. Implicit theories of intelligence predict achievement across an adolescent transition: A longitudinal study and an intervention. *Child Development,* Vol. 78, No. 1, p. 246–63.

Borghans, Lex, Duckworth, Angela Lee, Heckman, James J., & ter Weel, Bas. The economics and psychology of personality traits. Institute for the Study of Labor, Discussion Paper Series No. 3333.

Brehm, Sharon S., Kassin, Saul M., & Fein, Steven, eds. *Social Psychology,* 5th ed. Boston & New York: Houghton Mifflin Company, 2002.

Brendgen, Mara, Boivin, Michel, Vitaro, Frank, Bukowski, William M., Dionne, Ginette, Tremlay, Richard E., & Perusse, Daniel. 2008. Linkages between children's and their friends' social and physical aggression: Evidence for a gene-environment interaction? *Child Development,* Vol. 79, No. 1, pp. 13–29.

Brickman, Philip, Coates, Dan, & Janoff-Bulman, Ronnie. 1978. Lottery winners and accident victims: Is happiness relative? *Journal of Personality and Social Psychology,* Vol. 36, pp. 918–27.

Bruer, John T. *The Myth of the First Three Years: A New Understanding of Early Brain Development and Lifelong Learning.* New York: The Free Press, 1999.

Buehlman, Kim Therese, Gottman, John Mordechai, & Katz, Lynn Fainsilber. 1992. How a couple views their past predicts their future: Predicting divorce from an oral history interview. *Journal of Family Psychology,* Vol. 5, pp. 295–318.

Bukowski, William M., Newcomb, Andrew F., & Hartup, Willard W. *The Company They Keep: Friendship in Childhood and Adolescence.* New York: Cambridge University Press, 1996.

Buss, David M. The evolution of love. In *The New Psychology of*

*Love,* Sternberg, Robert J., & Karen Weis, eds. New Haven & London: Yale University Press, 2006, pp. 65–86.

Carey, Benedict. Bad behavior does not doom pupils, studies say. *New York Times.* November 13, 2007.

Caspi, Avshalom. 2000. The child is the father of the man: Personality continuities from childhood to adulthood. *Journal of Personality and Social Psychology,* Vol. 78, pp. 158–72.

Caspi, Avshalom, & Silva, Phil A. 1995. Temperamental qualities at age three predict personality traits in young adulthood: Longitudinal evidence from a birth cohort. *Child Development,* Vol. 66, pp. 486–98.

Caspi, Avshalom, Moffitt, Terrie E., Morgan, Julia, Rutter, Michael, Taylor, Alan, Arseneault, Louise, Tully, Lucy, Jacobs, Catherine, Kim-Cohen, Julia, & Polo-Tomas, Monica. 2004. Maternal expressed emotion predicts children's antisocial behavior problems: Using monozygotic-twin differences to identify environmental effects on behavioral development. *Developmental Psychology,* Vol. 40, pp. 149–61.

Ceci, Stephen J. *On Intelligence: A Bioecological Treatise on Intellectual Development.* Cambridge, MA: Harvard University Press, 1996.

Clark, David A., Beck, Aaron T., & Alford, Brad A. *Cognitive Theory and Therapy of Depression.* U.S.A.: John Wiley & Sons, 1999.

Coie, John D. Toward a theory of peer rejection. In *Peer Rejection in Childhood,* Asher, Steven R., & Coie, John D., New York: Cambridge University Press, 1990, pp. 365–401.

Coie, John D., & Kupersmidt, Janis B. 1983. Behavioral analysis of emerging social status in boys' groups. *Child Development,* Vol. 54, pp. 1400–1416.

Cole, Michael, Cole, Sheila R., & Lightfoot, Cynthia. *The Development of Children,* 5th ed. Worth Publishers, 2005.

Coles, Robert. *The Moral Intelligence of Children.* New York: Random House, 1997.

Collins, Nancy L., & Read, Stephen J. 1990. Adult attachment, working models, and relationship quality in dating couples. *Journal of Personality and Social Psychology*, Vol. 58, pp. 644–63.

Coplan, Robert J., Rubin, Kenneth H., Fox, Nathan A., Calkins, Susan D., & Stewart, Shannon L. 1994. Being alone, playing alone, and acting alone: Distinguishing among reticence and passive and active solitude in young children. *Child Development*, Vol. 65, pp. 129–37.

Corsaro, William A. *The Sociology of Childhood*, 2nd ed. Newbury Park, CA: Pine Forge Press, 2005.

Cramer, Phebe, & Tracy, Allison. 2005. The pathway from child personality to adult adjustment: The road is not straight. *Journal of Research in Personality*, Vol. 39, pp. 369–94.

Creswell, Julie, & Thomas, Landon, Jr., "The Talented Mr. Madoff," *New York Times*, January 24, 2009, p. B1.

Cui, Ming, Fincham, Frank D., & Pasley, Kay B. 2008. Young adult romantic relationships: The role of parents' marital problems and relationship efficacy. *Personality and Social Psychology Bulletin*, Vol. 34, pp. 1226–35.

Cytryn, Leon, & McKnew, Donald. "What is childhood depression?" In *Growing Up Sad: Childhood Depression and Its Treatment*. U.S.A.: W. W. Norton & Company, 1996.

Damon, William. *The Moral Child: Nurturing Children's Natural Moral Growth*. New York: The Free Press, 1988.

Damon, William. *Greater Expectations: Overcoming the Culture of Indulgence in Our Homes and Schools*. New York: Free Press Paperbacks, 1995.

DeLoache, Judy S., Simcock, Gabrielle, & Macari, Suzanne. 2007. Planes, trains, automobiles, and tea sets: Extremely intense interests in very young children. *Developmental Psychology*, Vol. 43, No. 6, pp. 1579–86.

De Waal, Frans. *Good Natured: The Origins of Right and Wrong in Humans and Other Animals*. Cambridge, MA: Harvard University Press, 1996.

Diamond, Adele, & Amso, Dima. 2008. Contributions of neuroscience to our understanding of cognitive development. *Current Directions in Psychological Science*, Vol. 17, pp. 136–41.

Diamond, Lisa M. 2003. What does sexual orientation orient? A biobehavioral model distinguishing romantic love and sexual desire. *Psychological Review*, Vol. 110, pp. 173–92.

Diener, Carol I., & Dweck, Carol S. 1978. An analysis of learned helplessness: Continuous changes in performance, strategy, and achievement cognitions following failure. *Journal of Personality and Social Psychology*, Vol. 36, No. 5, pp. 451–62.

Doherty, William R., Hatfield, Elaine, Thompson, Kari, & Choo, Patricia. 1994. Cultural and ethnic influences on love and attachment. *Personal Relationships*, Vol. 1, pp. 391–98.

Dovidio, John F., Piliavin, Jane Allyn, Schroeder, David A., & Penner, Louis A. *The Social Psychology of Prosocial Behavior*. Mahwah, N.J.: Lawrence Erlbaum Publishers, 2006.

Driscoll, Richard, Davis, Keith E., & Lipetz, Milton E. 1972. Parental interference and romantic love: The Romeo and Juliet effect. *Journal of Personality and Social Psychology*, Vol. 24, pp. 1–10.

Dubow, E.F., et al. 2006. Middle childhood and adolescent contextual and personal predictors of adult educational and occupational outcomes: A mediational model of two countries. *Developmental Psychology*, Vol 42., No. 5, pp. 937–49.

Duckworth, Angela L. (Over and) Beyond high-stakes testing. *American Psychologist*, Vol. 64, No. 4, pp. 279–80.

Duncan, Greg J., Dowsett, Chantelle J., Claessens, Amy, Magnuson, Katherine, Huston, Aletha C., Klebanov, Pamela, Pagani, Linda S., Feinstein, Leon, Engel, Mimi, Brooks-Gunn, Jeanne, Sexton, Holly, Duckworth, Kathryn, & Japel, Crista. 2007. School readiness and later achievement. *Developmental Psychology*, Vol. 43, pp. 1428–46.

Dunn, Judy. The beginnings of moral understanding: Development in the second year. In Jerome Kagan & Sharon Lamb, eds. *The Emergence of Morality in Young Children.* Chicago & London: The University of Chicago Press, 1987, pp. 91–112.

Dutton, Donald G., & Aron, Arthur P. 1974. Some evidence for heightened sexual attraction under conditions of high anxiety. *Journal of Personality and Social Psychology,* Vol. 4, pp. 510–17.

Dweck, Carol S. 1975. The role of expectations and attributions in the alleviation of learned helplessness. *Journal of Personality and Social Psychology,* Vol. 31, pp. 674–85.

Dweck, Carol S. 2008. Can personality be changed? The role of beliefs in personality and change. *Current Directions in Psychological Science,* Vol. 17, pp. 391–94.

Eisenberg, Nancy, Michalik, Nichole, Spinrad, Tracy L., Hofer, Claire, Kupfer, Anne, Valiente, Carlos, Liew, Jeffrey, Cumberland, Amanda, & Reiser, Mark. 2007. The relations of effortful control and impulsivity to children's sympathy: A longitudinal study. *Cognitive Development,* Vol. 22, pp. 544–67.

Elliott, Elaine S., & Dweck, Carol S. 1988. Goals: An approach to motivation and achievement. *Journal of Personality and Social Psychology,* Vol. 54, No. 1, pp. 5–12.

Emmons, Robert A., & Crumpler, Cheryl A. 2000. Gratitude as a human strength: Appraising the evidence. *Journal of Social and Clinical Psychology,* Vol. 19, p. 56.

Emmons, Robert A., & Michael E. McCullough, eds. *The Psychology of Gratitude.* New York: Oxford University Press, 2004.

Feshbach, Norma Deitch. Empathy training: A field study in affective education. In *Aggression and Behavior Change: Biological and Social Processes,* Seymour Feshbach & Adam Fraczek, eds. Praeger Publishers, 1979.

Feshbach, Norma Deitch. Sex differences in empathy and social behavior in children. In *The Development of Prosocial Behavior,* Nancy Eisenberg, ed. Academic Press, 1982.

Feshbach, Norma Deitch. 1983. Learning to care: A positive approach to child training and discipline. *Journal of Clinical Child Psychology*, Vol. 12, pp. 266–71.

Fox, Nathan A., Henderson, Heather A., Rubin, Kenneth H., Calkins, Susan D., & Schmidt, Louis A. 2001. Continuity and discontinuity of behavioral inhibition and exuberance: Psychophysiological and behavioral influences across the first four years of life. *Child Development*, Vol. 72, pp. 1–21.

Fox, Nathan A., Nichols, Kate E., Henderson, Heather A., Rubin, Kenneth, Schmidt, Louis, Hamer, Dean, Ernst, Monique, & Pine, Daniel S. 2005. Evidence for a gene-environment interaction in predicting behavioral inhibition in middle childhood. *Psychological Science*, Vol. 16, pp. 921–26.

Freeman, Leslie J., Templer, Donald I., & Hill, Curt. 1999. The relationship between adult happiness and self-appraised childhood happiness and events. *The Journal of Genetic Psychology*, Vol. 160, pp. 46–54.

Friend, Angela, DeFries, John C., & Olson, Richard K. 2008. Parental education moderates genetic influences on reading disability. *Psychological Science*, Vol. 19, pp. 1124–30.

Gardner, Howard, Csikszentmihalyi, Mihaly, & Damon, William. *Good Work: Where Excellence and Ethics Meet*. New York: Basic Books, 2001.

Gilbert, Daniel. *Stumbling on Happiness*. New York: Alfred A. Knopf, 2006.

Gillham, Jane E., Peivich, Karen J., Jaycox, Lisa H, & Seligman, Martin E.P. 1995. Prevention of depressive symptoms in schoolchildren: Two year follow-up. *Psychological Science*, Vol. 6, No. 6, pp. 343–51.

Gladwell, Malcolm. *Outliers*. New York: Little, Brown, and Company, 2008.

Gladwell, Malcolm. Late bloomers: Why do we equate genius with precocity? *The New Yorker*, October 20, 2008.

Gladwell, Malcolm. Most likely to succeed. *The New Yorker*, December 15, 2008.

Golombok, Susan. *Parenting: What Really Counts?* London & New York: Routledge, 2000.

Greene, Joshua D., Sommerville, R. Brian, Nystrom, Leigh E., Darley, John M., & Cohen, Jonathan D. 2001. An fMRI investigation of emotional engagement in moral judgment. *Science*, Vol. 293, pp. 2105–8.

Greene, Joshua D., Cushman, Fiery A., Stewart, Lisa E., Lowenberg, Kelly, Nystrom, Leigh E., & Cohen, Jonathan D. 2009. Pushing moral buttons: The interaction between personal force and intention in moral judgment. *Cognition,* in press.

Grevan, Corina U., Harlaar, Nicole, Kovas, Yulia, Chamorro-Premuzic, Tomas, & Plomin, Robert. 2009. More than just IQ: School achievement is predicted by self-perceived abilities—but for genetic rather than environmental reasons. *Psychological Science*, Vol. 20, pp. 753–62.

Grusec, Joan E., & Redler, Erica. 1980. Attribution, reinforcement, and altruism: A developmental analysis. *Developmental Psychology*, Vol. 16, No. 5, pp. 525–34.

Hallowell, Edward M. *The Childhood Roots of Adult Happiness: Five Steps to Help Kids Create and Sustain Lifelong Joy.* New York: Ballantine Books, 2002.

Hampson, Sarah E. *The Construction of Personality: An Introduction.* New York: Routledge & Kegan Paul, 1982.

Hampson, Sarah E. 2008. Mechanisms by which childhood personality traits influence adult well-being. *Current Directions in Psychological Science,* Vol. 14, No. 4, pp. 264–68.

Hampson, Sarah E., & Goldberg, Lewis R. 2006. A first large cohort study of personality trait stability over the 40 years between elementary school and midlife. *Journal of Personality and Social Psychology*, Vol. 91, pp. 763–79.

Hane, Amie Ashley, Cheah, Charissa, Rubin, Kenneth H., & Fox, Nathan A. 2008. The role of maternal behavior in the relation between shyness and social reticence in early childhood and social withdrawal in middle childhood. *Social Development*, Vol. 17, pp. 795–811.

Hane, Amie Ashley, Fox, Nathan A., Henderson, Heather A., & Marshall, Peter J. 2008. Behavioral reactivity and approach-withdrawal bias in infancy. *Developmental Psychology*, Vol. 44, pp. 1491–96.

Harris, Paul. Testimony and moral judgment. Personal correspondence.

Hart, Betty, & Risley, Todd R. *Meaningful Differences in the Everyday Experience of Young American Children*. Baltimore: Paul H. Brookes Publishing Co., 1995.

Hatfield, Elaine, Schmitz, Earle, Cornelius, Jeffrey, & Rapson, Richard L. 1988. Passionate love: How early does it begin? *Journal of Psychology and Human Sexuality*, Vol. 1, pp. 35–51.

Hatfield, Elaine, & Rapson, Richard L. *Love, Sex, and Intimacy: Their Psychology, Biology, and History*. New York: Harper Collins College Publishers, 1993.

Hatfield, Elaine, & Rapson, Richard L. 1994. Historical and cross-cultural perspectives on passionate love and sexual desire. *Annual Review of Sex Research*, Vol. 4, pp. 67–97.

Haworth, Claire M.A., Dale, Phillip S., & Plomin, Robert. 2009. The etiology of science performance: Decreasing heritability and increasing importance of the shared environment from 9 to 12 years of age. *Child Development*, Vol. 80, No. 3, pp. 662–73.

Hazan, Cindy, & Shaver, Phillip. 1987. Romantic love conceptualized as an attachment process. *Journal of Personality and Social Psychology*, Vol. 52, pp. 511–24.

Hoffman, Martin L. *Empathy and Moral Development: Implications for Caring and Justice*. New York: Cambridge University Press, 2000.

Hussar, Karen, & Harris, Paul L. Children who choose not to eat meat: A demonstration of early moral decision-making. *Social Development*. In press.

Iyer, Pico. The doctor is within. The Opinionater, *New York Times*, July 22, 2009.

Jaffee, Sara R., Caspi, Avshalom, Moffitt, Terrie E., Polo-Tomas, Monica, & Taylor, Alan. 2007. Individual, family, and neighborhood factors distinguish resilient from non-resilient maltreated children: A cumulative stressors model. *Child Abuse & Neglect*, Vol. 31, pp. 231–53.

Jaycox, Lisa H., Reivich, Karen J., Gillham, Jane, & Seligman, Martin E.P. 1994. Prevention of depressive symptoms in school children. *Behavior Research Therapy*, Vol. 32, No. 8, pp. 801–16.

Judge, Timothy A., & Hurst, Charlice. How the rich (and happy) get richer (and happier): Relationship of core self-evaluations to trajectories in attaining work success. *Journal of Applied Psychology*, Vol. 93:4, pp. 849–63.

Kagan, Jerome. *The Second Year*. U.S.A.: Harvard University Press, 1981.

Kagan, Jerome. *The Nature of the Child*. New York: Basic Books, 1984.

Kagan, Jerome. 2008. In defense of qualitative changes in development. *Child Development*, Vol. 79, pp. 1606–24.

Kagan, Jerome, & Nancy Snidman. *The Long Shadow of Temperament*. Cambridge, Massachusetts, and London, England, Belknap Press of Harvard University Press: 2004.

Kaufman, James C., & Agars, Mark D. 2009. Being creative with the predictors and criteria for success. *American Psychologist*, Vol. 64, No. 4, pp. 280–81.

Kazdin, Alan E. *Parent Management Training: Treatment for Oppositional, Aggressive, and Antisocial Behavior in Children and Adolescents*. New York: Oxford University Press, 2005.

Knee, C. Raymond, Canevello, Amy, Bush, Amber L., & Cook, Astrid. 2008. Relationship contingent self-esteem and the ups and downs of romantic relationships. *Journal of Personality and Social Psychology*, Vol. 95, pp. 608–27.

Kochanska, Grazyna. 1997. Multiple pathways to conscience for children with different temperaments: From toddlerhood to age 5. *Developmental Psychology,* Vol. 33, No. 2, pp. 228–40.

Kochanska, Grazyna, Askan, Nazan, & Nicholas, Kate E. 2003. Maternal power assertion in discipline and moral discourse contexts: Commonalities, differences, and implications for children's moral conduct and cognition. *Developmental Psychology,* Vol. 39, pp. 949–63.

Kochanska, Grazyna, Askan, Nazan, Prisco, Theresa R., & Adams, Erin E. 2008. Mother-child and father-child mutually responsive orientation in the first 2 years and children's outcomes at preschool age: Mechanisms of influence. *Child Development,* Vol. 79, pp. 30–44.

Kohlberg, Lawrence. *The Psychology of Moral Development.* New York: Harper & Row Publishers, 1984.

Kohnstamm, Geldolph A., Slotboom, Anne Marie, & Elphick, Eric. 1994. Conscientiousness in children. *Psychologica Belgica,* Vol. 34, pp. 207–29.

Kovacs, Maria, Joorman, Jutta, & Gotlib, Ian H. 2008. Emotion (dys)regulation and links to depressive disorders. *Child Development Perspectives,* Vol. 2, pp. 149–55.

Kovas, Yulia, Haworth, Claire M.A., Dale, Philip, & Plomin, Robert. 2007. The genetic and environmental origins of learning abilities and disabilities in the school years. *Monographs of the Society for Research in Child Development,* Vol. 72, No. 3.

Labile, Deborah, Panfile, Tia, & Makariev, Drika. 2008. The quality and frequency of mother toddler conflict: Links with attachment and temperament. *Child Development,* Vol. 79, pp. 426–43.

Lareau, Annette. *Unequal Childhoods: Class, Race, and Family Life.* Berkeley: University of California Press, 2003.

LaVoie, Joseph C. 1974. Cognitive determinants of resistance to deviation in seven-, nine-, and eleven-year-old children of low and high maturity of moral judgment. *Developmental Psychology,* Vol. 10, pp. 393–403.

Leadbeater, Bonnie J., & Hoglund, Wendy L.G. 2009. The effects of peer victimization and physical aggression on changes in internalizing from first to third grade. *Child Development,* Vol. 80, No. 3, pp. 843–59.

Lee, John Alan. 1977. A typology of styles of loving. *Personality and Social Psychology Bulletin,* Vol. 3, pp. 173–82.

Lee, John Alan. 1988. Love styles. In *The Psychology of Love,* Robert J. Sternberg & Michael L. Barnes, eds. New Haven and London: Yale University Press, 1988, pp. 38–67.

Lemelin, Jean-Pascal, Boivin, Michel, Forget-Dubois, Nadine, Dionne, Ginette, Seguin, Jean R., Brendgen, Mara, Vitaro, Frank, Tremblay, Richard E., & Peiusse, Daniel. 2007. The genetic environmental etiology of cognitive school readiness and later academic achievement in early childhood. *Child Development,* Vol, 78, No. 6, pp. 1855–69.

Lepper, Mark R., Greene, David, & Nisbett, Richard E. 1973. Undermining children's intrinsic interest with extrinsic reward: A test of the "overjustification" hypothesis. *Journal of Personality and Social Psychology,* Vol. 28, No. 1, pp. 129–37.

Lerner, Richard M. 1991. Changing organism-context relations as the basic process of development: A developmental contextual perspective. *Developmental Psychology,* Vol. 27, No. 1, pp. 27–32.

Lewis, Michael. 2005. The child and its family: The social network model. *Human Development,* Vol. 48, pp. 8–27.

Liben, Lynn S. 2008. Reflections on child development: The journal and the field. *Child Development,* Vol. 79, pp. 1597–99.

Liben, Lynn. 2008. Continuities and discontinuities in children and scholarship. *Child Development,* Vol. 79, pp. 1600–1605.

Lockhart, Kristi L., Nakashima, Nobuko, Inagaki, Kayoko, & Keil, Frank C. 2008. From ugly duckling to swan? Japanese and

American beliefs about the stability and origins of traits. *Cognitive Development*, Vol. 23, pp. 155–79.

Lyubomirsky, Sonja. *The How of Happiness: A Scientific Approach to Getting the Life You Want.* New York: The Penguin Press, 2008.

Lyubomirsky, Sonja, & Lepper, Heidi S. 1999. A measure of subjective happiness: Preliminary reliability and construct validation. *Social Indicators Research*, Vol. 46, p. 137.

Ma, Xin. 2000. A longitudinal assessment of antecedent course work in mathematics and subsequent mathematical attainment. *Journal of Educational Research*, Vol. 94, pp. 16–28.

Ma, Xin. 2005. Growth in mathematics achievement: Analysis with classification and regression trees. *Journal of Educational Research*, Vol. 99, pp. 78–86.

Malti, Tina, Gummerum, Michaela, Keller, Monika, & Buchmann, Marlis. 2009. Children's moral motivation, sympathy, and prosocial behavior. *Child Development*, Vol. 80, pp. 442–60.

Maron, Bradley A., Fein, Steven, Maron, Barry J., Hillel, Alexander T., El Baghdadi, Mariam M., & Rodenhauser, Paul. 2007. Ability of prospective assessment of personality profiles to predict the practice specialty of medical students. *Baylor University Medical Center Proceedings*, Vol. 20, pp. 22–26.

Miner, Jennifer L., & Clarke-Stewart, K., Alison. 2008. Trajectories of externalizing behavior from age 2 to age 9: Relations with gender, temperament, ethnicity, parenting, and rater. *Developmental Psychology*, Vol. 44, pp. 771–86.

Moffitt, Terrie E., & Caspi, Avshalom. 2001. Childhood predictors differentiate life-course persistent and adolescence-limited antisocial pathways among males and females. *Development and Psychopatholoy*, Vol. 13, pp. 355–75.

Nangle, Douglas W., & Erdley, Cynthia A., eds. *The Role of Friendship in Psychological Adjustment.* U.S.A.: Jossey-Bass, 2001.

Nangle, Douglas W., Erdley, Cynthia A., Newman, Julie E., Mason,

Craig A., & Carpenter, Erika M. 2003. Popularity, friendship quantity, and friendship quality: Interactive influences on children's loneliness and depression. *Journal of Clinical Child and Adolescent Psychology*, Vol. 32, pp. 546–55.

Nolen-Hoeksema, Susan, Girgus, Joan S., & Seligman, Martin E.P. 1986. Learned helplessness in children: A longitudinal study of depression, achievement, and explanatory style. *Journal of Personality and Social Psychology*, Vol. 51, pp. 435–42.

Nolen-Hoeksema, Susan, Girgus, Joan S., & Seligman, Martin E.P. 1992. Predictors and consequences of childhood depressive symptoms: A 5-year longitudinal study. *Journal of Abnormal Psychology*, Vol. 101, pp. 405–22.

Odgers, Candice L., Caspi, Avshalom, Nagin, Daniel S., Piquero, Alex R., Slutske, Wendy S., Milne, Barry J., Dickson, Nigel, Poulton, Richie, & Moffitt, Terrie E. 2008. Is it important to prevent early exposure to drugs and alcohol among adolescents? *Psychological Science*, Vol. 19, pp. 1037–44.

Olson, Kristina R., & Dweck, Carol S. 2009. Social cognitive development: A new look. *Child Development Perspectives*, Vol. 3, pp. 60–65.

Ozer, Daniel J., & Benet-Martinez, Veronica. 2006. Personality and the prediction of consequential outcomes. *Annual Review of Psychology*, Vol. 57, pp. 401–21.

Paciello, Marinella, Fida, Robert, Tramontano, Carlo, Lupinetti, Catia, & Caprara, Gian Vittorio. 2008. Stability and change of moral disengagement and its impact on aggression and violence in late adolescence. *Child Development*, Vol. 79, pp. 1288–1309.

Parker, Jeffrey G., & Asher, Steven R. 1993. Friendship and friendship quality in middle childhood: Links with peer groups acceptance and feelings of loneliness and social dissatisfaction. *Developmental Psychology*, Vol. 29, No. 4, pp. 611–21.

Parker, Jeffrey G., Rubin, Kenneth H., Price, Joseph, M., &

DeRosier, Melissa E. Peer relationships, child development, and adjustment: A developmental psychopathology perspective. *Developmental Psychopathology*, Vol. 2. Cicchetti, Dante, & Cohen, Donald J., eds. Oxford, England: John Wiley & Sons, 1995, pp. 96–161.

Pennebaker, James W., Dyer, Mary Anne, Caulkins, R. Scott, Litowitz, Debra Lynn, Ackreman, Phillip L., Anderson, Douglas B., & McGraw, Kevin M. 1979. Don't the girls get prettier at closing time: A country and western application to psychology. *Personality and Social Psychology Bulletin*, Vol. 5, pp. 122–25.

Pepler, Debra J., & Craig, Wendy M. 1995. A peek behind the fence: Naturalistic observations of aggressive children with remote audiovisual recording. *Developmental Psychology*, Vol. 31, No. 4, pp. 548–53.

Pollak, Seth D. 2008. Mechanisms linking early experience and the emergence of emotions: Illustrations from the study of maltreated children. *Current Directions in Psychological Science*, Vol. 17, pp. 370–76.

Pulkkinen, Lea, & Caspi, Avshalom, eds. *Paths to Successful Development: Personality in the Life Course*. Cambridge: Cambridge University Press, 2002.

Quinn, Paul C. 2008. In defense of core competencies, quantitative change, and continuity. *Child Development*, Vol. 79, pp. 1633–38.

Regents of the University of Minnesota, Institute of Childhood Development. 2000. Minnesota Longitudinal Study of Parents and Children: Overview. University of Minnesota. October 9, 2008. http://cehd.umn.edu/ICD/Parent-Child/PCPOverview.html.

Roberts, Brent W., Harms, Peter D., Caspi, Avshalom, & Moffitt, Terrie E. 2007. Predicting the counterproductive employee in a child-to-adult prospective study. *Journal of Applied Psychology*, Vol. 92, pp. 1427–36.

Roberts, Brent W., Kuncel, Nathan R., Shiner, Rebecca, Caspi, Avshalom, & Goldberg, Lewis R. 2007. The power of personality: The comparative validity of personality traits, socioeconomic status, and cognitive ability for predicting important life outcomes. *Perspectives on Psychological Science*, Vol. 2, No. 4, pp. 313–45.

Robins, Lee N., & Rutter, Michael. *Straight and Devious Pathways from Childhood to Adulthood.* Cambridge: Cambridge University Press, 1990.

Rubin, Kenneth H. *The Friendship Factor.* New York: Penguin Books, 2002.

Rubin, Zick. 1970. Measurement of romantic love. *Journal of Personality and Social Psychology*, Vol. 16, pp. 265–73.

Ruston, J. Phillipe, Fulker, David W., Neale, Michael C, Nias, David K.B., & Eysenck, Hans J. 1986. Altruism and aggression: The heritability of individual differences. *Journal of Personality and Social Psychology*, Vol. 50, pp. 1192–98.

Rutter, Michael. *Genes and Behavior: Nature-Nurture Interplay Explained.* Malden, MA: Blackwell Publishing, 2006.

Rutter, Michael, & Rutter, Marjorie. *Developing Minds: Challenge and Continuity Across the Life Span.* New York: Basic Books, 1993.

Sackett, Paul R., Borneman, Matthew J., & Connelley, Brian S. 2008. High-stakes testing in higher education and employment: Appraising the evidence for validity and fairness. *American Psychologist*, Vol. 53, No. 4, pp. 215–27.

Sackett, Paul R., Zedeck, Sheldon, & Fogli, Larry. 1988. Relations between measures of typical and maximum job performance. *Journal of Applied Psychology*, Vol. 73, No. 3, pp. 482–86.

Saegert, Susan, Swap, Walter, & Zajonc, R.B. 1973. Exposure, context, and interpersonal attraction. *Journal of Personality and Social Psychology*, Vol. 25, pp. 234–42.

Schweinhart, Lawrence J. How the High/Scope Perry Preschool Study Grew: A Researcher's Tale. High/Scope.http://www.high-scope.org/Content.asp?ContentId=232.

Schweinhart, Lawrence J., Montie, Jeanne, Xiang, Zongping, Barnett, W. Steven, Belfield, Clive R., & Nores, Milagros. *Lifetime Effects: The High/Scope Perry Preschool Study Through Age 40.* U.S.A.: High/Scope Press, 2005.

Seligman, Martin E.P. *The Optimistic Child: A Proven Program to Safeguard Children Against Depression and Build Lifelong Resilience.* Boston & New York: Houghton Mifflin Company, 1995.

Seligman, Martin, et al. 1984. Attributional style and depressive symptoms among children. *Journal of Abnormal Psychology,* Vol. 93, pp. 235–38.

Shaver, Phillip R., & Mikulincer, Mario. A behavioral systems approach to romantic love relationships: Attachment, caregiving, and sex. In *The New Psychology of Love,* Robert J. Sternberg & Karen Weis, eds. New Haven & London: Yale University Press, 2006, pp. 35–64.

Shaw, Brian F. 1977. Comparison of cognitive therapy and behavior therapy in the treatment of depression. *Journal of Consulting and Clinical Psychology,* Vol. 45, No. 4, pp. 543–51.

Shiner, Rebecca L., Masten, Ann S., & Roberts, Jennifer M. 2003. Childhood personality foreshadows adult personality and life outcomes two decades later. *Journal of Personality,* Vol. 71:6, pp. 1145–70.

Shiner, Rebecca L., Masten, Ann S., & Tellegen, Auke. 2002. A developmental perspective on personality in emerging adulthood: Childhood antecedents and concurrent adaptation. *Journal of Personality and Social Psychology,* Vol. 83, No. 5, pp. 1165–77.

Shonkoff, Jack P., & Phillips, Deborah A., eds. *From Neurons to Neighborhoods: The Science of Early Development.* Washington, D.C.: National Academy Press, 2000.

Shure, Myrna B., & Aberson, Bonnie. Enhancing the process of resilience through effective thinking. In *Handbook of Resilience in Children,* Sam Goldstein & Robert B. Brooks, ed. U.S.A.: Springer, 2005, pp. 373–94.

Shurkin, Joel N. *Terman's Kids: The Groundbreaking Study of How the Gifted Grow Up.* New York: Little, Brown, and Company, 1992.

Sigelman, Carol, & Rider, Elizabeth. *Life-Span Human Development,* 5th ed. Florence, Ky.: Wadsworth Publishing, 2006, p. 361.

Silva, Phil A., & Stanton, Warren R., eds. *From Child to Adult: The Dunedin Multidisciplinary Health and Development Study.* New York: Oxford University Press, 1996.

Simonton, Dean Keith, & Song, Anna V. 2009. Eminence, IQ, physical and mental health and achievement domain: Cox's 282 geniuses revisited. *Psychological Science,* Vol. 20, pp. 429–34.

Simpson, Jeffry A. 1990. Influence of attachment styles on romantic relationships. *Journal of Personality and Social Psychology,* Vol. 59, pp. 971–80.

Smiley, Patricia A., & Dweck, Carol S. 1994. Individual differences in achievement goals among young children. *Child Development,* Vol. 65, pp. 1723–43.

Snyder, Mark, Tanke, Elizabeth D., & Berscheid, Ellen. 1977. Social perception and interpersonal behavior: On the self-fulfilling nature of social stereotypes. *Journal of Personality and Social Psychology,* Vol. 35, pp. 656–66.

Spencer, John. P., & Perone, Sammy. 2008. Defending qualitative change: The view from dynamic systems theory. *Child Development,* Vol. 79, pp. 1639–47.

Spencer, Steven J., & Walton, Gregory M. Identity safe environments: How positive environments can unlock latent ability. Presentation, Williams College, Williamstown, Mass., 2009.

St. Petersburg-USA Orphanage Research Team. 2008. The effects of early social-emotional and relationship experience on the development of young orphanage children. *Monographs of the Society for Research in Child Development,* Vol. 73, No. 3.

Sternberg, Robert J. *The Triangle of Love.* New York: Basic Books, Inc., 1987.

Stevenson, Leslie, & Haberman, David L. *Ten Theories of Human Nature,* 3rd ed. New York: Oxford University Press, 1998.

Stipek, D., Recchia, S., & McClintic, S. 1992. Self evaluation in young children. *Monographs of the Society for Research in Child Development,* Vol. 57, pp. 1–95.

Subbotsky, Eugene V. *The Birth of Personality.* New York: Harvester Wheatsheaf, 1993.

Sulloway, Frank J. *Born to Rebel: Birth Order, Family Dynamics, and Creative Lives.* New York: Pantheon Books, 1996.

Swensen, Clifford H., Jr. 1961. Love: A self-report analysis with college students. *Journal of Individual Psychology,* Vol. 17, p. 167.

Swensen, C.H. 1972. The behavior of love. In *Love Today,* H.A. Otto, ed. New York: Association Press, pp. 86–101.

Taumoepeau, Mele, & Ruffman, Ted. 2008. Stepping stones to others' minds: Maternal talk relates to child mental state language and emotion understanding at 15, 24, and 33 months. *Child Development,* Vol. 79, pp. 284–302.

Tremblay, Richard E., Hartup, Willard W., & Archer, John. *Developmental Origins of Aggression.* New York: The Guilford Press, 2005.

Ullman, Ellen. My secret life. *New York Times.* January 2, 2009.

Underwood, Bill, & Moore, Bert S. The generality of altruism in children. In *The Development of Prosocial Behavior,* Nancy Eisenberg, ed. Academic Press, 1982.

Wachs, Theodore D., Black, Maureen M., & Engle, Patrice L. 2009. Maternal depression: A global threat to children's health, development, and behavior and to human rights. *Child Development Perspectives,* Vol. 3, pp. 51–59.

Walton, Gregory M., & Spencer, Steven J. Latent ability: Grades and test scores systematically underestimate the intellectual ability of negatively stereotyped students. *Psychological Science,* in press.

Warneken, Felix, & Tomasello, Michael. 2008. Extrinsic rewards undermine altruistic tendencies in 20-month-olds. *Developmental Psychology,* Vol. 44, pp. 1785–88.

Werner, Emmy E., Bierman, Jessie M., & French, Fern E. *The Children of Kauai: A Longitudinal Study from the Prenatal Period to Age 10.* Honolulu: University of Hawaii Press, 1971.

Werner, Emmy E., & Smith, Ruth S. *Overcoming the Odds: High Risk Children from Birth to Adulthood.* Ithaca, N.Y.: Cornell University Press, 1992.

Werner, Emmy E., & Smith, Ruth S. *Journeys from Childhood to Midlife: Risk, Resilience, and Recovery.* Ithaca, N.Y., and London: Cornell University Press, 2001.

Wigfield, Alan, & Eccles, Jacquelynne, S., eds. *Development of Achievement Motivation.* Academic Press, 2002.

Wright, Margaret O'Dougherty, & Masten, Ann S. Resilience processes in development. In Sam Goldstein & Robert B. Brooks, eds. *Handbook of Resilience in Children.* U.S.A.: Springer, 2005.

Zahn-Wexler, Carolyn, Cummings, E. Mark, & Iaonnotti, Ronald. *Altruism and Aggression: Biological and Social Origins.* New York: Cambridge University Press, 1986.

Zernike, Kate. The cool factor: Never let them see you sweat. *New York Times.* November 30, 2008.

Zins, Joseph E., & Elias, Maurice J. Social and emotional learning. In *Children's Needs III.* National Association of School Psychologists, 2006.

# Acknowledgments

Many smart and generous people shared their experiences and thoughts with me as I worked on this book. In particular, I want to thank Chris Moore, Margery Franklin, Lucy Prashker, Susanne King, Katherine Bouton, Bill Damon, Judy Deloache, and Paul Harris. Once again, Betty Prashker gave me just the right advice at just the right time.

Marlene Sandstrom and I talk about children and development all the time. Where my ideas are good, no doubt, she had something to do with it. Where they fall short, it's probably because she finally had to kick me out of her office and do something else.

I thank my wonderful agent, Neeti Madan. She's provided terrific support and guidance and seems to know exactly when I should say yes and when I should say no. Now I understand why people feel they cannot get on without their agents.

I thank my smart and delightful editor at Simon & Schuster,

Sarah Durand. She's been a complete pleasure to work with and made the difficult process of writing much smoother. I know this book is better because of her.

I adore my students at Williams. I am grateful to three in particular who helped me find material, read portions of the manuscript, and gave me feedback before anyone else. They are Kristen Baldiga, Laura Corona, and Kate Anderson.

My husband, Tom Levin, is part of everything I do and think. He's part of this book as well, and I thank him for that.

Watching my sons, Jake, Will, and Sam, grow up to be such strong, smart, funny, courageous, accomplished, and loving men has been the greatest pleasure of my life. It has also provided me with many insights about childhood.

From the bottom of my heart, I thank all of the mothers and fathers, brothers and sisters, sons and daughters, grandparents, uncles, and aunts whose life stories fill these pages. If the book is any good, it's because their lives offered such riches.

I dedicate this book to my mother, Tinka, and my sisters, Kathy and Jenno. Luckily for me, our lives are intertwined. I wouldn't be me without them, and neither would *Red Flags or Red Herrings?*

# Index